Programming Tools
Shareware

PC-SIG's Best Books
Windows 3 Shareware Utilities
DOS Shareware Utilities
Programming Tools Shareware
Business Applications Shareware
The PC-SIG Encyclopedia of Shareware
4th Edition

Programming Tools Shareware

Ed DiGiovanna

Windcrest®/McGraw-Hill

FIRST EDITION
SECOND PRINTING

Library of Congress Cataloging-in-Publication Data

Programming tools shareware / by PC-SIG, Inc.
     p.   cm.
    Includes index.
    ISBN 0-8306-2489-9 (pbk.)
    1. Shareware (Computer software)   2. Microcomputers—Programming.
I. PC-SIG, Inc.
QA76.76.S46P76   1991
005.365—dc20   91-23986
                                           CIP

TAB Books offers software for sale. For information and a catalog, please contact
TAB Software Department, Blue Ridge Summit, PA 17294-0850.

Acquisitions Editor: Ron Powers
Book Editor: David M. McCandless
Director of Production: Katherine G. Brown
Book Design: Jaclyn J. Boone
Cover Design: Sandra Blair Design, Harrisburg, PA   WP1

Contents

_____PART ONE_____
LEARNING TOOLS

_____**PART TWO**_____

COMPANION TOOLS

PART THREE

USER INTERFACE TOOLS

13   *Screen Debut*   243

_____PART FOUR_____

OTHER TOOLS

14   *PopText*   259

Foreword

Programming. It's a strange and mysterious art to those who aren't involved with it—a bizarre world of memory addresses, interrupts, and line after cryptic line of what programmers call code. To the programmer, however, the world of programming is a realm of endless fascination, a place where the fearless creator can build a program from the ground up—limited only by his or her imagination and the tools he or she possesses. For, just like the general contractor who builds your house, a programmer needs good, solid tools to create a quality product. When it comes to programming tools, the world of shareware provides an almost infinite variety to choose from.

Of course, you can find programming tools in the conventional retail marketplace, but they can be very expensive. The selection is also limited because big companies only want to provide things that they believe will be profitable to them. The shareware marketplace, on the other hand, doesn't worry nearly as much about profit and thus produces a variety of products.

This means that you'll find programming tools in shareware that you could never buy in any store. Shareware programming tools also tend to be much less expensive, with some items (like source code) often being absolutely free. The factors of greater selection and lower price make shareware very appealing to programmers trying to expand their collection of programming tools.

Programming Tools Shareware gives you an inside look at some of the very best programming tools available in shareware, focusing on a wide range of tools for use with the C and Turbo Pascal programming languages. You'll examine excellent packages like the Programmer's Productivity Pak from Falk Data Systems, Window Boss from Star Guidance

Consulting, the TSR routines of TesSeRact by Innovative Data Concepts, and much, much more. From compilers to source code libraries, *Programming Tools Shareware* highlights some of the most valuable tools, explains how to use them, and gives you information on obtaining them. You'll even find a disk at the back of the book containing some excellent tools to try out.

Over the years I've worked with many shareware authors, and a good number of them use some of the various programming tools discussed in these pages. It is my pleasure to welcome you to *Programming Tools Shareware*. I believe you'll find it both interesting and beneficial.

Michael E. Callahan
(aka Dr. File Finder)
Editor-in-Chief, *Shareware Magazine*
Elizabeth, Colorado

Introduction

If you have written more than one program in your time, you probably have started developing a toolkit. Your toolkit is that collection of routines or program segments (i.e., tools) that you keep reusing in nearly all of your programs. Anyone who has been programming for a while has collected a number of these tools. Some of them may be scalpels; some may be hammers. But each is useful in its own way. You will find that the longer you engage in programming, the larger and more refined your toolkit will become. Some of your tools will be special routines specific to your own applications. Others will be more general and could be used in nearly any type of program. In the latter case, most of what you need will already have been done by other programmers.

The fact is, in order to program effectively and expeditiously, you MUST have a good set of programming tools at hand. But for most of us, that isn't so easy. Not only does it take years and years of programming experience to develop your own comprehensive set of programming tools, but many of the routines you will write yourself are inferior compared to commercial software. This is because you simply do not have the time and resources to write robust code and to fully test it.

Programmers in general, being creative people, tend to prefer composing their own code rather than reusing code written by others—even if that code fits their needs exactly. However, the pragmatic programmer (you should read that as "successful programmer") knows that it is never worth the effort, and especially the time, reinventing the installation program or the windowing routine. While the intellectual challenge of writing one's own routines may be stimulating and instructive, in today's rapid paced software market it can also be ruinous. That is why there are so many programming tools available on the commercial market. These tools can be extremely valuable to programmers. Unfortunately, the people who market these tools know it. As a result, it is usually extremely expensive to purchase and license commercially available programming tools.

The perfect alternative is shareware. Shareware programming tools can give you all the performance of the top quality commercial products at a fraction of the cost—usually without any royalties. In addition, many shareware authors offer the source code to their registered users.

This book presents a collection of tools that can be used by just about any programmer. The purpose is to show you just what is available to you in the shareware world and to help you choose which of the tools will be of value to you. The documentation included is comprehensive. However, with some of the tools, the fine details of individual functions would fill several more books, and must be left to the documentation included on the distribution disks. The vast majority of tools in this book are written for use with Pascal and C Languages. The most prominent compilers for these languages are Microsoft C (including Quick C), and Borland's Turbo C and Turbo Pascal. Many of the tools will work with other compilers, perhaps requiring some modification. Some of the tools can also be used with assemblers.

For the most part, the discussions in this book assume that you know at least the basics of programming in general, and that you are familiar in particular with the languages discussed. If you are not familiar with programming at all, you might want to start by looking at the Pascal Tutorial in Chapter 1.

The shareware programs in this book have all been supplied through the PC-SIG library. PC-SIG is the largest distributor of shareware and public domain software in the world. Currently, the PC-SIG library offers over 2000 programs, and it is growing every day.

Included with this book is a disk containing several of the programming tools featured in the book. This will allow you to evaluate these tools first hand, right away. Remember that these tools are only for evaluation. If you want to keep using them, you'll have to register them. All of the necessary registration information is included in the documentation.

It is important to emphasize that you must always register any shareware product that you decide to put into use. This is the only way that we can ever expect the shareware concept to continue working. Aside from that, paying the registration fee usually entitles you to some additional benefits. These often include a disk with the latest version of the program, technical support, and notification of program updates.

The book is arranged in four parts in which the tools have been categorized. Typically, software products are difficult to categorize because there is just too much variety. Programming tools are no exception. Thus, the categories are somewhat arbitrary. Some software packages would fit in several categories, and some really don't fit into any.

Part One starts at what is presumably the beginning: learning the programming languages. Part Two contains some tools that are designed to help you while you're writing your programs. Perhaps the most important section is Part Three, User Interface Tools. User interfaces are the most difficult programming chores. At the same time, the quality of your user interface is probably the most important factor in determining the success of your software. Part Four is the "miscellaneous chapter." Included in this chapter are a number of routines that would classify as user interface tools. But there are also various other tools, including those for accessing low-level machine functions, mouse control, and terminate and stay resident programming.

Part One

Learning tools

1

Pascal Tutorial

Program title   Pascal Tutorial   *(Disk 579 and 580)*

Special requirements   There aren't really any requirements. However, you will probably want to make hard copies of the tutorial, which of course will require a printer. If you want to compile the sample programs, you will need a copy of Turbo Pascal 3.0 or later (note the *Turbo*). Other Pascal compilers could be used, but you might need to modify the programs.

If you're new to programming or just new to Pascal, Pascal Tutorial is an excellent place to start: it's a complete course in Pascal programming, consisting of a sixteen-chapter book on disk along with nearly 100 sample Pascal programs. The book centers around the example programs, with the best way to learn being to study the examples and then compile and run them. You can learn even more by making your own modifications and observing the results. The book emphasizes developing a good programming form. Figure 1-1 and FIG. 1-2 show the author's examples of bad and good programming style.

Pascal Tutorial is written specifically for Turbo Pascal but can apply to any version of Pascal in general.

Chapter 12 of the Tutorial refers to some figures that unfortunately cannot be included in the text files. However, a printed copy of Chapter 12 including the figures is available from Coronado Enterprises. In fact, the entire Tutorial is available in printed form (although at an extra cost). See "Registration" at the end of this chapter for more details.

```
program Ugly_Programming_Style;begin  Write('Programming style ')
;Write                   ('is a matter of ');
Writeln('personal choice');Write('Each person ');
Write('can choose ');Writeln
('his own style');Write('He can be ');Write
    ('very clear, or ');
Writeln('extremely messy');end.



( Result of execution

Programming style is a matter of personal choice
Each person can choose his own style
He can be very clear, or extremely messy

}
```

1-1 Bad programming form.

```
program Good_Programming_Style;

begin

    Write('Programming style ');
    Write                 ('is a matter of ');
    Writeln                            ('personal choice');

    Write('Each person ');
    Write                 ('can choose ');
    Writeln                        ('his own style');

    Write('He can be ');
    Write             ('very clear, or ');
    Writeln                            ('extremely messy');
end.


( Result of execution

Programming style is a matter of personal choice
Each person can choose his own style
He can be very clear, or extremely messy

}
```

1-2 Good programming form.

About the author

Gordon Dodrill, the author of these tutorials, began programming in 1961 using Fortran on an IBM 1620. Since then, he has been involved with designing digital logic for satellite application. In 1983 (being somewhat burned out with logic design), he began a study of some of the more recent programming languages and has since made a complete career shift into software development. After learning Pascal, he studied C, followed by Modula-2, Ada, and (more recently) C++. Rather than simply learning the syntax of each new language, he has studied and applied the latest methods of software engineering. Gordon is currently employed by a large research and development laboratory where he continues to study, teach, and apply the newer programming languages.

Getting started

As with any software, you should first backup the distribution diskettes and store the originals away in a safe place. Use only these copies for all operations.

Before you begin studying Pascal, you will want to print out a copy of the tutorial text. The file named PRINTEXT.BAT is designed to help you do this; simply type the name

```
PRINTEXT
```

at the DOS prompt and all of the tutorial text will be printed for you. This batch file uses the executable file named PRNTTEXT.EXE to print the files. PRNTTEXT.EXE inserts 8 spaces at the beginning of each printout line for neat formatting and will print about 100 pages.

If you want a printout of the example Pascal files, you can use the PRINTALL.BAT file included; simply type

```
PRINTALL
```

at the command prompt with the printer on and lots of paper in place (this will print about 150 pages). You might want to edit a copy of the PRINT-ALL.BAT file so that it prints only part of the files initially and prints the remainder only as you come to them in the lessons.

PRINTALL.BAT uses the file LIST.EXE to actually do the printing. LIST.EXE is written in Pascal and compiled with Turbo Pascal (the difference is because Borland International does not require a licensing fee for distributing executable files.)

Tutorial topics

Listed next are the topics covered in the tutorial. The corresponding Pascal example programs are shown with short descriptions.

What is a computer program?

Getting started in Pascal.

TRIVIAL.PAS	The minimum Pascal program.
WRITESM.PAS	Write something out.
WRITEMR.PAS	Write more out.
PASCOMS.PAS	Pascal comments illustration.
GOODFORM.PAS	Good formatting example.
UGLYFORM.PAS	Ugly formatting example.

The simple Pascal data types.

INTVAR.PAS	Integer variables.
INTVAR2.PAS	More integer variables.
ALLVAR.PAS	All simple variable types.
REALMATH.PAS	Real variable math example.

INTMATH.PAS	Integer variable math example.
BOOLMATH.PAS	Boolean variable math example.
CHARDEMO.PAS	Character variable demonstration.
CONVERT.PAS	Data type conversion.
NEWINT4.PAS	New integer types, v4.0 and v5.x
NEWREAL4.PAS	New real types, v4.0 and v5.x

Pascal loops and control structures.

LOOPDEMO.PAS	Loop demonstration.
IFDEMO.PAS	Conditional branching.
LOOPIF.PAS	Loops and Ifs together.
TEMPCONV.PAS	Temperature conversion.
DUMBCONV.PAS	Poor variable names.
REPEATLP.PAS	Repeat until structure.
WHILELP.PAS	While structure.
CASEDEMO.PAS	Case demonstration.
BIGCASE.PAS	Bigger case example

Pascal procedures and functions.

PROCED1.PAS	Simple procedures.
PROCED2.PAS	Procedures with variables.
PROCED3.PAS	Multiple variables.
PROCED4.PAS	Scope of variables.
PROCED5.PAS	Procedure calling procedures.
FUNCTION.PAS	An example function.
RECURSON.PAS	An example with recursion.
FORWARD.PAS	The forward reference.
PROCTYPE.PAS	The procedure type.
FUNCTYPE.PAS	The function type.

Arrays, types, constants, and labels.

ARRAYS.PAS	Simple arrays.
ARRAYS2.PAS	Multiple arrays.
TYPES.PAS	Example of types.
CONSTANT.PAS	Example of constants.
LABELS.PAS	Label illustration.

Strings and string procedures.

STRARRAY.PAS	Pascal strings.
STRINGS.PAS	Turbo Pascal strings.
WHATSTRG.PAS	What is a string?

Scalars, subranges, and sets.

ENTYPES.PAS	Enumerated types.
SUBRANGE.PAS	Scaler operations.
SETS.PAS	Set operations.
FINDCHRS.PAS	Search for characters.

Records.

SMALLREC.PAS	A small record example.
BIGREC.PAS	A large record example.
VARREC.PAS	A variant record example.

Standard input/output.

WRITELNX.PAS	Generalized output statements.
READINT.PAS	Read integers from keyboard.
READREAL.PAS	Read reals from keyboard.
READCHAR.PAS	Read characters from keyboard.
READARRY.PAS	Read an array from keyboard.
READSTRG.PAS	Read a string from keyboard.
PRINTOUT.PAS	Print some data on the printer.

Files.

READFILE.PAS	Read and display this file.
READDISP.PAS	Read and display any file.
READSTOR.PAS	Read and store any file.
READINTS.PAS	Read an integer data file.
INTDATA.TXT	Integer data file.
READDATA.PAS	Read a mixed data file.
REALDATA.TXT	Real data file.
BINOUT.PAS	Write a binary file.
BININ.PAS	Read a binary file.

Pointers and dynamic allocation.

POINT.PAS	First pointer example.
POINT4.PAS	Pointers with ver 4.0 & 5.x.
POINTERS.PAS	Example program with pointers.
DYNREC.PAS	Dynamic record allocation.
LINKLIST.PAS	An example linked list.

Units in Turbo Pascal 4.0 and 5.x

AREAS.PAS	Areas of geometric shapes.
PERIMS.PAS	Perimeters of geometric shapes.
GARDEN.PAS	User of above units.
SHAPES4.PAS	User of above units.

Complete example programs.

AMORT1.PAS	Start of amortization program.
AMORT2.PAS	Better amortization program.
AMORT3.PAS	Usable amortization program.
AMORT4.PAS	Neat amortization program.
AMORT5.PAS	Complete amortization program.
LIST3.PAS	List Pascal programs (v3.0).
LIST4.PAS	List Pascal programs (v4 and v5).
LIST.EXE	Ready to use list program.

TIMEDATE.PAS	Get time and date (v3.0).
TIMEDAT4.PAS	Get time and date (v4 and v5).
SETTIME.PAS	Set a file's time and date.
SHAPES3.PAS	Calculate areas of shapes.
OT3.PAS	Directory list (v3.0).
OT4.PAS	Directory list (v4 and v5).
OT.DOC	How to use OakTree.

Encapsulation and inheritance.

ENCAP1.PAS	First encapsulation.
ENCAP2.PAS	More encapsulation.
INHERIT1.PAS	First inheritance.
VEHICLES.PAS	An object in a unit.
CARTRUCK.PAS	Descendant objects.
INHERIT2.PAS	Inheritance in use.
INHERIT3.PAS	Pointers and arrays.

Virtual methods.

VIRTUAL1.PAS	No virtual yet.
VIRTUAL2.PAS	Virtual methods in use.
VIRTUAL3.PAS	Virtuals and pointers.
PERSON.PAS	An ancestor object.
SUPERVSR.PAS	Descendant objects.
EMPLOYEE.PAS	Using Virtual methods.

Registration

The registration fees are listed here. Coronado Enterprises also has completed tutorials on Ada, Modula-2, C, and C++; you can inquire about them if you are interested.

$39.95 covers the price for the

☐ Registration fee
☐ Printed version of the Pascal tutorial in a loose-leaf binder including pointer diagrams

$20.00 covers the price for the

☐ Registration fee for the Pascal
☐ Printed version of Chapter 12 with the graphics included

$15.00 covers the price for the

☐ Registration fee only

Mail to

Coronado Enterprises
12501 Coronado Ave NE
Albuquerque, NM 87122

2
C and Turbo C Tutorials

Program title   C Tutorial   *(Disk 577 and 578)*
                    Turbo C Tutorial   *(Disk 816 and 817)*

Special requirements   There are no special requirements. However, you will need a printer if you want hard copies. Also, you will find it helpful to have a C compiler (thus allowing you to compile and run the sample programs).

If you're really serious about applications programming, it will be worth your while to learn C. Of all the high-level languages, C compiles into the tightest and fastest code, making it ideal for applications. It is not, however, a beginner's language. Of all the high-level languages, C is also perhaps the least forgiving. If you don't know anything about programming, you will be better off learning the fundamentals with another language like Pascal. (Perhaps you should consider looking at Pascal Tutorial first.)

C Tutorial is written by Gordon Dodrill, the author of Pascal Tutorial, and thus (not surprisingly) is arranged in very much the same format as Pascal Tutorial. Like Pascal Tutorial, C Tutorial relies heavily on example programs, including about 80 of them. C Tutorial addresses the C language in general, while Turbo C Tutorial is aimed specifically towards Borland's Turbo C. Both emphasize MS-DOS applications and are still applicable to C programming with other operating systems.

Getting started

Before you can begin studying C, you will want a printout of the tutorial text; the file PRINTEXT.BAT will do this for you. Simply type the name

    PRINTEXT

at the DOS prompt and the tutorial text will be printed out. PRINTEXT .BAT uses the executable file PRNTTEXT.EXE to print the files, which inserts 8 spaces at the beginning of each printed line for neat formatting. About 115 pages will be printed.

If you want a printout of all of the sample C files, run the PRINT-ALL.BAT file. Simply type

    PRINTALL

at the command prompt with the printer on and lots of paper in place (about 150 pages will be printed). You might want to edit a copy of PRINT-ALL.BAT so that it only prints part of the files initially and prints the remainder only when you come to them in the lessons.

To actually do the printing, PRINTALL.BAT uses the LIST.EXE file, which is a program written in Pascal and compiled with Turbo Pascal (because Borland International does not require a licensing fee for distributing executable files). After you gain experience, you can debug both LIST.C and LISTF.C and then compile them for use with your particular printer. You do not need to print out the C example files, but you might find a hardcopy convenient sometimes.

Tutorial topics

Listed next are the topics covered in the tutorial. The corresponding C example programs are shown with short descriptions.

Getting started.

FIRSTEX.C	The first example program.

Program structure.

TRIVIAL.C	The minimum program.
WRTSOME.C	Write some output.
WRTMORE.C	Write more output.
ONEINT.C	One integer variable.
COMMENTS.C	Comments in C.
GOODFORM.C	Good program style.
UGLYFORM.C	Bad program style.

Program control.

WHILE.C	The While loop.
DOWHILE.C	The Do-While loop.
FORLOOP.C	The For loop.

IFELSE.C	The If and If-Else construct.
BREAKCON.C	The Break and Continue.
SWITCH.C	The Switch construct.
GOTOEX.C	The Goto statement.
TEMPCONV.C	The temperature conversion.
DUMBCONV.C	Poor program style.

Assignment and logical compare.

INTASIGN.C	Integer assignments.
MORTYPES.C	More data types.
LOTTYPES.C	Lots of data types.
COMBINE.C	Combining different types.
COMPARES.C	Logical compares.
CRYPTIC.C	The cryptic constructs.

Functions, variables, and prototyping.

SUMSQRES.C	First functions.
SQUARES.C	Return a value.
FLOATSQ.C	Floating returns.
SCOPE.C	Scope of variables.
RECURSON.C	Simple recursion program.
BACKWARD.C	Another recursion program.
FLOATSQ2.C	Floating returns with prototypes.

Defines and macros.

DEFINE.C	Defines.
MACRO.C	Macros.
ENUM.C	Enumerated type.

Strings and arrays.

CHRSTRG.C	Character strings.
STRINGS.C	More Character strings.
INTARRAY.C	Integer array.
BIGARRAY.C	Many arrays.
PASSBACK.C	Getting data from functions.
MULTIARY.C	Multidimensional arrays.

Pointers.

POINTER.C	Simple pointers.
POINTER2.C	More pointers.
TWOWAY.C	Two-way function data.
FUNCPNT.C	A pointer to a function.

Standard input/output.

SIMPLEIO.C	Simplest standard I/O.
SINGLEIO.C	Single character I/O.
BETTERIN.C	Better form of single I/O.

INTIN.C	Integer input.
STRINGIN.C	String input.
INMEM.C	In-memory I/O conversion.
SPECIAL.C	Standard error output.

File input/output.

FORMOUT.C	Formatted output.
CHAROUT.C	Single character output.
READCHAR.C	Read single characters.
READTEXT.C	Read single words.
READGOOD.C	Better read and display.
READLINE.C	Read a full line.
ANYFILE.C	Read in any file.
PRINTDAT.C	Output to the printer.

Structures.

STRUCT1.C	Minimum structure example.
STRUCT2.C	Array of structures.
STRUCT3.C	Structures with pointers.
NESTED.C	Nested structure.
UNION1.C	An example union.
UNION2.C	Another union example.
BITFIELD.C	Bitfield example.

Dynamic allocation.

DYNLIST.C	Simple dynamic allocation.
BIGDYNL.C	Large dynamic allocation.
DYNLINK.C	Dynamic linked-list program.

Character and bit manipulation.

UPLOW.C	Upper/lowercase text.
CHARCLAS.C	Character classification.
BITOPS.C	Logical bit operations.
SHIFTER.C	Bit-shifting operations.

Example programs.

DOSEX.C	DOS call examples.
WHATNEXT.C	Ask question in batch file.
LIST.C	Source code lister.
VC.C	Visual calculator.

Registration

Registration fees for C Tutorial and Turbo C Tutorial are as follows:

$39.95 covers the price for the

☐ Registration fee

☐ Printed version of the C or Turbo C tutorial in a loose-leaf binder including pointer diagrams
☐ A special discount offer for additional tutorials

$20.00 covers the price for the

☐ Registration fee for the C or Turbo C
☐ Printed version of Chapters 8 and 12 with the graphics included

$15.00 covers the price for the

☐ Registration fee only

Mail to

Coronado Enterprises
12501 Coronado Ave NE
Albuquerque, NM 87122

3
P-ROBOTS

Program title   P-ROBOTS   *(Disk 1386)*

Special requirements   You will need at least 384K of memory and DOS 2.1 or later.

P-ROBOTS (pronounced "pee-robots") is a game based on computer programming in Pascal. To win the game, you must design and program a "robot" that can triumph over similar robots (which are designed and programmed by other programmers) in a real-time battle of wits and flying missiles. You control your robot by writing a procedure in Pascal that specifies your robot's behavior and strategy in its efforts to vanquish up to three other robots in a battle to the death. A variety of predefined P-ROBOTS Pascal functions and procedures allow your robot to track its position on the battlefield, monitor its health or damage condition, and calculate the distance and angle to opponents from its current battlefield position (among other things). Each robot is equipped with a cannon that fires missiles and a motorized drive mechanism that allows it to either close in and kill a hapless opponent or flee from a fierce foe.

    P-ROBOTS offers an excellent way for the novice programmer to sharpen his/her Pascal skills and have fun at the same time. However, P-ROBOTS does assume that the robot designer/programmer already knows the funda-mentals of Pascal programming.

    For the experienced programmer, P-ROBOTS offers a chance to see just how well you program in a programming environment where "bad" code can lead to graphic and ignoble defeat and "brilliant" code can bring triumph and glory.

In addition to being enjoyed in thousands of homes, P-ROBOTS has been successfully used in a number of classroom settings—from high school Pascal programming classes to graduate level courses in Artificial Intelligence. "The competitive environment that P-ROBOTS creates has really sparked my students' desire to learn. Our weekly robot contests are great fun and enjoyed by all—including me," said one high school Pascal teacher. Another teacher has offered his Pascal students a unique reward: any student that can design and program a robot that consistently beats the teacher's robot is excused from taking the final exam.

P-ROBOTS comes with these files on disk:

P-ROBOTS.EXE   The main program executed whenever you hold a P-ROBOTS contest.

PR-DEMO.BAT   A batch file demonstrating a typical P-ROBOTS contest between three robots.

????????.PR   Other Pascal source code files for other robots. All P-ROBOTS robots *must* have .PR file extensions; without it, P-ROBOTS will not compile the robot and enter it in any robot contests.

Getting started

To watch a typical P-ROBOTS contest, just execute the batch file PR-DEMO. What you will see will be the Pascal source code for three robots being read from the disk and compiled by P-ROBOTS. After the program has compiled successfully (without any errors), you then will see a battle between these three robots. The battle will last between one and four minutes, and you will be able to watch the individual robots move around the battlefield, fire their missiles, and get hit when missiles explode too close to them on the screen. (See FIG. 3-1 for a view of the screen and the battlefield.)

The battlefield is 1000×1000 meters in size, with the coordinates (0,0) representing the lower left-hand corner of the screen. The border of the battlefield has a "fence" or "wall" around it that will both stop and damage any robot foolish enough to run into it. On the battlefield, each robot is represented by a number from 1 to 4 (with 4 being the maximum number of robots in any one contest). Flying missiles will be represented on the screen by + symbols, and explosions are represented as a flurry of lines and corners (look back at FIG. 3-1).

Beside the battlefield are several status areas where information about each robot is displayed. The number preceding the robot's name is its symbol on the screen. (For example, the number 2 represents the robot M66 in the earlier display.) The D% field shows the percentage of damage incurred by the robot so far; when the damage percentage reaches 100%, the robot dies. The Sc field shows the direction in degrees (from 0 to 359) that the robot's scanner is currently pointed; the scanner is used both to

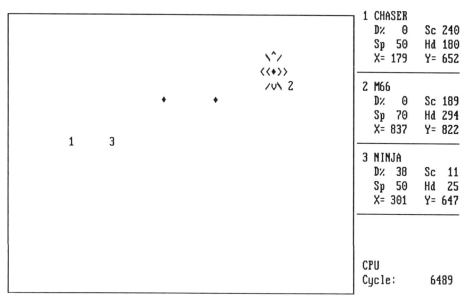

3-1 A typical P-ROBOTS battlefield scene.

detect the presence of enemy robots and to aim missiles at them. The Sp field show the robot's current speed; a speed of 0 means that the robot is standing still, and a speed of 100 (the maximum) suggests a robotic "warp drive." The Hd field show the robot's current heading (i.e., the direction it is moving); like the scanner field, the heading is shown in degrees from 0 to 359. The X= and Y= fields show the robot's current X and Y coordinates (respectively) on the battlefield; the X-axis runs from 0 on the left to 999 on the right side of the battlefield, while the Y-axis runs from 0 at the bottom on the screen to 999 at the top.

All angles or directions in P-ROBOTS are calculated in degrees from 0 to 359 using the traditional compass directions you undoubtedly learned in geometry class. Due east is 0 degrees, while north is 90 degrees (see FIG. 3-2 for help).

3-2 Direction convention used by P-ROBOTS.

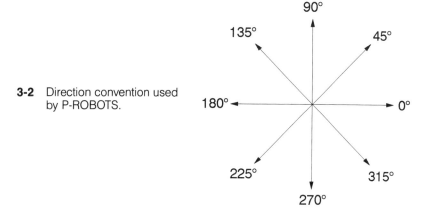

Running a contest

Sooner or later, you will grow tired of just watching the Demo match and will want to see contests between other robots—perhaps even between your own robot creations. There are two types of contests: single games and matches. In single game mode, the game is played with animated "graphics" where the progress of the battle can be watched on the screen. Match play is when you want to run a series of contests (maybe as many as 100) between the same group of robots to see what the winning percentages are for each contestant. Match play does not display the actual battles but just shows the summary of wins and losses as each individual game is played (which makes it ideal for playing overnight).

To simply stop a P-ROBOTS game (either a single game or a match), just hit Ctrl-Break.

To run a single game, just give at the DOS prompt the command

    P-ROBOTS Robot1 Robot2 .. Robot3

where Robot1, Robot2, and Robot3 are the names of your robots. For example, to run a single game between robots Ninja, HotShot, Wimp, and Blaster, you simply would enter the command

    P-ROBOTS NINJA HOTSHOT WIMP BLASTER

Likewise, to run a single game just between HotShot and Wimp, you would enter the command

    P-ROBOTS HOTSHOT WIMP

You also can test your robot against a "default" robot built into the P-ROBOTS program named Target. Target just sits in the center of the battle-field waiting to get shot at. However, Target does shoot back—so be warned that beating Target is not totally a trivial exercise.

Target is an excellent opponent for testing new robots. To test a robot against Target, merely type input the name of that robot; Target is loaded automatically. For example, to test a robot named Fred against Target, just give the command

    P-ROBOTS FRED

Target will be loaded up to fight Fred because no other robots were mentioned in the command.

To invoke a series of contests (i.e., match play), append a /MNNN behind the normal single play command, where NNN represents the number of games you want to play in the match. For example, /M50 would cause 50 games to be played in the match, and /M100 would cause 100 games to be played. Thus, to run a series of 20 games between Ninja, HotShot, Wimp, and Blaster, enter the command

    P-ROBOTS NINJA HOTSHOT WIMP BLASTER /M20

Likewise, to run a series of 10 games just between HotShot and Wimp, enter the command

```
P-ROBOTS HOTSHOT WIMP /M10
```

Important: The actual files on the disk containing the source code for the various robots *must* have a .PR file extension. However, when you invoke the game, you don't need to use the extension when referring to the robots.

Controlling your robot's movement

To move your robot, you must use the special procedure `Drive` that is built into the P-ROBOTS version of the Pascal language. The `Drive` procedure would be used in your program as

```
Drive (degree,speed);
```

This command moves your robot in the direction specified by `degree` and at the speed indicated by the `speed` parameter. The direction is restricted by `Drive` to be between 0 and 359 (i.e., degree := degree MOD 360;) and the speed is restricted to be between 0 and the maximum of 100. Calling the `Drive` procedure with a speed of 0 will stop your robot.

For example,

```
Drive(90,100);    (* drive north at top speed *)
Drive(heading,0); (* slow down and stop *)
```

In an attempt to simulate some degree of reality, a robot's speed does not change instantly but rather must go through periods of acceleration and deceleration. For example, stopping a robot travelling at the maximum speed of 100 will require between 100 and 200 meters of stopping room. Conversely, "flooring" a robot up to a speed of 100 from a standing stop will also take between 100 and 200 meters of running room.

In addition, your robot cannot "turn on a dime." You must be moving at a speed of either 50 or less to change directions. Attempting to turn while going over 50 will "overheat" your robot's drive motor, and your robot will simply coast to a stop on its current heading.

To monitor the status of your movement on the battlefield, the P-ROBOTS version of Pascal has several special built-in functions.

The Speed function returns the current speed of your robot (from 0 to 100). Remember that the value returned by Speed might not always be the same as the last parameter used in the last call to Drive because of acceleration and deceleration.

An example of how the Speed function might be used is as follows:

```
Drive(270,100);           (* start driving, due south *)
;;;                       (* other instructions *)
```

```
IF Speed = 0              (* check if stopped-current
                          speed = 0 *)
   THEN Drive(90,20);     (* Probably, ran into the south
                          border *)
                          (* Go north at speed of 20 *)
```

The Loc_X and Loc_Y functions return your robot's X and Y coordinates (respectively) on the battlefield. The following code demonstrates these functions:

```
Drive (45,50);            (* start driving in north-east-
                          erly direction *)
WHILE (Loc_X < 900) AND (Loc_Y < 900) DO Drive(45,50);
                          (* i.e., just keep driving until
                          we are close to a border *)
Drive (45,0);             (* slow down and stop *)
```

Attacking other robots

The main offensive weapons available to your robot are its scanner and its cannon. Both of these weapons are controlled by using special built-in capabilities of the P-ROBOTS Pascal language.

The scanner is an "electronic eye" enabling your robot to look for enemy robots in any chosen direction from 0 to 359 degrees. The scanner has a maximum resolution of +/– 10 degrees, which allows your robot to quickly scan the battlefield at a low resolution and then use finer resolution to pinpoint a foe's precise position. The scanner would be accessed by a reference to the Scan function, as follows:

```
Scan(degree,resolution)
```

Scan invokes the robot's scanner at the specified degree and resolution, returning an integer value of 0 if no enemy robots are within the scan range or an integer value (greater than 0) representing the distance to the nearest robot in the scan area. The value passed as the parameter degree is restricted to the range of 0 to 359. Likewise, the resolution is restricted to the range of +/– 10 degrees.

Some examples of Scan are as follows:

```
Enemy := Scan(180,10);        (* scans the area from
                              170 to 190 degrees *)
Dist_To_Foe := Scan(180,2);   (* scans from 178 to 182
                              degrees *)
Target_Range := Scan(90,0);   (* scan 90 degrees, with
                              no variance *)
```

Once an enemy robot is found with the scanner, you would use your robot's cannon to fire a missile at the enemy. To fire the cannon, simply use P-ROBOTS special Cannon procedure:

```
Cannon(degree,range);
```

Cannon will fire a missile in the direction specified by the parameter `degree` and to a distance specified by the value of `range` (up to the maximum range of 700). You have an unlimited number of missiles, so you do not have to worry about running out. However, it will take some time to reload between firing missiles; thus, the number of missiles in the air at any one time is limited to two. Also, the cannon is mounted on an independent turret and therefore can fire in any direction, regardless of the robot's current movement direction.

For example, the chunk of code in FIG. 3-3 will cause your robot to constantly scan for enemies and blast away at them as long as they are in sight. When they are no longer in sight (or in range), the scanner will move to the next 20 degree segment of the circle.

```
Angle := 0; (* initialize to east *)
REPEAT
  Enemy_Range := Scan(Angle,10); (* Get range to target -- if any *

  WHILE (Enemy_Range > 40) AND (Enemy_Range <= 700) DO
    BEGIN (* Enemy in sight and in range *)
      Cannon(Angle,Enemy_Range); (* Blast it! *)
      Enemy_Range := Scan(Angle,10); (* Still there? *)
    END;
    Angle := Angle + 20; (* move search to next segment *)
UNTIL Dead or Winner;
```

3-3 Code for a simple robot.

The `Dead` and the `Winner` words in the UNTIL statement are special predefined Boolean functions in P-ROBOTS. `Dead` will have a value of FALSE while your robot is still alive (i.e., its damage is less than 100%) and TRUE when it finally dies. Similarly, `Winner` will be TRUE if your robot is the last survivor of the battle and FALSE otherwise.

If your robot utilized the basic "Sitting Duck" strategy given earlier, its opponents would undoubtedly make short work of it. To improve our strategy, then, your robot needs some way to determine if it is under attack. Fortunately (and not surprisingly), P-ROBOTS has another special function that can assist us—the Damage function. Whenever you use this function in your code, it will return an integer value of your robot's current damage percentage. If this value changes, we then know that the robot is under attack and probably should run for safety.

Using the code in FIG. 3-4 as an example, let's see how the Damage function could be used to make the previous code a little smarter. The Move reference would call a separate procedure (shown a little later) that would move the robot to another hopefully safer position on the battlefield.

```
Old_Damage := Damage; (* Get initial value of damage *)
Angle := 0; (* initialize to east *)
REPEAT
  Enemy_Range := Scan(Angle,10); (* Get range to target -- if any *)
  WHILE (Enemy_Range > 40) AND (Enemy_Range <= 700) DO
    BEGIN (* Enemy in sight and in range *)
      Cannon(Angle,Enemy_Range); (* Blast it! *)
      Enemy_Range := Scan(Angle,10); (* Still there? *)
    END;
  Angle := Angle + 20; (* move search to next segment *)
  IF Damage > Old_Damage THEN
    BEGIN (* Under attack *)
      Old_Damage := Damage; (* Get latest Damage value *)
      Move; (* Get out of here!! *)
    END;
UNTIL Dead or Winner;
```

3-4 This robot is a little smarter.

Other special P-ROBOTS functions and procedures

Time

The built-in Time function returns the current time as measured by the P-ROBOTS' CPU cycles. By using this function, you should be able to calculate the speed of your enemies. The value returned by this function is restricted to being in the range 0 to 32767 and when it gets to 32767 it starts again at zero. An example of how you might get this value is as follows:

```
Start_Time := Time;
```

Distance

Because your robot will frequently find it useful to be able to calculate distances from one point on the battlefield to another, P-ROBOTS provides a built-in function to do so:

```
Distance(X1,Y1,X2,Y2)
```

This code would return the integer distance from the point (X1,Y1) to the point (X2,Y2).

Angle_To

The Angle_To function will return the angle to a point on the battlefield from your robot's current position. The value returned will be an integer in degrees from 0 to 359. As an example of how both the Distance and Angle_To functions might be used, consider the procedure in FIG. 3-5 that will move your robot to the point (X,Y) on the battlefield.

```
PROCEDURE GoTo(X, Y : Integer);(* Go to location X,Y *)
  VAR
    Heading  : Integer;
BEGIN       (* Find the heading we need to get to the desired spot. *)
  Heading := Angle_To(X, Y);

  (* Keep traveling at top speed until we are within 150 meters. *)
  WHILE (Distance(Loc_X, Loc_Y, X, Y) > 150) DO Drive(Heading, 100);

  (* Cut speed, and creep the rest of the way. *)
  WHILE (Distance(Loc_X, Loc_Y, X, Y) > 20) DO Drive(Heading, 20);

  (* Stop driving, should coast to a stop. *)
  Drive(Heading, 0); (* I.E., Stop *)
END; (* GoTo(X,Y) *)
```

3-5 This code will move the robot to (X,Y) using the Distance and Angle_To functions.

Random

The function Random(limit) returns a random integer between 0 and limit. As an example, the procedure in FIG. 3-6 will move your robot to a random spot on the battlefield.

Notice that the Move procedure makes use of the GoTo(X,Y) procedure developed in the previous example.

```
PROCEDURE Move; (* Move to a random spot on the playing field. *)
  VAR
    x, y      : Integer;
BEGIN
  x := Random(900) + 50;
  y := Random(900) + 50;
  GoTo(x, y);
END; (* Move *)
```

3-6 Use of the Random function.

Trig functions

P-ROBOTS has several standard Trig functions that will be of value to a clever robot. For example,

Sin(degree)

will return the real value of the Sin of an angle of degree (where degree is an integer from 0 to 359). Likewise,

Cos(degree)

will return the real value of the Cos of an angle of degree (where degree is an integer from 0 to 359). In addition,

ArcTan(ratio)

will give the angle in integer degrees that has a Tan of ratio.

Inflicting damage

Your robot can be damaged by only two things: collisions and missiles. The level of damage is as follows:

2%   A collision with either another robot (with both robots in a collision receiving damage) or with one of the battlefield walls. A collision also causes the robot to stop cold (i.e., its speed is reduced instantly to 0).

3%   A missile explodes within a 40-meter radius.

5%   A missile explodes within a 20-meter radius.

10%   A missile explodes within a 5-meter radius.

Damage is inflicted on ALL robots (including the aggressor) within these distances. Thus, even if one of your *own* missiles explodes within 40 meters of your robot, your robot will still take damage. Thus, using sloppy programming logic, you can nuke your own robot—effectively committing suicide—by ordering it to fire missiles too close to itself. One example of treacherous code is as follows:

```
Drive(Angle,100);
WHILE (Loc_X < 999) DO Cannon(Angle,Scan(Angle,10));
```

Damage is cumulative and cannot be repaired. However, a robot does not lose any mobility, fire potential, etc., at high damage levels. In other words, a robot at 99% damage performs just as well as a robot with no damage. However, when the damage level reaches 100%, your robot is dead and out of the current competition.

Putting it all together

Now that we know the basics, let's look at a simple robot. Figure 3-7 contains the code for a robot named HotShot.

Robot programming rules

HotShot in FIG. 3-7 demonstrates several standards for programming a robot. All robots must be modeled after these following standards:

- Your robot should be in a "self-contained" procedure with the following basic structure:

```
PROCEDURE RoboName;
{"Global" variables}
FUNCTION A;
    ....
PROCEDURE B;
    ....
FUNCTION Z;
```

```
PROCEDURE HotShot;
(* Author: David Malmberg

Strategy:  Stay in one place.  Find a foe.  Take a shot.
Keep improving aim and shooting until foe is lost from sights.
Then move sights (scanning) to adjacent target area.  If hit,
then move to another random position on playing field.  If the
Robot scans two complete circles (720 degrees) without finding
a foe in shooting range, move to another spot on the field.
(This will avoid "stand-offs" where opponents stay just out of
range of one another.)

This Robot should be VERY effective against foes which are
stopped or are moving slowly.  It will be less effective
against Robots traveling at high speeds.    *)

VAR (* HotShot "Global" variables *)
  Angle,          (* Scanning angle *)
  Last_Damage,  (* Robot's last damage value *)
  Range,          (* Range/Distance to foe *)
  Sweep,          (* "Sweep count" when = 36, have scanned 720 degrees *)
  Delta           (* Scanning arc *)
                : Integer;

  PROCEDURE GoTo(X, Y : Integer);
    (* Go to location X,Y on playing field. *)
    VAR
      Heading  : Integer;
  BEGIN        (* Find the heading we need to get to the desired spot. *)
    Heading := Angle_To(X, Y);

    (* Keep traveling at top speed until we are within 150 meters. *)
    WHILE (Distance(Loc_X, Loc_Y, X, Y) > 150) DO Drive(Heading, 100);

    (* Cut speed, and creep the rest of the way. *)
    WHILE (Distance(Loc_X, Loc_Y, X, Y) > 20) DO Drive(Heading, 20);

    (* Stop driving, should coast to a stop. *)
    Drive(Heading, 0); (* I.E., Stop *)
  END; (* GoTo(X,Y) *)

FUNCTION Hurt  : Boolean;
  (* Checks if Robot has incurred any new damage. *)
  VAR
    Curr_Damage  : Integer;
    Answer       : Boolean;
BEGIN
    Curr_Damage := Damage;
    Answer := (Curr_Damage > Last_Damage);
    Last_Damage := Curr_Damage;
    Hurt := Answer;
END; (* Hurt *)

PROCEDURE Move;
  (* Move to a random spot on the playing field. *)
  VAR
    x, y       : Integer;
BEGIN
```

3-7 A complete robot.

BEGIN {RoboName Main}

....

END; {RoboName Main}

Failure to follow this basic structure will send the P-ROBOTS program as well as your robot to a fiery death.

- A robot should have its procedure named *exactly* the same as the file containing the code for the robot, except for the .PR extension. (For example, the procedure for the HotShot robot is named "Hot-Shot" and is in a file named HOTSHOT.PR.) Again, failure to follow this rule will crash your robot program.

- In the "main" routine for your robot, you must have some kind of "infinite" loop (i.e., a loop repeated endlessly). In the sample robot HOTSHOT, this loop is the REPEAT ... UNTIL structure:

```
REPEAT (* Until Dead or Winner *)
....
UNTIL Dead OR Winner;
```

Another infinite loop that works equally well is as follows:

```
WHILE (NOT Dead) AND (NOT Winner) DO
BEGIN
....
END;
```

In addition, your robot source code should be very well documented with comments.

Advanced P-ROBOT features

The latest versions of P-ROBOT include many advanced features:

- Animation speed options
- Protective shields
- Fuel constraints
- Robot teams
- Obstructions on the battlefield
- Intelligence options

Note: All of these new features are optional. Your old version 1.0 robots can still be used just as they have always been used.

Controlling the animation speed

Because not all computers operate at the same speed, it is very desirable to be able to control the animation speed of the robot contest. You can do this using another command line parameter, the /SN parameter (where N can be either 1, 2, 3, or 4). A value of 1 corresponds to the slowest animation speed, while 4 corresponds to the fastest. Normally, the default setting is at 4 (i.e., the fastest speed), which will typically look fine on an 8086 or 80286 computer. If you are using a 386 machine, however, you will probably want to use one of the slower animation speeds. As an example, to run a single game between the robots Ninja, HotShot, Wimp, and Blaster at a moderately slow animation speed (let's choose a speed of 2), just enter the command

```
P-ROBOTS NINJA HOTSHOT WIMP BLASTER /S2
```

If you are playing a series of contests (i.e., match play), you should not slow down the speed because these games are not displayed or animated anyway.

Protective shields

In P-ROBOTS 2.0, your robot can use a protective shield with the command RaiseShield. When your robot's shield is up, your robot will not incur any damage from collisions or cannon explosions. The shield may then be lowered with the command LowerShield. The status of your robot's shield can be determined by using the built-in Boolean function ShieldRaised, which will return a value of TRUE or FALSE based on your robot's shield condition. For example, you might want to use the following statement in a robot program:

```
IF NOT ShieldRaised THEN RaiseShield;
```

Of course, there must be a catch to using your Shield; otherwise, every robot would run around as invulnerable as Superman, completely negating the purpose of the game. As explained in the next section, your robot begins with a limited amount of fuel that powers its movement, attacks, and defenses: using the Shield extensively will drain the robot's fuel and eventually leave it as a defenseless pile of scrap metal.

Note: Unlike the expansive Starship Enterprise, your robot has only one Shield (i.e., singular), not multiple Shields (plural). If you use "Shields" (plural) in your robot programs, you will get a compiler error for an "UNKNOWN IDENTIFIER."

Fuel constraints

At one time, the earlier versions of P-ROBOTS favored robots that used brute force rather than raw cunning: all other things being equal, robots that fired in quantity seemed to beat robots that fired less but more accurately. In an attempt to even up this game imbalance, the P-ROBOTS programmers have added fuel constraints to the confusion. Under these constraints, robots that fire indiscriminately will waste valuable fuel, ultimately running out of power and finding themselves defenseless at the mercy of their wiser and more fuel-efficient opponents.

When you run a contest using the fuel constraint option, each robot will begin with 1000 "jiggers" of fuel. During the contest, fuel is used at the following rates:

- Firing a missile takes 3 jiggers
- Traveling 100 meters takes 5 jiggers
- Throwing up a shield for 200 CPU cycles takes 1 jigger

In addition, the Shield will use more fuel if it must absorb damage. If your robot's Shield is up and your robot would have incurred damage from a missile or a collision, the Shield will use fuel jiggers equal to twice the amount of damage your robot would have taken had its Shield been down. For example, with the Shield up, absorbing a direct missile hit uses 20 jiggers of fuel (10% damage for a direct hit times 2 equals 20 jiggers); likewise, absorbing the impact of a collision with another robot uses 4 jiggers of fuel (because 2% damage for a collision times 2 equals 4 jiggers). Thus, considering this, your robot should prudently avoid missiles and collisions even if its Shield is raised.

The number of jiggers of each robot's fuel is displayed continuously next to the robot's name on the screen. This value also can be accessed from within a robot program by using the built-in function Fuel. For example, you might want to use the following logic in a robot program to begin a special "End-Game" strategy when your fuel gets low:

```
IF Fuel < 200 THEN End_Game;
```

Several other built-in P-ROBOTS functions might be useful when you have fuel constraints. Specifically, LimitedFuel will return a TRUE or FALSE based upon whether the contest your robot is playing in has fuel constraints or not. The built-in function Meters is like an odometer on a car, only it returns the number of meters your robot has traveled since the beginning of the contest. For example, you might want to use the following command in your robot's program to invoke your "End-Game" strategy:

```
IF LimitedFuel
    THEN IF (Meters > 20000) OR (Fuel < 200) THEN End_Game;
```

To run a robot contest with fuel constraints, you must use an /F command-line parameter when invoking the contest. Thus, to run a single game with fuel constraints between the robots Ninja, Wimp, and Blaster, you would enter the following command at the DOS prompt:

```
P-ROBOTS NINJA WIMP BLASTER /F
```

If you want to run a series of 50 matches with fuel constraints between the same group of robots, you would add an /M50 parameter to the command:

```
P-ROBOTS NINJA WIMP BLASTER /F /M50
```

Running out of fuel   When your robot runs out of fuel, it reacts similarly to a car without gas: it stops cold and can no longer move, it can no longer fire its cannon, and it can no longer maintain a raised shield. In other words, it is totally and absolutely defenseless. Other robots still possessing fuel will make quick work of any robot unfortunate enough to become such a "sitting duck." If all of the robots in the game run out of fuel, the game ends and the robot with the least damage (i.e., the strongest of the survivors) is declared the winner.

An example using a shield and fuel

Figure 3-8 provides a coded example of how the HotShot robot might be modified to use its shield and consider fuel constraints.

```
PROCEDURE HotShot2;
{
Author: David Malmberg

Strategy:  Stay in one place.  Find a foe.  Take a shot.
Keep improving aim and shooting until foe is lost from sights.
Then move sights (scanning) to adjacent target area.
If the Robot scans a complete circle (360 degrees) without
finding a foe in shooting range, move to another spot on the
field.  (This will avoid "stand-offs" where opponents stay
just out of range of one another.)  RaiseShield when standing
still and lower them when moving.

When damage gets to 70 (or more) or fuel (if using fuel) gets
below 200 adopt an "End-Game" strategy of moving to the lower
left corner, lower shield, and continue to scan and shoot in
the corner's 90 degree range.

This Robot should be VERY effective against foes which
are stopped or are moving slowly.  It will be less effective
against Robots traveling at high speeds.

 This Robot has been designed to utilize Fuel (if it is available)
to power its Shield.  However, it has NOT been designed to deal
effectively with Obstructions.
}

VAR { HotShot2 "Global" variables }
  Angle, { Scanning angle }
  Range, { Range/Distance to foe }
  Sweep, { "Sweep count" -- when = 18, Robot has scanned 360 degrees }
  Delta            : Integer; { Scanning arc }

  PROCEDURE GOTO(x, y : Integer);
    { Go to location X,Y on playing field. }
  VAR Heading      : Integer;
  BEGIN
    { Find the heading we need to get to the desired spot. }
    Heading := Angle_To(x, y);

    { Keep traveling at top speed until we are within 150 meters }
    WHILE (distance(loc_x, loc_y, x, y) > 150) DO drive(Heading, 100);

    { Cut speed, and creep the rest of the way. }
    WHILE (distance(loc_x, loc_y, x, y) > 20) DO drive(Heading, 20);

    { Stop driving, should coast to a stop. }
    drive(Heading, 0); {I.E., Stop}
  END; {GoTo(X,Y)}

  PROCEDURE Move;
    { Move to a random spot on the playing field. }
  VAR x, y         : Integer;
```

3-8 This robot uses a shield and considers the fuel constraint.

3-8 Continued.

```
BEGIN
  Sweep := 0; { Reset Sweep counter to zero. }
  x := Random(900)+50;
  y := Random(900)+50;
  GOTO(x, y);
END; {Move}

PROCEDURE Aim( VAR Ang : Integer; VAR Arc : Integer);
  (* Improve aim by doing a binary search of the target area.
     I.E., divide the target area in two equal pieces and redefine
     the target area to be the piece where the foe is found.
     If the foe is not found, expand the search area to the
     maximum arc of plus or minus 10 degrees. *)
BEGIN
   (* Divide search area in two. *)
   Arc := Arc DIV 2;
   (* Check piece "below" target angle. *)
   IF Scan(Ang - Arc, Arc) <> 0
     (* If foe found, redefine target angle. *)
     THEN Ang := Ang - Arc
     (* If not found, then check piece "above" target angle. *)
     ELSE IF Scan(Ang + Arc, Arc) <> 0
            (* If foe found, redefine target angle. *)
            THEN Ang := Ang + Arc
            ELSE Arc := 10;
   (* If foe not found in either piece, expand search arc to +/- 10 *)
END; (* Aim *)

PROCEDURE End_Game;
  Special strategy for "End Game" }
BEGIN {End_Game}
  GoTo(0,0); {Lower Left Corner}
  Angle := 10; {Sweep arc from 0 to 90 degrees only}
  REPEAT
    Delta := 10; { Start with widest scanning arc. }
    Range := scan(Angle, Delta);
    WHILE (Range > 40) AND (Range < 700) DO
      { Must be far enough away to avoid self-damage. }
      BEGIN
        Aim(Angle, Delta); { Improve aim. }
        cannon(Angle, Range); { Fire!! }
        Range := scan(Angle, Delta); { Is foe still in sights? }
      END;
    Angle := Angle+20; { Look in adjacent target area. }
    IF Angle > 90 THEN Angle := 10;
  UNTIL Dead OR Winner;
END; {End_Game}

BEGIN {HotShot2 Main}
  RaiseShield;
  Angle := 0;
  GoTo(500, 500); { Move to center of field. }
  Sweep := 0; { Initialize Sweep counter to zero. }
  REPEAT { Until Dead or Winner }
    Delta := 10; { Start with widest scanning arc. }
    Range := scan(Angle, Delta);
    WHILE (Range > 40) AND (Range < 700) DO
      { Must be far enough away to avoid self-damage. }
      BEGIN
        Sweep := 0; { Found foe, so reset Sweep to zero }
        Aim(Angle, Delta); { Improve aim. }
        cannon(Angle, Range); { Fire!! }
        Range := scan(Angle, Delta); { Is foe still in sights? }
      END;
    Angle := Angle+20; { Look in adjacent target area. }
    Sweep := 0; (* Reset Sweep counter to zero. *)
    x := Random(900) + 50;
    y := Random(900) + 50;
    GoTo(x, y);
END; (* Move *)
```

```
PROCEDURE Aim( VAR Ang : Integer; VAR Arc : Integer);
  (* Improve aim by doing a binary search of the target area.
     I.E., divide the target area in two equal pieces and redefine
     the target area to be the piece where the foe is found.
     If the foe is not found, expand the search area to the
     maximum arc of plus or minus 10 degrees. *)
  BEGIN
    (* Divide search area in two. *)
    Arc := Arc DIV 2;
    (* Check piece "below" target angle. *)
    IF Scan(Ang - Arc, Arc) <> 0
      (* If foe found, redefine target angle. *)
      THEN Ang := Ang - Arc
      (* If not found, then check piece "above" target angle. *)
      ELSE IF Scan(Ang + Arc, Arc) <> 0
             (* If foe found, redefine target angle. *)
             THEN Ang := Ang + Arc
             ELSE Arc := 10;
    (* If foe not found in either piece, expand search arc to +/- 10 *)
  END; (* Aim *)

BEGIN (* HotShot Main *)
  (* Start scanning for foes in center of field. *)
  Angle := Angle_To(500, 500);
  Sweep := 0; (* Initialize Sweep counter to zero. *)
  REPEAT (* Until Dead or Winner *)
    Delta := 10; (* Start with widest scanning arc. *)
    Range := Scan(Angle, Delta);
    WHILE (Range > 40) AND (Range < 701) DO
      (* Must be far enough away to avoid self-damage. *)
      BEGIN
        Sweep := 0; (* Found foe, so reset Sweep to zero *)
        Aim(Angle, Delta); (* Improve aim. *)
        Cannon(Angle, Range); (* Fire!! *)
        Range := Scan(Angle, Delta); (* Is foe still in sights? *)
      END;
    Angle := Angle + 20; (* Look in adjacent target area. *)
    Sweep := Sweep + 1;
    IF Hurt OR (Sweep = 36) THEN Move;
    (* If hit or have scanned two full circles, move elsewhere. *)
  UNTIL Dead OR Winner;
END; (* HotShot Main *)
    Sweep := Sweep+1;
    IF Sweep >= 18 THEN
      BEGIN { If robot has scanned a full circle, move elsewhere. }
        LowerShield; {Don't need shield (as much) when moving}
        Move;
      END;
    RaiseShield; {Standing still so use shield}
    {"End" game strategy}
    IF (Fuel < 200) OR (Damage > 70) THEN End_Game;
  UNTIL Dead OR Winner;
END; {HotShot2 Main}
```

Robot teams

One of the most intriguing features of P-ROBOTS is the idea of allowing two robots to act as members of the same team and communicate with each other during the course of the battle.

Note: For consistency and better understanding, if your robot is a member of a two-robot team, the other team member is referred to as your robot's *Ally*. Similarly, within your Ally's robot program, your robot would be referred to as its Ally.

Robot teams can use the following special built-in P-ROBOTS functions:

AllyLoc_X	Returns the current X coordinate of your Ally.
AllyLoc_Y	Returns the current Y coordinate of your Ally.
AllyDamage	Returns your Ally's current Damage level.
AllySpeed	Returns your Ally's current Speed.
AllyHeading	Returns your Ally's current Heading.
AllyMeters	Returns your Ally's current Meters.
AllyFuel	Returns your Ally's current Fuel level.
AllyShieldRaised	Returns TRUE or FALSE depending upon whether your Ally's shield is raised or not.
AllyDead	Returns TRUE or FALSE depending upon whether your Ally is Dead or not.
AllyAlive	Returns TRUE or FALSE depending upon whether your Ally is Alive or not.

In addition to using these built-in functions to examine your Ally's status, your robot (in v2.0) can exchange information by accessing the "global" array COMM[1..20]. All robots may access this array, both to retrieve and store values in any of its 20 elements. Be warned however, that stuffing "garbage" into COMM's elements to sabotage the communication between opposing team members is NOT considered fair play!!

One other piece of information is necessary in order for two robots to work together effectively as a team—there must be some way to tell if a robot is friend or foe. To do this, define a special function called Object-Scanned, which is reset whenever your robot scans the battlefield. The value returned by ObjectScanned will be one of four specially defined values/constants: Nothing, Ally, Enemy, or Obstruction. For example, when part of a team, to make sure that you only fire your cannon at enemy robots, you might want to use statements like the following:

```
Dist := Scan(Angle, Delta);
IF ObjectScanned = Enemy THEN Cannon(Angle, Dist);
{Blast 'Em!!}
```

To tell the P-ROBOTS compiler that you have an Ally and are part of a team, you must include a statement within your robot's program that looks like this:

```
TeamAlly = "TagTeam2";
```

This statement tells the P-ROBOTS compiler that your Ally is named "TagTeam2". To work correctly, the robot TagTeam2 must have a similar statement within its program that identifies your robot's name as its Ally.

An example of a robot team Figure 3-9 is an example of one member of a robot team. Notice that this robot and its Ally (named "TagTeam2") communicate by passing information through COMM[10] and COMM[11].

```
PROCEDURE TagTeam1;

TeamAlly = "TagTeam2";   (* This statement MUST be included for teams!! *)

{
 Author: David Malmberg

  Strategy: Go to a random corner, raise shield, and blast away at any
            robot in range.  Improve aim after every successful scan.
            If the robot scans 20 times unsuccessfully, move to another
            random corner.  Lower shields when moving; raise them when
            stopped.

            This robot can act individually or as part of a team with
            another robot that follows an identical strategy, i.e.,
            TagTeam2.  If operating as a team, the two robots communicate
            their corners to each other by setting COMM[10] to TagTeam1's
            corner and COMM[11] to TagTeam2's corner.  They try to always
            pick different random corners.  Operating from different
            corners, the two robots should be able to cover most of the
            battlefield very well.

            WARNING: This Robot has NOT been designed to deal with
            Obstructions effectively.  However, it has been designed to
            use its Shield (if possible).
}

CONST
  NW_Corner = 1;
  NE_Corner = 2;
  SW_Corner = 3;
  SE_Corner = 4;

VAR { TagTeam1 "Global" variables }
  CornerX : ARRAY[1..4] OF Integer; {X coordinate of Corners}
  CornerY : ARRAY[1..4] OF Integer; {Y coordinate of Corners}
  StartAngle : ARRAY[1..4] OF Integer; {Starting scan angles for Corners}
  Corner, { Current Corner }
  Times,  { Number of times robot has scanned without success for enemy }
  Angle,  { Scanning angle }
  Delta,  { Scanning angle width }
  Range   { Range/Distance to foe }  : Integer;

  PROCEDURE Initialize;
  { Set up Corner data }
  BEGIN
    CornerX[NW_Corner] := 10;
    CornerY[NW_Corner] := 990;
    StartAngle[NW_Corner] := 270;

    CornerX[NE_Corner] := 990;
    CornerY[NE_Corner] := 990;
    StartAngle[NE_Corner] := 180;

    CornerX[SW_Corner] := 10;
    CornerY[SW_Corner] := 10;
    StartAngle[SW_Corner] := 0;
    CornerX[SE_Corner] := 990;
    CornerY[SE_Corner] := 10;
    StartAngle[SE_Corner] := 90;
  END; {Initialize}

  PROCEDURE GOTO(x, y : Integer);
    { Go to location X,Y on playing field. }
  VAR Heading    : Integer;
  BEGIN
    LowerShield; {Moving target is hard to hit - so lower shield}

    { Find the heading we need to get to the desired spot. }
    Heading := Angle_To(x, y);
```

3-9 A robot tag-team.

3-9 Continued.

```
    { Keep traveling at top speed until we are within 150 meters }
    WHILE (distance(loc_x, loc_y, x, y) > 150) DO Drive(Heading, 100);

    { Cut speed, and creep the rest of the way. }
    WHILE (distance(loc_x, loc_y, x, y) > 20) DO Drive(Heading, 20);

    { Stop driving, should coast to a stop. }
    Drive(Heading, 0); {I.E., Stop}

    RaiseShield; {Still target is easy to hit - so raise shield}
  END; {GoTo(X,Y)}

  PROCEDURE Aim( VAR Ang : Integer; VAR Arc : Integer);
  (* Improve aim by doing a binary search of the target area.
     I.E., divide the target area in two equal pieces and redefine
     the target area to be the piece where the foe is found.
     If the foe is not found, expand the search area to the
     maximum arc of plus or minus 10 degrees. *)
  BEGIN
    Arc := Arc DIV 2; (* Divide search area in two. *)
    (* Check piece "below" target angle. *)
    IF Scan(Ang - Arc, Arc) <> 0
      (* If foe found, redefine target angle. *)
      THEN Ang := Ang - Arc
      (* If not found, then check piece "above" target angle. *)
      ELSE IF Scan(Ang + Arc, Arc) <> 0
              (* If foe found, redefine target angle. *)
              THEN Ang := Ang + Arc
              ELSE Arc := 10;
    (* If foe not found in either piece, expand search arc to +/- 10 *)
  END; (* Aim *)

PROCEDURE Do_Corner;
{ Scan and shoot from corner }
BEGIN {Do_Corner}
  Times := 0; {Count of unsuccessful scans}
  Angle := StartAngle[Corner] + 10; {Starting angle for scanning}
  REPEAT
    Delta := 10; { Start with widest scanning arc. }
    Range := scan(Angle, Delta);
    WHILE (Range > 40) AND (Range < 700) DO
      { Must be far enough away to avoid self-damage. }
      BEGIN
        Aim(Angle, Delta); { Improve aim. }
        IF ObjectScanned = Enemy THEN cannon(Angle, Range); { Fire!! }
        Range := scan(Angle, Delta); { Is foe still in sights? }
      END;
    Angle := Angle + 20; { Look in adjacent target area. }
    IF (Angle > (StartAngle[Corner] + 90))
      THEN Angle := StartAngle[Corner] + 10;
    Times := Times + 1;
  UNTIL Times > 20; { Leave after 20 unsuccessful scans }
END; {Do_Corner}

BEGIN {TagTeam1 Main}
  Initialize;
  COMM[11] := 0; {Set Ally's corner (if any) to zero}
  COMM[10] := 0; {Communicate my corner to Ally}
  REPEAT
    REPEAT
      Corner := Random(3) + 1; {Pick a corner}
    UNTIL Corner <> COMM[11]; {Need different corner than Ally}
    COMM[10] := Corner; {Communicate my corner to Ally (if any)}
    GoTo(CornerX[Corner], CornerY[Corner]);
    { Move to selected corner. }
    Do_Corner;
  UNTIL Dead OR Winner;
END; {TagTeam1 Main}
```

Obstructions on the battlefield

Another feature of P-ROBOTS is the possibility of randomly placed Obstructions on the battlefield. This option is selected by using the /ON command-line parameter, where N can be 1, 2, or 3—corresponding to 1, 2, or 3 Obstructions. Each Obstruction will be a randomly sized and placed rectangle.

Be warned however, that using Obstructions in your battles will slow down the speed of the battle considerably. The logic required for P-ROBOTS to deal with Obstructions is fairly extensive and very computationally intense. Thus, the more Obstructions your battle has, the slower it will run.

If your robot runs into one of these Obstructions, it will be stopped cold and incur Damage (if its Shield is down), just as if it ran into one of the battlefield walls. A scanner will not be able to see beyond an Obstruction, nor can the robot shoot a missile past an Obstruction. Therefore, a robot can "hide" from enemy scanners and missile by "hugging" the walls of an Obstruction. More often than not, a scanner will only "see" the Obstruction and not the robot.

Obstructions add a whole new dimension to the possible problems and opportunities that a robot may face.

Your robot will be able to determine where the Obstructions are by scanning and then checking the value returned by the function Object-Scanned. For example, you might use the following Boolean function to determine if the direction your robot is traveling (denoted below by the variable Heading) is clear of Obstructions for the next 100 meters:

```
FUNCTION ClearAhead : Boolean;
BEGIN
    ClearAhead := (Scan(Heading,2) > 100)
        OR (ObjectScanned <> Obstruction);
END; {ClearAhead}
```

An example dealing with obstructions   Figure 3-10 is our old friend, Hot-Shot, adapted to deal with the problem of Obstructions by using logic to move around them. Notice, that we can no longer use the same routine we have been using to go to point (X,Y) on the battlefield—now, the chosen point could be inside an Obstruction and our robot would commit suicide by repeatedly "banging its head" against the Obstruction's wall. To see a solution to this problem, look specifically at the procedure Ramble in the listing.

Intelligence options

P-ROBOTS also allows you to vary the intelligence of your robots' "on-board" computers. You can select this option by using the /IN command-line parameter, where N can be an integer from 1 to 10. What this option

```
PROCEDURE HotShot3;
(
 Author: David Malmberg

 Strategy:  Stay in one place.  Find a foe.  Take a shot.
 Keep improving aim and shooting until foe is lost from sights.
 Then move sights (scanning) to adjacent target area.
 If the Robot scans a complete circle (360 degrees) without
 finding a foe in shooting range, move to another spot on the
 field.  (This will avoid "stand-offs" where opponents stay
 just out of range of one another.)  RaiseShield (if available)
 when standing still and lower them when moving.

 When damage gets to 70 (or more) or fuel (if using fuel) gets
 below 200 adopt an "End-Game" strategy of moving to the lower
 left corner, lower shield, and continue to scan and shoot in
 the corner's 90 degree range.

 This Robot should be VERY effective against foes which
 are stopped or are moving slowly.  It will be less effective
 against Robots traveling at high speeds.

 This Robot has been designed to utilize Fuel (if it is available)
 to power its Shield.  It has also been designed to deal with
 Obstructions (if any) by moving around them.
)

VAR ( HotShot3 "Global" variables )
  Angle, ( Scanning angle )
  Range, ( Range/Distance to foe )
  Sweep, ( "Sweep count" -- when = 18, Robot has scanned 360 degrees )
  Delta       : Integer; ( Scanning arc )

  PROCEDURE GOTO(X, Y : Integer);
    ( Go to location X,Y on playing field. )
  VAR Heading    : Integer;
  BEGIN
  ( WARNING:  If the point X,Y is inside an Obstruction then )
  ( executing this routine will cause the Robot to commit )
  ( suicide by repeatedly running into the wall of the Obstruction. )

    ( Find the heading we need to get to the desired spot. )
    Heading := Angle_To(x, y);

    ( Keep traveling at top speed until we are within 150 meters )
    WHILE (distance(loc_x, loc_y, x, y) > 150) DO drive(Heading, 100);

    ( Cut speed, and creep the rest of the way. )
    WHILE (distance(loc_x, loc_y, x, y) > 20) DO drive(Heading, 20);

    ( Stop driving, should coast to a stop. )
    drive(Heading, 0); (I.E., Stop)
  END; (GoTo(X,Y))

  PROCEDURE Ramble(X, Y : Integer);
    ( Move to X, Y (if possible) on the playing field )
    ( by avoiding Obstructions - if any.               )

VAR Heading, Tries, Dist : Integer;
BEGIN
  Tries := 0;
  Heading := Angle_To(X, Y);
  Drive(Heading, 50); (Start off toward X,Y)
  Dist := Scan(Heading, 5);
  REPEAT
    IF ObjectScanned = Obstruction
      THEN BEGIN
```

3-10 How a robot can handle obstructions.

```
        REPEAT
          Heading := Heading + 10;
          Dist := Scan(Heading, 5);
        UNTIL ObjectScanned <> Obstruction;
        Drive(Heading, 50); {Minimum speed to turn freely}
      END;
    Heading := Angle_To(X, Y);
    Dist := Scan(Heading, 5);
    Tries := Tries + 1;
  UNTIL (ObjectScanned <> Obstruction) OR (Tries > 20);
  IF (ObjectScanned <> Obstruction) THEN GOTO(X,Y);
END; {Ramble}

PROCEDURE Move;
  { Move to a random spot on the playing field. }
VAR x, y         : Integer;
BEGIN
  Sweep := 0; { Reset Sweep counter to zero. }
  x := Random(900)+50;
  y := Random(900)+50;
  Ramble(x, y);
END; {Move}

PROCEDURE Aim(VAR Ang : Integer; VAR Arc : Integer);
{
 Improve aim by doing a binary search of the target area.
 I.E., divide the target area in two equal pieces and redefine
 the target area to be the piece where the foe is found.
 If the foe is not found, expand the search area to the
 maximum arc of plus or minus 10 degrees.
}
BEGIN
  IF ObjectScanned = Enemy
    THEN BEGIN
      Arc := Arc DIV 2; { Divide search area in two. }
      IF scan(Ang-Arc, Arc) <> 0 { Check piece "below" target angle. }
        THEN Ang := Ang-Arc { If foe found, redefine target angle. }
        ELSE IF scan(Ang+Arc, Arc) <> 0 { Check piece "above" Ang. }
          THEN Ang := Ang+Arc { If foe found, redefine target angle. }
          ELSE Arc := 10;
      { Foe not found in either piece, expand search area to max arc. }
    END
    ELSE Arc := 10;
END; {Aim}

PROCEDURE End_Game;
{ Special strategy for the "End Game" }
BEGIN {End_Game}
  Ramble(0,0); {Lower Left Corner}
  Angle := 10; {Sweep arc from 0 to 90 degrees only}
  REPEAT
    Delta := 10; { Start with widest scanning arc. }
    Range := scan(Angle, Delta);
    WHILE (Range > 40) AND (Range < 700) AND (ObjectScanned = Enemy)
      DO { Must be far enough away to avoid self-damage. }
        BEGIN
          Aim(Angle, Delta); { Improve aim. }
          IF ObjectScanned = Enemy
            THEN cannon(Angle, Range); { Fire!! }
          Range := scan(Angle, Delta); { Is foe still in sights? }
        END;
    Angle := Angle+20; { Look in adjacent target area. }
    IF Angle > 90 THEN Angle := 10;
  UNTIL Dead OR Winner;
END; {End_Game}

BEGIN {HotShot3 Main}
  RaiseShield;
  Angle := 0;
  Ramble(500, 500); { Move to center of field -- if possible. }
  Sweep := 0; { Initialize Sweep counter to zero. }
```

```
      REPEAT { Until Dead or Winner }
        Delta := 10; { Start with widest scanning arc. }
        Range := scan(Angle, Delta);
        WHILE (Range > 40) AND (Range < 700) AND (ObjectScanned = Enemy)
          DO { Must be far enough away to avoid self-damage. }
            BEGIN
              Sweep := 0; { Found foe, so reset Sweep to zero }
              Aim(Angle, Delta); { Improve aim. }
              IF ObjectScanned = Enemy
                THEN cannon(Angle, Range); { Fire!! }
              Range := scan(Angle, Delta); { Is foe still in sights? }
            END;
        Angle := Angle+20; { Look in adjacent target area. }
        Sweep := Sweep+1;
        IF Sweep = 18 THEN
          BEGIN { If robot has scanned a full circle, move elsewhere. }
            LowerShield; {Don't need shield (as much) when moving}
            Move;
          END;
        RaiseShield; {Standing still so use shield}
        {"End" game strategy}
        IF (Fuel < 200) OR (Damage > 70) THEN End_Game;
      UNTIL Dead OR Winner;
    END; {HotShot3 Main}
```

really does is vary the number of instructions your robots' on-board computers can execute in any given amount of time during the game. For example, with the lowest intelligence setting (i.e., a value of 1), your robots' on-board computer might execute 10 instructions during the time it travels 10 meters; at the highest intelligence setting (of 10), 100 instructions might be executed during the same 10-meter travel period. Obviously, at higher intelligence settings, your robot will be able to perform more calculations and make more effective use of complex strategies and algorithms.

For example, to run a single game between the robots: Ninja, Wimp, and Blaster with an intelligence setting of 5 (i.e., very smart robots), you would enter the following command at the DOS prompt:

P-ROBOTS NINJA WIMP BLASTER /I5

If you want to have a series of 50 matches with the same intelligence setting between the same group of robots, you would add a /M50 parameter to the command as follows:

P-ROBOTS NINJA WIMP BLASTER /I5 /M50

The default intelligence setting is 1—both the lowest value and the standard setting used in P-ROBOTS 1.0. You should not think of this lowest setting as signifying "dumb" or "stupid" robots; robots operating at an intelligence level of 1 are still quite smart. To use an analogy from personal computing, you might think of an intelligence setting of 1 as having each robot in the game equipped with an Intel 8088 microprocessor, running at 4.77 megahertz—i.e., the same speed and processor used in the original IBM PC back in 1981. By comparison, using an intelligence setting of 10 is like putting a 33 megahertz 80386 in your robot.

However, a price must be paid for increased robot intelligence—the apparent speed of the game slows down. At higher intelligence settings, the computer you run P-ROBOTS on must execute more instructions (on your robot's behalf) while the robot travels 10 meters, and the game will appear to take longer for your robot to travel that same 10 meters. This might or might not be a problem for you depending upon the speed of the computer you are using to play P-ROBOTS.

One other potential problem occurs when using various intelligence settings in P-ROBOTS: the inconsistent performance of your robots. For example, you might have a robot that beats everything in sight at higher intelligence levels and gets beat by everything in sight at lower levels—or vice versa. Unfortunately, you cannot have it both ways. I advise you to select an intelligence level that plays at an acceptable display/animation speed on your computer and then stick to it.

Compiler errors

The Pascal compiler in P-ROBOTS will report any syntax or logic errors encountered during the compilation process and then terminate without playing the game. You'll be able to find the robot(s) source code listing with errors marked in the file LISTING.TXT on the disk/directory where P-ROBOTS is being run. Because P-ROBOTS is going to write to the disk, you must NOT have a write-protect tab on the disk, or you will get a fatal error whenever you try to run the program. This file should be printed out and studied and your corrections made to your robot source files. Do NOT make your corrections on the LISTING.TXT file! The compiler only compiles robot files (i.e., files with a .PR extension).

If your robot(s) source code did not have any errors (at least, that the compiler could detect), the LISTING.TXT file will not be created, the P-ROBOTS program will execute normally, and the contest between the various robots will be played.

The compiler will report the following errors by number:

   0   UNDEFINED IDENTIFIER
   1   MULTIPLE DEFINITION OF THIS IDENTIFIER
   2   EXPECTED AN IDENTIFIER
   3   PROGRAM MUST BEGIN WITH "PROGRAM"
   4   EXPECTED CLOSING PARENTHESIS ")"
   5   EXPECTED A COLON ":"
   6   INCORRECTLY USED SYMBOL
   7   EXPECTED IDENTIFIER OR THE SYMBOL "VAR"
   8   EXPECTED THE SYMBOL "OF"
   9   EXPECTED AN OPENING PARENTHESIS "("
  10   EXPECTED IDENTIFIER, "ARRAY" OR "RECORD"
  11   EXPECTED AN OPENING BRACKET "["
  12   EXPECTED A CLOSING BRACKET "]"

13   EXPECTED ".." WITHOUT INTERVENING BLANKS
14   EXPECTED A SEMICOLON ";"
15   BAD RESULT TYPE FOR A FUNCTION
16   EXPECTED AN EQUAL SIGN "="
17   EXPECTED BOOLEAN EXPRESSION
18   CONTROL VARIABLE OF THE WRONG TYPE
19   MUST BE MATCHING TYPES
20   "OUTPUT" IS REQUIRED IN PROGRAM HEADING
21   THE NUMBER IS TOO LARGE
22   EXPECT PERIOD ".", CHECK BEGIN-END PAIRS
23   BAD TYPE FOR A CASE STATEMENT
24   ILLEGAL CHARACTER
25   ILLEGAL CONSTANT OR CONSTANT IDENTIFIER
26   ILLEGAL ARRAY SUBSCRIPT (CHECK TYPE)
27   ILLEGAL BOUNDS FOR AN ARRAY INDEX
28   INDEXED VARIABLE MUST BE AN ARRAY
29   EXPECTED A TYPE IDENTIFIER
30   UNDEFINED TYPE
31   VAR WITH FIELD SELECTOR MUST BE RECORD
32   EXPECTED TYPE "BOOLEAN"
33   ILLEGAL TYPE FOR ARITHMETIC EXPRESSION
34   EXPECTED INTEGER FOR "DIV" OR "MOD"
35   INCOMPATIBLE TYPES FOR COMPARISON
36   PARAMETER TYPES DO NOT MATCH
37   EXPECTED A VARIABLE
38   A STRING MUST HAVE ONE OR MORE CHAR
39   NUMBER OF PARAMETERS DO NOT MATCH
40   INVALID "TeamAlly" NAME FORMAT
41   ILLEGAL PARAMETERS TO "WRITE"
42   PARAMETER MUST BE OF TYPE "REAL"
43   PARAMETER MUST BE OF TYPE "INTEGER"
44   EXPECTED VARIABLE OR CONSTANT
45   EXPECTED A VARIABLE OR PROCEDURE
46   TYPES MUST MATCH IN AN ASSIGNMENT
47   CASE LABEL NOT SAME TYPE AS CASE CLAUSE
48   ARGUMENT TO STD. FUNCTION OF WRONG TYPE
49   THE PROGRAM REQUIRES TOO MUCH STORAGE
50   ILLEGAL SYMBOL FOR A CONSTANT
51   EXPECTED BECOMES ":="
52   EXPECTED "THEN"
53   EXPECTED "UNTIL"
54   EXPECTED "DO"
55   EXPECTED "TO" OR "DOWNTO"
56   EXPECTED "BEGIN"
57   EXPECTED "END"
58   EXPECTED ID, CONST, "NOT" OR "("

59   "INPUT" IS REQUIRED IN PROGRAM HEADING
60   ILLEGAL (CONTROL) CHARACTER PRESENT IN SOURCE

Not all of the above error messages will be used in P-ROBOTS because the compiler has been modified to not allow certain kinds of Pascal statements. For example, because P-ROBOTS does not allow READs and WRITEs, you will not get the above error messages normally associated with READ and WRITE. If you attempt to READ or WRITE in a P-ROBOTS program, you will get an error message number 0—"UNDEFINED IDENTIFIER".

Also, remember not to use Pascal "reserved" words as variable or procedure names (i.e., variables named BEGIN, ARRAY, DO, FOR, etc.) because they will cause strange error messages.

On very rare occasions, you might get another kind of compiler error if the robots' source code you are currently trying to compile is so "verbose" that it causes one of the compiler's tables to overflow. When this happens, you will be given an error message identifying which specific table has overflowed. The limits for these tables are as follows:

400   Identifiers (variables, constants, procedures, and functions)
40   Procedures or functions
40   Real constants
60   Arrays
7   Levels of "nested" procedures or functions
5000   "Compiled" P-code instructions

These limits apply to the total number of identifiers (etc.) for all of the robots you have in the current contest.

Run-time errors

When using P-ROBOTS, you can get two kinds of run-time errors. The first kind (and probably the most frequent) is an error occurring within the P-ROBOTS program itself when you try to do something that the P-code compiler within P-ROBOTS objects to— like trying to divide by zero. The second kind of run-time error is generated by Turbo Pascal and is due to situations like not having enough memory or disk space to run the P-ROBOTS program. Each of these types of errors will be discussed below.

P-ROBOTS run-time errors   It is possible that the P-ROBOTS compiler will detect an error during the game. These are known as *run-time* errors and will terminate the game as well as trigger the printing of an error message. The following kinds of run-time errors will be caught and reported:

- **Divide by 0**
    For example, if Delta_X had a value of zero in the following program statement, you would get a "Divide by 0" error:

    ```
    Target_Angle := ArcTan(Delta_Y/Delta_X);
    ```

- **Undefined case**

    For example, if the variable X had a value of 12 in the next example, you would get an "Undefined case" error:

```
CASE X OF
   1 : .....
   2 : .....
   3 : .....
         .
         .
  10 : .....
END; {CASE}
```

- **Invalid index**

    For example, a reference to the tenth element of an array (i.e., Spot[10]) that was only defined to have the elements one through five (i.e., `Spot : ARRAY[1..5] OF INTEGER;`) would cause an "Invalid index" error.

- **Storage overflow**

    You would only get a "Storage overflow" error if one (or more) of your robots in the current contest was making too many recursive calls to the same procedure or function or was evaluating a large number of very, very complex assignment statements so that the robot's "stack" space was exceeded. If you get this error, check your overall robot logic—there must be a better way to accomplish your purpose.

Turbo Pascal run-time errors   Here are the run-time errors that might be generated by Turbo Pascal:

- **101—Disk write error**

    You would get this error (probably) because you did not have enough room on your disk to contain the complete LISTING.TXT file (i.e., the error listing) and your disk became full.

- **203—Heap overflow error**

    You probably don't have enough free memory. P-ROBOTS needs at least 384K of free memory (i.e, after counting all of the memory residents programs).

Common problems

If P-ROBOTS is not doing what you think it should do, check for these common problems:

- Leaving a write-protect tab on the game disk will cause a fatal crash. There must be a way for the LISTING.TXT file (i.e., the error listing) to be written on the disk. Also, make sure you have enough disk space to contain the LISTING.TXT file (20K of available disk space should be plenty of room).

- Your robot must be a self-contained Pascal PROCEDURE with the same name as the file (but without the .PR extension).

- Your robot must have an "infinite" loop in the "main" routine.

- Don't commit robot "suicide" by firing your cannon for a range of zero. For example, this code will cause your robot to commit suicide:

```
Drive(Angle,100);
WHILE (Loc_X < 999) DO Cannon(Angle,Scan
(Angle,10));
```

- You must have at least 384K of free memory in order to run P-ROBOTS. If you don't have enough memory, you will get a Turbo Pascal run-time error number 203.

The P-ROBOTS Pascal language

"Normal" Pascal

P-ROBOTS allows a relatively rich subset of the "normal" Pascal language, including the following:

- Predefined types include REAL, INTEGER, and BOOLEAN. CONSTANTs, RECORDs, and user-defined TYPEs are allowed, as well as ARRAYs.

- Comments may be added to a program by enclosing text with braces { }, or (* *) pairs.

- Variable and other identifier names can have up to 10 significant characters.

- Arithmetic operators include +, −, *, /, DIV, and MOD. Comparison operators include >, <, < >, =, < =, and > =. Boolean operators include AND, OR, and NOT.

- Control statements/structures include CASE, FOR-TO-DO, FOR-DOWNTO-DO, IF-THEN, IF-THEN-ELSE, REPEAT-UNTIL, and WHILE-DO.

- Procedures and functions are allowed to have parameters. If a procedure or function has parameters, these parameters may be passed by value or by reference (i.e., a VAR parameter). Procedures and functions may be "nested" to a maximum of seven levels. Recursion is allowed.

- Predefined functions include TRUE, FALSE, ABS, SQR, ODD, SUCC, PRED, ROUND, TRUNC, SIN, COS, EXP, LN, SQRT, ARC-

TAN, and RANDOM. All of these functions have the same interpretation in P-ROBOTS as in standard Pascal, except for the various Trig functions (which, in P-Robots, use degrees rather than radians).

- The following are NOT allowed in P-ROBOTS and will generate error messages: CHAR, STRING, enumerated types, subranges, pointers, variant records, PACKED, sets, IN, files, input, output, GET, PUT, READ, WRITE, WITH, LABEL, and GOTO.

Unique P-ROBOTS Pascal procedures and functions

Listed here are procedures and functions specific to P-ROBOTS:

Alive	Returns a TRUE or FALSE depending upon whether your robot is alive or not.
AllyAlive	Returns TRUE or FALSE depending upon whether your Ally is alive or not.
AllyDamage	Returns your Ally's current Damage level.
AllyDead	Returns TRUE or FALSE depending upon whether your Ally is dead or not.
AllyFuel	Returns your Ally's current Fuel level.
AllyHeading	Returns your Ally's current Heading.
AllyLoc_X	Returns the current X coordinate of your Ally.
AllyLoc_Y	Returns the current Y coordinate of your Ally.
AllyMeters	Returns your Ally's current Meters.
AllyShieldRaised	Returns TRUE or FALSE depending upon whether your Ally's shield is raised or not.
AllySpeed	Returns your Ally's current Speed.
Angle_To(X,Y)	Return to angle in degrees from your robot's current position to the point (X,Y) on the battlefield.
Cannon(degree, range);	Fires a missile at an angle of degree and for a distance of range.
Damage	Returns the value of your robot's current damage level.
Dead	Returns a TRUE or FALSE depending upon whether your robot is dead or not.
Distance(X1,Y1, X2,Y2)	Returns the distance in meters from the point (X1, Y1) on the battle field to the point (X2, Y2).
Drive(degree, speed);	Causes your robot to move in the direction given by degree at a specified speed.
Fuel	Returns the current value of your robot's fuel level in jiggers.

LimitedFuel	Returns TRUE or FALSE depending upon whether your current battle has fuel constraints or not.
LowerShield;	Causes your robot's shield to be lowered.
Meters	Returns the cumulative number of meters that your robot has traveled during the current battle.
ObjectScanned	Returns the type of object that was found by the most recent Scan call (if any). The result returned can have one of these predefined constant values: Nothing, Ally, Enemy, or Obstruction.
RaiseShield;	Causes your robot's shield to be raised.
Random(limit)	Returns a random integer in the range of 0 to limit.
Scan(degree, resolution)	Returns the distance in meters to any other robot or obstruction within the "viewing" arc/angle of degree +/- resolution. If nothing is scanned, then Scan returns a value of 0.
ShieldRaised	Returns TRUE or FALSE depending upon whether your robot's shield is up or down.
Time	Returns the current CPU cycle count and can be used to time various events, speeds, etc., within your robot program.

Registration

Registration entitles you to the following:

☐ Notice of all future P-ROBOTS upgrades
☐ Latest version of the program, with a collection of the most recent and best robots.
☐ Turbo or Quick Pascal source code for P-ROBOTS
☐ Turbo or Quick Pascal source code for the multi-tasking Pascal compiler used as the basis for developing P-ROBOTS
☐ Telephone support

To register P-Robots, send $25.00 to

Softworks
43064 Via Moraga
Mission San Jose, CA 94539
(415) 659-0533

Part Two

Companion tools

4
ProPak

Program title   ProPak   *(Disk 2339 and 2340)*

Special requirements   A hard disk is recommended. EMS and/or XMS memory is helpful but not required. (See "Memory requirements" in this chapter.)

The Programmer's Productivity Pack—ProPak—is a software package designed to provide the utilities and reference tools most frequently needed by programmers. What's more, each individual tool or "attachment" within the ProPak package was designed to be the best, most powerful, most flexible, and easiest-to-use tool in its category.

For instance, the Programmer's Calculator (only one of the tools built into ProPak) is the best Programmer's Calculator on the market, bar none! Integrating all of these tools into one program and placing them at your disposal at one time makes the time you spend programming more productive than ever.

ProPak has many features that all programmers will find useful. Unfortunately, ProPak is too extensive to be fully explained here. The following sections briefly outline the available features and offer more detailed information about a few of them. Still, this is intended only as a sample to help you decide if ProPak will be useful to you.

ProPak provides you with

- A Programmer's Calculator that works simultaneously in decimal, binary, hexadecimal, and octal
- Addition, subtraction, multiplication, integer division, and modulus mathematical functions

- SHL, SHR, ROL, ROR, SAL, SAR, RCL, and RCR bit manipulation functions
- AND, NOT, OR, and XOR logical functions
- Exchange word and exchange double word functions
- An ASCII and color attribute chart
- A keystroke reference utility that returns both the BIOS scan codes and the dBASE INKEY( ) values
- Keystroke recording and playback that allows up to 100 keystroke recordings of 1,000 keystrokes each
- A screen grabber utility that grabs text from the screen and plays it back like a keystroke recording
- A screen capture facility that allows filtering for screen or printer
- Access to the DOS background PRINT facility
- A screen blanking facility that will park your hard disk (or disks) while the screen is blanked
- A pop-up DOS shell capability allowing you to shell to DOS from any program with as much as 600K bytes of memory available in the DOS shell
- Complete control of all the hotkeys, colors, sound effects, file extensions, memory usage, and more—through PCustom, the customizing program

All this and more, and all in one smoothly integrated package. The Programmer's Productivity Pack includes tools that can run stand-alone, as memory-resident (even with Sidekick), as memory-resident with swapping, or as a background task in a multitasking environment. And because ProPak provides you with the ability to customize every detail, it not only helps you to be more productive but also gives you the freedom to adapt it to your particular needs and preferences.

The Programmer's Productivity Pack can handle dual monitor systems, EMS and XMS memory, multitasking systems like DESQview and TaskView/OmniView, and more. Each version can be easily and safely unloaded from memory when the need arises. You can even unload it with three different methods.

The Programmer's Productivity Pack is even compatible with Borland's Sidekick, to the extent that it can be safely loaded *after* Sidekick.

All things considered, the Programmer's Productivity Pack should become one of your most often used utilities, and you might find yourself wondering how you ever got along without it.

Memory requirements

The actual memory requirements will vary depending upon which of the two versions you use, how swapping is handled, the amount of memory you reserve for keystroke recordings, etc.

The swapping version, ProSwap, retains only about 7K of memory while resident (and swapped out). The minimum memory requirement for ProPak is about 96K.

ProPak is shipped with 2K (2,048 bytes) of memory set aside for keystroke recordings.

The customizing program, PCustom, requires 256K of RAM.

ProSwap uses as little memory as possible. ProSwap can swap itself to disk, to EMS memory, or to XMS memory. All this flexibility means that ProSwap is the ideal choice when memory is scarce.

In order to conserve as much of your precious memory as possible, ProPak makes extensive use of overlays (whereas ProSwap does not).

You can do a number of things to maximize ProPak's performance and customize its memory usage. The biggest improvement will be obtained through the use of EMS memory. If you have EMS memory and allow ProPak to use it, the entire overlay file will be placed into EMS memory. This means two things. First, the overlay file on disk will no longer be needed, which will save you one file handle. Secondly, reading the necessary sections of the overlay file will occur much faster because it will be a simple memory transfer rather than a disk access (thus, the size of the overlay buffer can remain minimal). This also conserves the maximum amount of RAM (random access memory) for the use of your other programs.

ProPak

ProPak is distributed on either two 5.25" 360K floppy diskettes or one 2.5" 720K diskette, and/or in a compressed format.

Files included with ProPak

The following files are included in the Programmer's Productivity Pack:

PROPAK.EXE is the MS-DOS memory-resident version of the Programmer's Productivity Pack. ProPak uses overlays extensively. Early versions required a separate overlay file called ProPak.OVR. Beginning with v2.50, the overlay file is appended to the tail-end of the ProPak.EXE file.

PROSWAP.EXE is the flexible-loading version. ProSwap can run as a memory-resident "swapping" version, a standard memory-resident version, a background task under DESQview or OmniView/TaskView, or as a stand-alone program under MS-DOS.

PCUSTOM.EXE is the customizing program that will enable you to customize both versions of ProPak. In fact, you can even customize both versions at the same time.

PCUSTOM.EXE does not need to be present to make changes in the program "on the fly." You can always make changes in memory using the Modify Options submenu within the ProPak Control Center. The customizing program *must* be used, however, if you want the changes to be permanent (i.e., written to disk and available to you the next time you turn on your computer). Changes made from within ProPak are not permanent because they are made in memory and thus lost when you unload ProPak or turn off your computer. Both methods of customizing are simple to use whenever needed.

Those files make up the Programmer's Productivity Pack, but several other files are also included on the distribution diskettes.

You will find a file called ANSWERS.TXT that answers the most commonly asked questions concerning the use of the Programmer's Productivity Pack.

With this information you can decide which version or versions will be the most useful to you. Whichever files you decide to use, it is recommended that they all be placed into the same subdirectory—preferably in your DOS path. If the concept of directories or paths is new to you, please read Appendix C at the back of the *User's Guide*. More information is available from your *MS-DOS User's Guide*.

By the way, PCustom (the customizing program) is not required for the operation of ProPak or ProSwap but is nice to have on hand. Unless disk space is at a premium, keep it available at all times.

ProPak and your keyboard

Knowing how ProPak uses your keyboard can help you get the most out of it. ProPak is able to use more key combinations than most software, for two reasons.

When ProPak is installed, it hooks into the BIOS keyboard interrupts (Interrupts 09h and 16h), adding several extra capabilities to them. These additional features are much more apparent to those of you not having enhanced keyboards; ProPak is able to recognize many key combinations normally usable only with an enhanced keyboard. Also, for users of enhanced keyboards, ProPak is able to use about a dozen key combinations not normally recognized by the BIOS alone. This enhancement to normal keyboard functionality is at a very low level, meaning that you do not have to do anything special to obtain this benefit.

On a higher level, ProPak goes to extreme lengths to recognize keys logically according to the context in which they are typed. For instance, if you are using the Programmer's Calculator without NumLock turned on and then press the Up arrow key, you most probably wanted to type the number 8. Thus, the Calculator reads this input as the "8" rather than as the Up arrow. This ability to read keys in context makes ProPak very easy to use. (Coincidentally, referring back to the Calculator example, even the number 5 key—the center key on the numeric keypad—is read as 5 and not as center.)

By being aware of ProPak's efforts to make your keyboard more functional, you can often think of additional ways to improve your productivity.

After all, who knows more about the kinds of things you use your computer for than you?

Loading ProPak

When you have chosen which files you want to use and have installed them on your system, all you must do is use them.

Note: From now on, Programmer's Productivity Pack in general will be referred to as ProPak.

To load ProPak into memory, type

PROPAK

at the DOS prompt.

As soon as the program is read from disk, you will be given a screen full of information. The upper portion of the screen provides you with information concerning EMS memory, including the presence or absence of EMS memory, the status of EMS memory as reported by the Expanded Memory Manager, and (most importantly) whether or not ProPak is using EMS memory for its overlay file.

The lower portion of the screen provides detailed information regarding how much normal RAM memory is being used by ProPak, as well as an approximate breakdown of HOW it is being used. Here is a brief explanation of each of these values:

Program Segment Prefix (PSP) MS-DOS always places a 256-byte chunk of memory at the beginning of each program it executes. This 256-byte area contains information that the program can use or refer to during execution.

Environment Block (at least) This is the area of memory where MS-DOS stores any global parameters (i.e., strings, like your path command, any "SET=?" strings, etc). ProPak does not know how much memory is reserved for the environment block but does know how much of the environment block is actually in use storing parameters.

CODE (??,???) DATA (??,???) "CODE" refers to the memory used for machine instructions. "DATA" refers to the memory used for storing internal variables, data structures, etc.

Internal stacks A *stack* is a storage area used by your computer to keep track of information on a temporary basis. ProPak has five internal stacks, one for each of the tools accessed with a hotkey. To minimize memory usage, ProPak uses a sophisticated scheme allowing one internal stack to "overflow" onto another internal stack safely.

Overlay buffer The overlay buffer is very similar to the CODE area mentioned above and contains machine instructions needed by ProPak to perform various tasks. However, it does not always contain the same information but only the machine instructions needed at any given time. Machine instructions not currently needed remain on the disk in the .OVR file (or in EMS memory, if it is in use). This technique is commonly used to conserve memory.

HEAP (where dynamic storage occurs) The *HEAP* is simply an area of memory set aside for use by ProPak as needed. For example, when you pop up ProPak, it saves an area of the screen before overwriting the area (which is how ProPak is able to restore your screen when it is finished). This screen area is saved on the HEAP.

If this information is confusing to you, don't worry; you don't need to memorize any of these values. This information is here for those who like to know exactly how much memory is being used by ProPak, as well as for what it is being used. Pressing any key will clear the screen and return you to the DOS prompt.

ProPak is a memory-resident program. This means that when you first run the program, it will install itself in memory and then return control to DOS. Thus, when you find yourself back at the DOS prompt after pressing any key, don't worry—you're doing just fine.

Once you are back at the DOS prompt, you will see two key combinations listed. These keys will activate ProPak when pressed. One will pop up the Programmer's Calculator and the other will pop up the Control Center. These activation keys are called *hotkeys*.

ProSwap

ProSwap is an extremely flexible program containing the most used features of the Programmer's Productivity Pack.

- ProSwap can be loaded as a swapping memory-resident version that swaps most of itself out of memory when not in use. When loaded in this fashion, ProSwap retains only about 7K of memory while resident. ProSwap can swap itself to XMS memory, EMS memory, a RAM disk, or a hard disk.

- ProSwap can be loaded as a traditional memory-resident program (no swapping).

- ProSwap can also be run as a stand-alone DESQview aware program that does not remain memory resident.

ProSwap has one additional capability not found in ProPak: a pop-up DOS shell capability. When activated, this capability swaps the currently running program out, freeing as much memory as possible, and then loads a secondary copy of the command processor and places you at the DOS prompt. This capability enables you to shell to DOS from programs that do not have this capability built in.

Note: To use the pop-up DOS shell capability, you must have MS-DOS 3.0 or later. If you are using an earlier version of DOS, you must disable the DOS shell capability (using PCustom) before you can use ProSwap.

Loading ProSwap

To start ProSwap, simply type

```
PROSWAP
```

at the DOS prompt. This will start ProSwap in its default (normal) mode. Several command-line options are available and described here in detail. Before I discuss the command-line options, however, you should be aware of some limitations.

ProSwap is designed to provide you with as much usable memory as possible while resident. To accomplish this, ProSwap must be able to swap itself into and out of memory. Thus, because of this swapping behavior, you must avoid several things:

- ProSwap cannot be loaded into "high" memory using utilities such as QRAM, QEMM, 386MAX, or any similar utility.

- ProSwap should not be loaded before programs containing hardware interrupt handlers (such as network shells, multitasking operating systems, and communications programs). If you are going to use ProSwap in these environments, you should load it after the network shell or multitasking operating system is installed.

- It is possible to load ProSwap and still run communications programs like ProComm or TAPCIS, provided you follow some simple guidelines. Do *not* pop ProSwap up over your communications program while it is online, uploading or downloading, or waiting to answer an incoming call. When ProSwap pops up, it swaps the current application out—essentially trading places with it in memory. This will cause a problem if the other program was trying to deal with com ports or some other hardware-related activity. Of course, if you are using a program like ProComm or TAPCIS and the program is not online or waiting to answer an incoming call, then you can safely pop up ProSwap.

- ProSwap will not pop up over a program operating in graphics mode and does not know how to save and restore a graphics screen. To prevent problems, ProSwap will simply beep and refuse to pop up when your video system is in graphics mode.

In addition, some important restrictions apply to the pop-up DOS shell capabilities:

- You cannot pop to a DOS shell while you are at the DOS command line, due to the way DOS handles its internal stacks. You're probably wondering "Why would I want to shell to the DOS command line when I'm already at the DOS command line?". Well, there's really no reason to do this, so this isn't much of a limitation. Still, strangely enough, this is one of the first things users try to do when they start experimenting with ProSwap.

- This same conflict arises if you pop up a TSR from the DOS command line and then try to pop to a DOS shell using ProSwap. Even though you popped up another TSR, technically you are still at the DOS command line.

- The DOS programs DEBUG and EDLIN are very similar to the DOS command line in terms of how internal DOS stacks are managed. Because of this, you cannot pop to a DOS shell from within DEBUG or EDLIN.

- It is possible, under a multitasking system such as DESQview, for ProSwap to not recognize that you are at the DOS command line. Be very careful when using ProSwap under a multitasking operating system—don't try to pop to a DOS shell from the DOS command line.

- Finally, the most important restriction: do *not* install another memory-resident program while you are within the ProSwap DOS shell. When you exit from the DOS shell, ProSwap will swap the new memory-resident program out and the results will not be pretty.

When ProSwap is swapping to disk, it must be absolutely guaranteed that it will have access to its swap files when swapping itself into or out of memory. This requirement, coupled with the speed issue, means that ProSwap's swap file cannot be located on removable media such as a floppy diskette. ProSwap checks for this and will refuse to load if you specify a floppy drive as the location for the swap files. Even though the media is technically removable, however, you may still use a Bernoulli drive as the location for the swap files.

ProSwap command-line options

Here is a brief list of each option, followed by a detailed description of each option:

-D	Force swapping to Disk only.
-E	Force swapping to EMS memory only.
-H	Help (same as "-?").
-M	Minimize swap size (XMS and Disk only).
-N	No swapping (TSR mode—same as -T).
-P	Preserve mouse state within the DOS shell.
-S	Stand-alone (nonresident), DESQview aware mode.
-T	TSR mode (no swapping—same as -N).
-U	Unload the previously loaded copy of ProSwap from memory.
-X	Force swapping to XMS memory only.

-?   Show a list of all available command-line options and return to the DOS command line (help—same as -H).

(D) Force swapping to disk only   Forces ProSwap to swap to disk even if sufficient EMS or XMS memory is available. Swapping to disk is inevitably slower than swapping to EMS or XMS memory.

The speed of the swapping process can be further controlled by the -M option described later.

This option can be permanently controlled using PCustom.

(E) Force swapping to EMS memory only   Forces ProSwap to swap to EMS memory. If not enough EMS memory is available, then ProSwap will abort without attempting to swap to either disk or XMS memory.

This option can be permanently controlled using PCustom.

(H) Help   Displays a list of command line options and returns to DOS without going resident. This can be accomplished using any command-line option not recognized by ProSwap.

This option is the same as -? described later.

(M) Minimize swap size   Applies only when ProSwap is swapping to disk or to XMS memory (is ignored when swapping to EMS memory).

When swapping to disk, two swap files are used; and when swapping to XMS memory, two blocks of memory are used. One is used for storing the memory under the control of ProSwap and the other is used for storing the memory under the control of the application being swapped out. This allows the swapping operation to occur as quickly as possible—at the expense of using more disk space or more XMS memory.

When the -M option is used, ProSwap will use only one file when swapping to disk or one memory block when swapping to XMS. In effect, the two swap images "trade places" with each other during the swapping operation.

This option causes ProSwap to use much less disk space or XMS memory. The price you pay for conserving these resources is speed; swapping takes much longer in this mode.

This option can be permanently controlled using PCustom.

(N) No swapping and (T) TSR mode   Because these options are identical, use the one easiest for you to remember.

When ProSwap is loaded in TSR mode, it will load just like ProPak. It will remain in memory until it is unloaded—no swapping will be performed. This means that it will pop-up instantly when a hotkey is pressed but will take much more memory away from your other programs. The pop-up DOS shell capability is not available in this mode.

This option can be permanently controlled using PCustom.

(P) Preserve mouse state   Most people won't pop to DOS from a program that uses a mouse and then run another program that uses a mouse. Thus, ProSwap usually does not need to preserve the mouse state when it pops to DOS and restore it when returning from DOS. Some newer mouse drivers are annoyingly slow at initializing (which happens every time you pop to DOS)—yet another reason why ProSwap does not normally preserve the state of the mouse.

This option tells ProSwap to preserve the mouse state before it shells to DOS and to restore the mouse state when it returns from the DOS shell. If you use a mouse often, you will want to start ProSwap with the -P option.

(S) Stand-alone mode Tells ProSwap to run like a traditional program (and thus not go memory resident). When you are finished using ProSwap and exit, you will return to DOS. In this mode ProSwap is DESQview aware and sends all screen output to the buffer provided by DESQview rather than directly to video memory.

This option can be permanently controlled using PCustom.

(U) Unload from memory Tells ProSwap to look for a copy of itself already loaded into memory and to unload that copy if found. When this option is used, ProSwap will unload the resident copy and then return to DOS.

This is the safest way to unload ProSwap from memory!

If ProSwap was not previously loaded, then this option is ignored. When this option is used, it should be the *only* option used.

(X) Force swapping to XMS memory only Forces ProSwap to swap to XMS memory. If not enough XMS memory is available, then ProSwap will abort without attempting to swap to either disk or EMS memory.

Note: XMS swapping is only available with XMS (Extended Memory Specification) extended memory—not with simulated extended memory or extended memory that doesn't conform to the XMS standard.

This option can be permanently controlled using PCustom.

(?) Help Displays a list of command-line options and returns to DOS without going resident. This can be accomplished using any command-line option not recognized by ProSwap.

This option is the same as -H described earlier.

ProSwap as a stand-alone program

By now, you have a good grasp of how a memory-resident program is loaded into memory. Now let's examine some of the differences between the memory-resident and the stand-alone or multitasking capabilities of ProSwap. ProSwap, when loaded with the /S option, is designed to run as a stand-alone program under MS-DOS or as a background task under DESQview or TaskView/OmniView.

The memory-resident versions of ProPak write directly to video memory when they output information to the screen, which has several advantages. First and foremost, writing directly to video memory is much faster than sending all screen output through the operating system. Additionally, direct screen writing allows ProPak to retain more control over the screen.

Programmers running ProSwap under DESQview or TaskView/Omni-View should consider the subject of "windows." In deciding how to set up ProSwap, you should be aware that some features use the entire screen. For instance, the ASCII and Color Attribute chart will use the entire 25, 43, or 50 lines available on the screen (depending upon the current video mode and hardware capabilities). Of course, before overwriting anything currently displayed on the screen, both versions of ProPak will copy the screen contents to their own internal buffer and then restore the screen before exiting. If you specify a window size smaller than the entire screen, sometimes ProSwap will write outside the boundaries of that window. It will always restore it when it is finished, however, so don't worry.

When ProSwap is running under a multitasking system, it might not be the only program using the screen. If another program is using the screen, it would be very rude for ProSwap to overwrite the other program's output. To avoid this, ProSwap sends its screen output to the "virtual screen" provided by the multitasking system rather than directly to video memory. This allows the multitasking system to retain control over which application has access to the actual screen at any given time.

What this means to multitasking systems is that ProSwap is very considerate of any other programs that might be running simultaneously.

Another consideration is that these multitasking systems provide their own keyboard macro (keystroke recording and playback) capabilities, and their own screen cut and paste (screen grabber) facilities. This includes all the features contained in the Control Center. To conserve memory and avoid redundancy, ProSwap does not have those features already provided by the operating environment.

Unloading ProPak or ProSwap

If you are using ProPak, at the DOS prompt type

```
PROPAK -U
```

If you are using ProSwap, type PROSWAP instead of PROPAK; this will unload ProPak from memory (if it is safe to do so). For the safest way to unload ProPak, you may use -U, /U, \U, or U to unload ProPak from memory (the U may be upper- or lowercase).

Whether or not you are at the DOS prompt, you can unload ProPak from memory by popping up the Programmer's Calculator and pressing Alt-U and then Alt-U. That's right: press it twice. If you prefer, you can press Ctrl-U and then Ctrl-U. You could also pop up the Control Center and choose the Unload From Memory option.

If at any time you are unsure if ProPak is loaded in memory, simply try to install it again. It won't allow itself to be installed twice, instead giving you a message to the effect that it is already resident. Pressing the hotkeys will also tell you if it is resident or not.

ProPak utilities

ProPak's many utilities are useful and perform numerous varied tasks.

The Programmer's Calculator and attachments

The Programmer's Calculator built into ProPak is a very flexible and powerful Programmer's Calculator. As a matter of fact, there are currently no Programmer's Calculators available (even hand-held types) that provide all the features available in the ProPak Programmer's Calculator. It is especially useful to programmers when converting hex, binary, and decimal.

The ASCII and Color Attribute chart provides a wealth of information on the different ASCII characters, color attributes, monochrome attributes, and extended characters. Now you can press a key instead of leaving your work to find a reference book.

After you've tried the Keystroke Reference Center, you might ask yourself how you ever got along without it. A programmer's dream, all with BIOS scan codes and dBASE INKEY( ) values on screen at the touch of a key.

The Keystroke Reference Center

The Keystroke Reference Center is an elegant solution to a simple and yet common problem.

In virtually every program you write, you'll need to identify a keystroke in order to determine what action to execute next. In most cases, this keystroke will be identified by way of all or part of the *Scan Code* returned by the system's ROM BIOS. Other specialized application development tools or languages such as dBASE and its various counterparts (Clipper, FoxBase, QuickSilver, and others), return a key code different than the one normally returned by the ROM BIOS.

To further complicate matters, not all keyboards are the same. The world contains older 83 key PC/XT keyboards, the newer 84 key PC/AT style keyboards, and the 101/102 key "enhanced" keyboards, as well as the compact keyboards found on many laptop computers (many of which are configured to act like an enhanced keyboard by having the same key return different values according to various conditions).

What all this means is that most of us keep reference charts from books or technical manuals close at hand while programming. We then refer to these books when we need to know what value is returned from a specific key. Of course, these books or charts usually do not list all of the possible key combinations. Thus, we often end up writing a separate little utility to display the return value from each key pressed, which we then use whenever we need to find out the value of a particular key or key combination.

Needless to say, neither of these methods is an ideal solution. Incredibly, though, ProPak's interactive Keystroke Reference Center provides the solution to this common problem!

First, because ProPak is memory-resident, it is always available at the touch of a key. Second, because we don't always use the same languages and tools when developing applications, ProPak's interactive Keystroke Reference Center provides the information needed for the most common keystroke return values, the BIOS scan codes, and the dBASE INKEY( ) return codes, all simultaneously. Third, to take the solution a step further, the Keystroke Reference Center displays a "Portability Note" whenever a key or key combination requiring additional information is pressed.

To round out the Keystroke Reference Center, a live (real-time) display of each individual bit in the two BIOS keyboard status bytes is displayed in the lower half of the screen.

As another piece of information possibly of interest to you, ProPak modifies the normal keyboard interrupts (Int 09h and 16h) in order to identify and use more keystrokes than normally available through the BIOS services alone. Of course, if you press one of these special key combinations, a Portability Note will let you know about it.

Using the Keystroke Reference Center is as simple as it could possibly be. Instead of paging through a long chart, simply press the key or key combination that you are interested in, and you'll instantly have all the necessary information.

Park disk(s) and blank screen

You are probably aware that when the same characters are displayed in the same position on your screen for long periods of time, they tend to burn a permanent image of themselves into the phosphorescent coating of your screen. To avoid this, many people use automatic screen blanking programs that blank the screen after a predetermined period of keyboard inactivity. Such utilities are certainly useful and necessary, but many people feel that there is a better way to accomplish the same goal.

There are some very obvious disadvantages to those particular utilities. The screen is often blanked unexpectedly, which can sometimes be rather unsettling. While the screen is blank, it is not necessarily obvious whether or not the computer is turned on, which is an important consideration when more than one person might be using the machine. Also, Some of these utilities "eat" the next keystroke entered, while some do not. In addition, while you are away from your computer, your monitor is protected from screen burns but your hard disk is not protected against head crashes.

ProPak provides an alternative to the many "automatic" screen blanking programs. Most users prefer to stop using their older screen blanking programs once they start using ProPak.

ProPak never blanks your screen automatically (i.e., unexpectedly); you are always in control. Furthermore, when ProPak blanks your screen, it also displays a clock on the screen so that you know that the computer is actually turned on. This clock will never produce screen burns because it moves to a new position on the screen every 60 seconds. Thus, for every minute the clock is in a certain position, there are over three hours when that same position is blank. To top it all off, when ProPak blanks your screen, it also parks your hard disk by moving the read/write heads to the last cylinder. If you have two hard disks, both will be parked.

If you do not want to use the Disk Parking feature when you blank your screen, you can disable that part of the utility with PCustom.

ProPak's Screen Blanking and Disk Parking feature can be activated from either the Programmer's Calculator or from the ASCII and Color Attribute Chart. In either case, the Screen Blanking and Disk Parking feature is invoked by pressing P for Park. You can also use Ctrl-P or Alt-P.

Once activated, you may "unblank" the screen and return to where you left off merely by pressing any key.

The Control Center

The Control Center is present only in PROPAK.EXE. It is through the Control Center that you can customize many aspects of ProPak "on the fly" (i.e., while you are actually using ProPak). It is also through the Control Center that you have access to some of ProPak's most useful features.

The Control Center is too extensive to cover here. Please refer to the ProPak documentation for more detailed information.

The Screen Capture facility

This feature allows you to capture the screen's contents to a disk file, by copying the text on the screen to a disk file and putting a carriage return at the end of each line. Optionally, the screen can be filtered according to your needs, specified with PCustom or changed "on the fly" using the Modify Options choice of the Control Center.

The filtering is actually pretty straightforward. Characters like Form Feed and Line Feed that mess up the screen image when you print will be replaced with a dot ("."—or any character you choose using PCustom to customize ProPak). This way, the screen image's alignment remains unchanged, and at the same time, you save yourself the trouble of editing the file before printing it. It will be ready to go!

The Screen Capture feature can be activated from either the Programmer's Calculator and its attachments or the Control Center.

From the Programmer's Calculator and its attachments, the Screen Capture can be activated by either Ctrl-Enter or Alt-Enter. It will copy the contents of the screen exactly as they are at the time those keys are pressed. Thus, you can copy the Programmer's Calculator display (with or without the Quick Reference Menu), the ASCII and Color Attribute chart display, or the Keystroke Reference Center display as part of the screen.

From the Control Center, the Screen Capture feature is activated by selecting the Copy Screen to File option on the Control Center. When you select that option, ProPak first removes the Menu and then copies the underlying screen in its entirety.

You will be asked for the name of the file to copy the screen to; and then an extension of .SCN will automatically be appended to the filename. If you don't like the .SCN extension, you can change it with PCustom.

If a file by that name already exists in the current directory, you will be asked to confirm that you want to overwrite it. If the file does not exist, a new file with that name will be opened in the current directory.

If you're interested, I'll explain the actual process involved. First, the screen is copied to an internal array where the characters are separated from their corresponding attribute bytes. Then the array containing the characters will have a carriage return appended to the end of each line. Optionally, each character will be *filtered*, which simply means that each character will be examined and compared against a filter list. If the character matches one of the characters on the list, it will be replaced with the replacement character specified through PCustom. The default replacement character is a period. After this is completed, the filtered information will be written to the disk file.

The Print facility

ProPak Print facility lets you access the DOS background PRINT facility at all times. Through this option, you can submit files to be printed in the background or cancel files that have already been submitted.

This feature demands only two things. First, the DOS background PRINT program must be installed in memory (it is also a memory-resident program). Second, you must be using DOS 3.0 or later.

Using this facility, you can submit files to the DOS background PRINT facility by specifying a filename or even a mask containing wildcards. For instance, specifying *.TXT will open a window showing all the files with the extension .TXT; you must simply move the highlight bar over the file to submit and press Enter to submit it. This "point and shoot" procedure will place the file you specify into the queue of files waiting to be printed.

You can also cancel all files presently in the queue by selecting Cancel ALL Print Files from the DOS Print Control menu.

This feature is very easy to use and very handy to have available. It allows you to continue working with your computer while your files are being printed. Remember that this print command is not identical to printing a document from your word processor; it will only format the text according to any control codes embedded in the document.

If you have never used the DOS background PRINT facility, or if you don't remember all the command-line options available, then read on. The following discussion does not list every option available because you can refer to your DOS manual for a complete list, but I will cover the most common options.

The DOS background PRINT facility is a utility program included with each copy of MS-DOS. Memory-resident, it is loaded into memory by typing PRINT at the DOS prompt. When loading, PRINT will ask you for the name of the *list device*, which simply means the printing device. Usually PRN is the answer you want. But you could also specify LPT1, LPT2, AUX, etc. Consult your DOS manual for more information.

When loading PRINT into memory, you can change many of its default parameters by adding extra information on the command line (between the word PRINT and pressing the Enter key). The two options that you will most likely use are /B:n and /Q:n.

The /B option allows you to change the size of PRINT's built-in print buffer. This buffer can range from 1 to 32,767 bytes, with the default being 512. In actuality, a better value is 1,024—probably sufficient for your needs.

The /Q option allows you to change the number of files allowed in the *queue*, which is the waiting line. You can specify any number from 1 to 32 (although I recommend the maximum—32).

In both cases, the option is followed by a colon and a number specifying the setting you desire. By the way, PRINT is case-sensitive on this point, so be sure to use uppercase letters when entering the command-line parameters.

Here's an example of loading PRINT with a 1K buffer and a maximum of 32 files allowed in the queue at any one time (recommended):

```
PRINT /B:1024 /Q:32
```

As you can see, PRINT is fairly easy to use. Your DOS manual provides more complete information, including other available options.

PCustom: the customizing program

PCustom is ProPak's companion customizing program. You might never use it if ProPak is exactly to your liking the way you received it. But even if you're happy with ProPak, more likely you'd have done just one or two things differently. PCustom is your gateway to making those changes.

PCustom works by going into the actual executable file (for PROPAK .EXE), making changes internally, and then updating the special configuration file (file with the .CFG extension) for both ProPak and ProSwap. This makes the custom features "permanent" and the programs act as if they were actually custom written just for you. Don't let the word "permanent" scare you; you can change as many features as you want, as often as you want.

Registration

The registration fee for ProPak is $79.00. After becoming a registered user of ProPak, you are entitled to the following:

- ☐ A printed User's Guide and the most current version of ProPak on disk (in a sealed envelope).
- ☐ An ASCII poster set including a large 26" × 20", two-color poster depicting the entire ASCII and IBM extended character sets, as well as a smaller 8½" × 11" reproduction.
- ☐ The next version automatically sent to you on disk at no extra charge.
- ☐ Free technical support.
- ☐ Additional programs, utilities, and shareware packages.
- ☐ Discounts on other products from Falk Data Systems.
- ☐ Automatic notification of future changes, modifications, and new versions.
- ☐ Automatic notification of other products and releases from Falk Data Systems.
- ☐ The opportunity to get new versions sometimes weeks or months before non-registered users.
- ☐ The opportunity to have ALL future versions shipped to you automatically as soon as they are released.

To register, send queries to

Falk Data Systems
ProPak Technical Support
5322 Rockwood Court
El Paso, TX 79932

5
PXL

Program title   PXL   *(Disk 1304)*

Special requirements   Turbo Pascal 4.0. Can use with Turbo Pascal 3.0 if the precautions indicated in the description are taken.

Once upon a time, Borland's Turbo Pascal came with an unadvertised source lister called TLIST. Unfortunately, it had bugs. So it came to pass that PXL was written to do some of the things TLIST was supposed to do, as well as some things it didn't— and everyone rejoiced.

Here are PXL's main features:

- PXL lists a file with headers: by default, it puts filename (with user's ID) and creation date on page 1, and filename and page numbers thereafter. If you prefer, you instead can make your own header of up to five lines.
- If desired, PXL marks reserved words by underlining them.
- If desired, PXL numbers the lines and counts begin-end pairs.
- PXL will paginate automatically, but you can insert symbols in the file to control page breaks.
- PXL handles lines of up to 255 characters in both condensed and elite print.
- PXL will make a cross-reference of the identifiers in the source file.
- PXL will include in the listing (and cross-ref) files called with the {$I filename} directive.
- PXL can be run from a batch file without stopping for interaction. Should anything go wrong, it sets ERRORLEVEL to 1.

- PXL will feed out a blank page before listing, if requested.
- PXL will run on DOS 2.00 or later. If you must run it on an earlier version of DOS, you'll have to use an earlier version of PXL. (1.12 was the last DOS 1.10 version.)

If you leave the reserved words unmarked, of course, PXL will list any sort of plain ASCII file.

Files

PXL comes with the following files:

PXL.EXE is the working compilation. Run it from DOS.

PXL.WDS contains the list of reserved words PXL uses if you ask it to mark reserved words in the listing. It must be in the default directory or somewhere on the DOS path when you run PXL.

PXL.PRN contains the printer control codes PXL uses when it numbers the lines or marks the reserved words. As it comes, it contains the codes for an Epson FX-80 but can be changed by means of PXLINST. PXL.PRN must be in the default directory or somewhere on the DOS path when you run PXL.

PXLINST.EXE is an installation program putting the proper print control symbols in PXL.PRN. You don't need it to run PXL, but it's required if you must adapt PXL for your printer.

PXL.PAS, **PXLINIT.PAS**, **PXLMENU.PAS**, and **PXLLIST.PAS** contain the source code for PXL.EXE. You might need it if you must recompile to change colors.

PXLINST.PAS contains the source code for PXLINST.EXE.

PXL.ID and **PXL.HDR** are not on your disk; you make them yourself. PXL.ID can hold a personal ID if you want one in your header: just type your name in the Turbo Pascal editor and save it under "PXL.ID". When PXL finds such a file, it takes up to 24 characters from it for an ID. PXL.HDR can hold your own default header to replace PXL's standard one. (See the "Header" section.)

PXL can be run without its .WDS and .PRN files; although it can't mark reserved words, count begin-end pairs, and can print only plain pica, it can still number the lines and break up long ones. If you ask for anything PXL can't do, it will stop and complain. There is a way, though, of tinkering with the source code in PXL.PAS that enables it to run properly without the external data files—see the "Adapting PXL" section.

Running PXL

To run PXL, the two files PXL.WDS and PXL.PRN must be on the default disk or somewhere on your DOS path. If you want an ID in the header, you must make a PXL.ID file and keep it on the path or default disk too. You can run the program in different ways.

The interactive mode

For one, you can simply enter PXL from the DOS prompt. PXL will ask what file you want to list (adding the extension .PAS unless you tell it otherwise). It will search along the path and, if it finds the file, ask you to confirm the filename. Then PXL lets you choose how you want the file printed. You can ask for three characters (upper-and lowercase both work):

M *(Mark)* makes it underline the reserved words.

W *(Wide)* makes it use "condensed print" (if your printer is capable) to handle wide files without breaking up the lines. (In any mode, it will break up long lines as necessary and line up the continuation flush with the beginning of the original.)

L *(Linenumber)* makes PXL number the lines (using elite type if your printer has it, to keep the lines from folding). Also, if you use any of the above options, it will keep count of begin-end pairs and print the number of open Begin (or Repeat or Case) statements at each line.

P *(Plain)* signifies that you want none of these things; just leaving four blanks works as well. (Also, you could just hit Enter.)

X *(X-Ref)* makes PXL produce a cross-reference of the identifiers in your source code.

F *(Form-Feed)* makes PXL feed out a blank page before listing. To do this, however, the printer must form-feed on getting the FF (char 12) symbol. Unless it is told (in PXL.PRN) that the printer can do this, PXL will neither offer nor accept this option.

Used this way, PXL is gabby; it checks your choices, explains your errors, and lets you make corrections.

The command-line mode

The interactive mode is time-consuming. Instead, to take a shortcut, enter the information at the DOS prompt. If you enter

```
PXL filename
```

PXL will accept the filename, check to see if it exists, and skip its opening inquiries. For faster speed, enter

```
PXL filename xxxx
```

(where xxxx is any string of characters). PXL will pick the print style letters out of the string, show you what you've asked for, and ask for confirmation. If you want a plain vanilla printout (no line numbers, key words unmarked), put a P in the string. Order and casing don't matter, and additional stray characters are ignored.

Note: P will override anything else (except X). Thus, if you enter

```
PXL XYZ whelp
```

PXL will supply the suffix .PAS, notice the p, and ignore the other letters.

You'll get file XYZ.PAS, printed plain vanilla.

```
PXL xyz.pas MeltWax
```

would get you file XYZ.PAS with the works: condensed print (W), key words underlined (M), line numbers and begin-end counts (L), and a cross-reference (X).

```
PXL XYZ.DOC L
```

would print file XYZ.DOC with the lines numbered.

When you enter the data at the command line this way, PXL will look for your file. If the file is found, you get one screen asking you to confirm the filename and the print mode choices. If you say "Yes," it goes into its act. If you say "No" (or if it can't find your file), it reverts to the interactive mode, allowing you to correct your instructions.

However you start it, PXL keeps you informed about what it's doing (sending lines to the printer, scanning without printing, sending X-ref lines to printer, etc.). It gives you a running line count—to show that something's happening—and at the end of an X-ref printout, you get some statistics about your file.

The batch mode

If you want to run PXL from a batch file, put a line in your file just as you'd enter it in command-line mode but put the letters "BAT" (upper- or lowercase) in the instructions. In that case, PXL will not stop for interaction no matter what; if all is well, it will print out as instructed. If any hitch occurs, the file to print can't be found, the .PRN or .WDS file is not on the path, or if you press Esc during operation, it will set the ERRORLEVEL at 1. Your batch file can take account of that in deciding what to do next. This sample code takes the filename from the command line, executes PXL (printing the file with key words marked and lines numbered), and prints "ALL WELL" if the whole file has been printed or "ENDED BADLY" if anything went wrong:

```
echo off
pxl %1 ml bat
if errorlevel 1 goto Abort
echo             ALL WELL
goto end
:Abort
echo             ENDED BADLY
:end
```

The cross-reference

The cross-reference cites all the identifiers in your program with the line numbers in which they occur. They are printed with the upper/lowercase combination of their first occurrence. At the end of the identifier listing, you get a list of all the procedures and functions declared in the listing.

The cross-reference has two limitations:

- As far as PXL can tell, an identifier is a given combination of symbols. If you declare a variable like I:integer in several different procedures, they'll be lumped together in the X-ref listing. If you care about having an accurate list of the declared procedures, be careful not to use a procedure name as a local variable earlier in the program.

- Standard Pascal allows only numbers to be used as labels, while Turbo Pascal allows any legal identifier (which must start with a letter) as well. PXL ignores numbers, so it can't pick up labels like 99. If you want your labels listed, start them with a letter.

Include files

Files called with the {$I filename} Include directive will be included in the listing and cross-reference, provided that

- The {$I filename} directive begins in the first column of the code (if the directive starts anywhere else, PXL will simply ignore it).

- PXL can find it. If the filename specifies a path, say {$I B:PXL 2.INC}, it will look for the file first in the place specified and then search along the path. Whether it finds the file or not, it will print a message on the screen and in the printout showing what's happened.

This gives you two ways to control inclusion of files in your listing.

Note: As it does with the main file, PXL will add the suffix .PAS to the name of include files if none is given. To instruct it otherwise, put a period at the end of the filename.

Page format

Unless otherwise instructed, PXL will make a one-line header of its own devising and paginate automatically every 62 lines (including the header). You can instruct it otherwise, however.

Headers

The standard default header occupies one line. It puts the filename and the user's ID (if it can find a PXL.ID file) on the left. It puts the file date on the right of page 1; subsequent pages get the page number instead.

If you prefer a different default header, you can write your own. Keep it in a file called PXL.HDR anywhere on the path, and PXL will use it for its default header. You can still alter the header by putting instructions in your text.

There's a heavily commented header file on the disk under the name XXL.HDR. To see what it does, change its name to PXL.HDR and run PXL.

A PXL header can have up to five lines, a limit controlled by constant MaxHeader at the top of PXLLIST.PAS. You can change it at any point in the file. Each header line has three segments that must be separately specified, with each segment specifier having five parts:

- { (opening brace)

- One of the following symbols:

.HN	No header at all
.HnL	Left side of Header line #n
.HnC	Center of Header line #n
.HnR	Right side of Header line #n
.HnN	No Header line number n
.HPLnn	Print nn pages per line (not really a header instruction at all, but it can be used in PXL.HDR. See under "Pagination" later.

    n of course, stands for a numeral. The other symbols must be uppercase exactly as shown.

- A space. (That's *one* space. Spaces after the first one become part of the text of the header segment.)

- The text of the header segment. Within the text, you can use the following symbols:

.Fn	filename
.Fd	file date (in long form)
.Ft	file time (12-hr am/pm)
.Pd	present (or printout) date (mm/dd/yy)
.Pt	present (or printout) time (24 hr)
.Id	user ID (from PXL.ID)
#	page number (no period)

    These symbols are case-sensitive and must be upper/lower-case exactly as shown.

- } (closing brace)

Some remarks on this:

- Header instructions can appear anywhere in a line, but each one must begin and end on the same line.

- To empty a segment (that's previously been filled), put the closing brace right after the symbol and space: {.H2R} means empty right segment for 2nd header line. In general, to empty header lines:

{.HN}   Empties all the header lines (i.e., no header).
{.H2N} Empties the second (#2) header line.
{.H2L} Empties left segment of the second header line.

- PXL normally puts one blank line above and one blank line below the header. To force extra blank lines below the header, make a blank (not empty) header segment. {.H5L} would do it—note the extra spaces between L and }. The first space is eaten, the others become the left segment of header line 5.

- Normally, header instructions take effect on the next page after the instructions. To specify the opening header, you must put all the instructions for it at the top of your file. You can use several consecutive lines to do this, but there must be no blank lines between or before them. At the top of the file, you could (almost) specify the standard default header like this:

```
{.H1L File: .Fn [.Id]}
{.H1R .Ft, .Fd}
```

Then, there or anywhere in the first page's worth of text:

```
{.H1R Page #}
```

- Note: in PXL 1.41, specifying any header segments at all anywhere in the text canceled the default header. This has been changed. Beginning with PXL 1.42, new header specs change only the segments specified. Thus,

  - ~ To cancel the default header for a particular file, you must use {.HN}. Put that in the first line of the file to head off the default before it gets onto the page.

  - ~ If you don't want a default header at all—not ever—create a PXL.HDR file that contains no header instructions (a zero-byte file will do). So long as that's on the path, PXL will make no headers on its own. You can still insert header specs in the body of your file.

- You can differentiate between headers for the first page and for subsequent pages. Within PXL.HDR (and at the top of the text), the first specification for a given segment defines what's to go on the first page. A subsequent spec for that segment will be used for other pages. Thereafter, specifications simply supersede each other.

- If you need several default headers for different sorts of file, you could manage it by controlling the DOS PATH.

Pagination

To control page breaks, put the following symbols in the file:

{.PA} produces an absolute page advance. The line on which the symbol appears will be the first line of the new page.

{.CPnn} (where nn is a number) makes a conditional page break. If there isn't room for nn lines, it will start a new page at that point. Look at the PXL source code: it's peppered with these to keep the procedures whole.

Caution: This command specifies physical lines on the page. If you write lines long enough to fold, PXL will not make allowance for it and might run out of space on the page, splitting your block across the page break. If you write such lines, be sure to allow for it in specifying the nn.

{.HPLnn} (where nn is a number) specifies the number of lines PXL is to print on the page (including the header). The default is 62 lines on a 66-line page. This command will override the standard 4-line bottom margin. The default is controlled by variable BottomMargin, set in procedure SetUp in PXL.PAS.

Please note that this command specifies the number of lines to print, not the size of the paper. Make sure you don't overrun the paper by putting too large a number in HPL. Specify actual paper size (in lines) in Page Control using PXLINST. Even though it's not a header specification, an HPL instruction can be placed in PXL.HDR.

Stopping PXL

You can stop PXL at any point by pressing the Esc key. You might have to wait while it finishes the line it's working on and folds up the files, but don't panic: it will stop.

Adapting PXL

As it comes, PXL is designed to print source files from Turbo Pascal 4.0 on an Epson FX-80 from an IBM PC. If that's what you want to do, you can use PXL.EXE as it is. It can be adapted, however.

- Other Pascals (including earlier versions of Turbo Pascal) can also be accommodated by changing the reserved word list in PXL.WDS (see below).
- For other printers, it can be adapted by changing the print control symbols in PXL.PRN. See the instructions for other printers, later, for doing this.

For other Pascals

If your source code is in plain ASCII text files, the only difficulty about other Pascals ought to be the list of reserved words. (PXL would print the file, but it would mark only words reserved in Turbo Pascal.)

The list of reserved words is in the file PXL.WDS, so you only need to rewrite the PXL.WDS file to contain your Pascal's reserved words. Any text editor (like the Turbo Pascal editor) that makes plain ASCII files will do. Put one word on each line (without any extra blanks)—order and casing don't matter. PXL can handle up to 100 reserved words (there are 43 in Turbo Pascal 1.00, 44 in 2.00 and 3.00, and 48 in 4.00) and the words may be up to 10 characters long. If you need more than that, you'll have to rewrite the source code. The only things you'd have to change are in procedure SetUp at the beginning of the implementation of PXL.PAS and are identified with comments.

For other printers

The Epson MX and IBM printers resemble the FX-80; but with the standard PXL.PRN data, the line numbering mode may come out odd. Unless you use the W (condensed print) option, line numbering expects an elite font (which these printers lack). If you write lines long enough to fold, you should use PXLINST to change the print control symbols in PXL.PRN.

For other printers, consult your printer manual to see what you need. Again, use PXLINST to install the proper data as described in the next section.

PXLINST: editing print control symbols

To change the print control symbols, you must first work out what symbols you'll need. Then, with PXL.PRN on the default drive, run PXLINST.

Necessary symbols

PXL assumes that your printer can be made to underline and to compress its type to 12-character-per-inch "elite" and 17-character-per-inch "condensed" by sending it control codes of 1 to 3 characters. These characters must be in PXL.PRN on the default drive when you run PXL. Seven print control strings are required—start and stop for three type styles plus page control instructions:

Underlining If you prefer to mark your reserved words in some other way (boldface? italics?), put here whatever your printer needs for it.

Elite (12 characters per inch) type Normally, when PXL uses the symbols you put here, it assumes it will get 96 characters per line. Normally, it uses this font only when numbering the lines.

If your printer hasn't got an elite font (e.g., the IBM printer), you have a choice. If you put the symbols for condensed in both places, it will always use condensed for line numbering (adjusting the line lengths properly). What you should do is put nothing in PXL.PRN for elite. Then, PXL's L command will number the lines in plain pica, and WL (wide, line-numbering) will number them using condensed.

Condensed (17 characters per inch) typeface   This is the font invoked by the W (for *wide*) symbol. If your printer hasn't got a Condensed font, put nothing here. In that case, if you have something for Elite, PXL will use elite for both elite and condensed, lines cut to fit 96 characters per line. If you put nothing for Elite and nothing for Condensed, everything will come out in pica at 80 characters per line.

Page control   Here, it needs to be told whether your printer will feed out a new page when sent a Char #12 (FF) and, if not, how many lines it puts on a page. If you give it a 12 for "Page control," it will use Char #12 to form-feed. If you give it any other number, it will take that for the number of lines the printer gets to a page.

Look up the print control symbols in your printer manual and work out the ASCII numbers for them. PXLINST requires the numbers; it can't accept characters. Thus, to enter Esc-G, you would use the numbers 27, 71. 27 is the ASCII number for Escape, and 71 is the number for G. When you know what numbers you're going to need, put PXL.PRN on the default drive and run PXLINST.

Running PXLINST

Because it's an EXE file, PXLINST (like PXL) runs straight from DOS. When you run it, PXLINST gives you a screen showing the seven different instructions. If it finds PXL.PRN somewhere on your DOS path, it will show you what is currently in the file for each instruction and the Present Data you've set for them. It gives pretty good operating instructions.

1. Move the cursor to the line you want to change.

2. Enter the proper sequence of numbers (*numbers*, not characters), separating them with commas. Press Enter, and it will move on to the next instructions. You can use up to three ASCII numbers per instruction.

3. If you want nothing for a given instruction, press Enter alone. If your printer has none of these print options, enter nothing for everything but Page Control. PXL will then print plain vanilla, but it will break the lines appropriately, number them, give you begin/end counts, and make cross-references.

4. Make sure the Present Data display indicates what you wanted.

5. When the Present Data is what you want, press Esc to end the program. It will then ask whether you want the file rewritten with your new data. Up to this point, PXLINST hasn't actually changed the file. If you've made a mess, you can say "No."

If you happen to run PXLINST without PXL.PRN somewhere on the path, don't worry. It won't have any file data to show you, and it will start you out with Present Data of [nothing]; but you can enter the numbers you want, and PXLINST will create a new PXL.PRN file on the default disk.

Wide-carriage printers

PXL is designed to run on a narrow-carriage printer using 8.5 inch wide paper. If you have a wide printer that puts 133 pica characters on a line, you can make use of the full width by giving PXL deceitful printer data. The trick depends on the fact that condensed print on a narrow printer is designed to print 133 columns per line to handle printouts meant for a wide printer. So, when PXL thinks it's using condensed print, it makes wide lines.

Run PXLINST, and where it calls for condensed instruction symbols, put the instructions for plain pica. Give pica start instructions for both condensed start and condensed stop. The W (wide) option will now print wide lines in pica.

The L (line numbering) option (without a W) will still use elite and break lines at 84 columns of program text. If entering LW bores you and you want the L option in full width, give pica instructions for both elite and condensed. PXL will now think it has condensed for both of these and adjust its width accordingly.

Eliminating the data files

PXL can be made to run without the .PRN and .WDS data files by a simple alteration in PXL.PAS. The program already contains the necessary code for loading the print instructions and reserved word list internally.

You simply only need to set the value of DataFiles to False instead of True. (You do this in procedure SetUp in PXL.PAS. The comments there will show you what's what.) Of course, that will commit you to the TP4/Epson data in the code. If you want to change that, you must go deeper.

- Procedure LoadReserv in PXLMENU.PAS contains a list of key words in Turbo Pascal 4.00.

- Procedure GetPrinterData in PXLINIT.PAS has the print control symbols. Be careful to preserve the data form. (Essentially, it's the form of a Turbo Pascal string[3].) Each instruction takes four bytes.

The first (subscript 0) contains the number of following bytes significant in the instruction. Set unused bytes to $FF. This is exactly how the data would come in from PXL.PRN.

You should begin by using PXL with the external files because it's easier to experiment on printer data with PXLINST than by changing and recompiling PXL. When you know what numbers you need, you can make the necessary changes to GetPrinterData in PXLINIT.PAS, set DataFiles to False in PXL.PAS, and recompile.

If you set out to make this adaptation, it would be wise to make a copy of PXL first and experiment on the copy.

Screen colors

On a monochrome text monitor, PXL always runs in black and white. On other monitors, it normally uses color and three variables: NormalColor, FrameColor, and Background control the colors. FrameColor is used only for the ornamental rectangle. Everything else is in NormalColor. To set the colors to your liking, change the values in procedure SetUp in PXL.PAS.

Using PXL in a network

The batch mode (BAT) and form-feed (F) options were added in order to make PXL usable conveniently on a printer-sharing network. To illustrate this use of PXL, this section describes the use made of it with elementary classes in the PC Lab at Hartwick College in Oneonta, NY. The network was the University of Waterloo's JANET.

In this system, all utilities were kept on a virtual disk in Drive A. Students put their own programs on a real disk drive labelled D: by the network and kept a PXL.ID user ID file on their disks. They were taught to send printer output from their programs to the file D:OUT.PUT. To allow these beginning students to get their printouts with a minimum of confusion and a minimum of instruction, PXL was run from a batch file. To get printouts, they merely entered:

    A:NEWPRINT programfilename

Figure 5-1 is an annotated copy of NEWPRINT.BAT.

Registration

PXL is not copyrighted but is in the public domain and requires no registration. The program can be ordered from

R. N. Wisan
37 Clinton St.
Oneonta, NY 13820

```
ECHO OFF

REM List program marked, numbered, xref, and FF
REM (to avoid the network's printout header)
A:PXL D:%1 MLXF BAT

REM Check that program listing went well
IF ERRORLEVEL 1 GOTO ABORT

REM List output file plain w/o FF
A:PXL D:OUT.PUT BAT

REM Check that this went well
IF ERRORLEVEL 1 GOTO ABORT

REM All went well, so send to printer, and report success:
A:PRINTIT
ECHO D:%1 and OUT.PUT sent to printer
GOTO END

REM If all did not go well, abort printing, and report failure:
:ABORT
A:PURGE *
ECHO Error in listing.  Printout has been aborted.

:END

Note: PRINTIT is the network's print command.  PURGE * cancels
      everything sent to the print spool from this work station.
```

5-1 A batch file to allow PXL printouts on a network.

6
Personal C Compiler

Program title   Personal C Compiler   *(Disk 1337)*

Special requirements   None.

Personal C Compiler is for the 8088/8086 family of microprocessors. It accepts C source programs as input and produces object files. The model employed by the compiler efficiently utilizes the 8088/8086 architecture but limits a program to 64K of code and 64K of data. PCC is fast, powerful, and fully compatible with code written for DeSmet 2.51. Code for earlier versions of DeSmet should work with minimal adjustment.

PCC builds "small model" only: 64K of code, 64K of data (which can be bypassed), and 64K of stack executables from Kernighan and Ritchie standard C language source. It comes with compiler, Assembler, linker, library utility, standard library, debugger, editor, and sample files. PCC is not a bare bones system; it supports overlays, has an 8087 library, a library of supplemental screen I/O routines, and a special data type to break the 64K limit. The documentation is indexed, very complete, and a good learning tool for the beginning C programmer.

Most importantly, PCC produces small and efficient code very quickly; even though it is not a fancy "optimizing" compiler with lots of bells and whistles, it's all a true programmer really needs: it makes fast compact programs.

Some of the terms and conventions of PCC are a bit different from those in books on the C language, so we will quickly run through the terms used.

Common term	PCC term	Description
LINK	PCCL	Builds .EXE file
FILENAME.OBJ	FILENAME.O	Basis for .EXE file
FILENAME.ASM	FILENAME.A	Assembly source file
MASM or ASM	PCCA	8088/8086 Assembler
CC or CPP	PCC	Main Compiler (1st Pass)
CC1	PC2	Compiler Second Pass

Using code from other sources

There are many C compilers, as well as many variations of interpretation of what C syntax should be. In addition, there are the extensions to support I/O, machine specific functions, etc. Source NOT written for PCC or DeSmet 2.51 might need minor adjustments to be accepted by the PCC compiler and run properly.

In fact, finding, compiling and modifying source code is an excellent way to learn any language or compiler. Just be careful not to adopt bad habits from exposure to poorly written code.

Caution: PCC will accept any valid code you supply to it, as will any compiler. The code might well be valid, but the results of the code could be dangerous to the health and safety of your computer, monitor, or contents of your hard drive or floppies (and it WILL be at one time or another). Guard and maintain up-to-date copies of all files on your system. If your program or the compiler starts to act erratically (i.e., screen goes blank, video displays strange characters, the hardware makes noises, or other strange unexpected actions occur), *immediately turn off the power* to the computer and investigate carefully after you have the system rebooted.

Getting started

First things first. Copy all of the files from the distribution disk onto a set of working floppy diskettes or hard disk. The package is not copy-protected, so the MS-DOS COPY command can be used to copy the files. The package is distributed on a single double-sided (360K) diskette. The distribution diskette should never be used but should be kept as the backup copy of PCC.

Let's make sure the compiler files are intact. A source program called DUMP.C has been provided in this package. Place the files from PCC12B.ARC in a directory of your choice or on floppy disks per the later documentation. To compile DUMP.C, enter

    PCC DUMP

This will compile DUMP.C into an object module DUMP.O. To link DUMP.O with the required library functions in PCCS.S, enter

    PCCL DUMP

This will produce a file DUMP.EXE. To run DUMP.EXE, enter

```
DUMP DUMP.C
```

This will produce a hex and ASCII dump of DUMP.C on your screen. If DUMP runs correctly, then the compiler should be in good working order.

PCC files

The package is distributed as a compressed file, PCC.ARC, so that integrity checks might be run. PCC.ARC contains the following files:

BUF128.A	Source code for 128 byte-type-ahead TSR.
BUGS!.EXE	Arcade game (use BUGS! c for color displays).
DUMP.C	Source code for hex file display utility.
EXEC.O	The Exec( ) and Chain( ) functions.
LATER.C	Source code for a file-modification date-checking program.
LIFE.C	Source code for the game of Life.
MATH.H	Include file for the Standard Math package.
PC2.EXE	The second pass of the C compiler.
PCC.EXE	The first pass of the C compiler.
PCC7.S	The standard C function library with 8087 support. To use this library, rename it to PCCS.S.
PCCA.EXE	The assembler and third pass of the C compiler.
PCCL.EXE	The object file linker.
PCCS.S	The standard C function library with software floating-point support.
PCIO.A	Source code for the PC screen functions.
RAM.COM	RAM Disk driver for DOS 2.0 and later operating systems.
SETJMP.H	Include file for the setjmp( )/longjmp( ) functions.
STDIO.H	Include file for the Standard I/O package.

Basic system

The minimum files you need from PCC.ARC are PCC.EXE, PC2.EXE, PCCA.EXE, PCCL.EXE, and PCCS.S. The files STDIO.H and MATH.H contain useful declarations.

If you are working in a directory other than the one containing the PCC files, be sure to set the PATH environment variable to include the PCC directory.

Setting up DOS 2.x and later

For systems utilizing DOS 2.x or later versions of the operating systems, make sure that the ASCII text file CONFIG.SYS exists on your boot disk.

The file must contain the line

```
FILES=20
```

because PCC supports 20 open files, Q stdin, stdout, stderr, and 17 other files. The default number of eight is insufficient for the PCCL program.

If there is enough memory available, add the line

```
BUFFERS=20
```

to improve file performance in the operating system. 512 bytes are allocated for each specified buffer.

RAM disk

If you have a system with more than 256K of memory, then the Ram Disk driver RAM.COM can be used to create an extremely fast disk. To add a Ram Disk, copy the RAM.COM file from the distribution diskette to the system disk and add the line

```
DEVICE=RAM.COM n
```

to the CONFIG.SYS file. The parameter n is a decimal number from 32 to 650 indicating the size of the Ram Disk. The value is specified in units of one K (1024).

Reboot the system to install the Ram Disk. The drive letter used for this "disk drive" is dependent on the configuration of the system. DOS will install the Ram Disk at the first free device slot, which will probably be drive C for an IBM PC with two floppies and drive D for an XT. Sanyo 550/5 reserves the first four slots for its floppies, so the Ram Disk is drive E. To find where DOS has installed the Ram Disk, use

```
chkdsk x:
```

where x takes on the values C, D, etc. You will get either a disk error or a return showing the size of the Ram Disk. Once you find it, the Ram Disk will always be the same until you add other device drivers before it in the CONFIG.SYS file.

Completion codes

The PCC, PCCA, and PCCL programs set the completion code to

0 If no warnings or errors occurred.
1 If warnings were issued.
2 If errors occurred.

Batch files can take advantage of these values to stop execution or otherwise handle these exceptional cases.

The batch file in FIG. 6-1 will stop on a PCC or PCCL error. More complicated development situations can be handled with the program LATER

6-1 Batch files can use the error levels from PCC and PCCL.

```
PCC %1
if errorlevel 1 goto stop
PCCL %1
if errorlevel 1 goto stop
%1
:stop
```

that is supplied in source form in the file LATER.C. LATER takes a list of filenames as arguments, setting the ERRORLEVEL to 1 if the last file does not exist or if the last file has an earlier modification date than any other file in the list. It can only be used on systems with a battery backup clock or where users are careful about setting the date and time when the system is brought up. Assume a program is composed of the files MODA.C, MODB.C, MODC.C, and they include file MOD.H. The following .BAT file in FIG. 6-2 can be used to regenerate the program whenever a module changes.

This provides a service similar to the UNIX MAKE program. Only those files that need to be compiled will be compiled.

6-2 Example batch file using the LATER.EXE program.

```
later moda.c mod.h moda.o
     if errorlevel 1 PCC moda
          if errorlevel 1 goto stop
later modb.c mod.h modb.o
     if errorlevel 1 PCC modb
          if errorlevel 1 goto stop
later modc.c mod.h modc.o
     if errorlevel 1 PCC modc
          if errorlevel 1 goto stop
later moda.o modb.o modc.o mod.exe
     if errorlevel 1 PCCL moda modb modc -omod
:stop
```

Running the personal C compiler

To run the compiler, type the following line at the DOS prompt:

```
PCC <filename> [options]
```

<filename> is the name of the file containing the C source. If it does not include an extension, the extension .C is assumed.

Options: The casing of the option is not significant. Each option should be separated from other options by blanks and may be preceded with the dash (-) character.

A   Assembly output. This option indicates that the compiler should produce an assembly language source file instead of an object file. The name of the assembly language file will be the same as the name of the source file but will have the extension .A.

D<name>	Compiler drive specification. The compiler assumes that the files PC2.EXE and PCCA.EXE are in the default directory on the current drive. This option is used to inform the compiler that the files are on a different drive. For example, if the compiler is on drive M, then the option DM is needed. Under MS-DOS 2.0 and later versions of the operating system, this option is rarely needed because the system PATH variable is also used to find the other passes of the compiler.
I<name>	Include path name. This option overrides the default drive/directory for files included with the #include control. The directory name must end with a trailing backslash (\) character (e.g., -ic:\src\include\). See the "Forward References" for #include details.
N<defname>=<defvalue>	Specify #define name and value. Used to set debugging switches or constant values without editing the file. This option is equivalent to #define defname defvalue at the beginning of the program. To set <defname> to one, enter n<defname>, which is equivalent to #define defname 1. Spaces are not allowed.
O<filename>	Output filename. The compiler will produce an object file with the specified name. If the name lacks an extension, the extension .O will be added. The default object name is the same as the source name with the extension of .O.
T<drive>	Specifies the drive that the compiler should use for its temporary files. If not specified, the compiler will build its temporary files on the default drive. If this drive is close to being full, the T option should be used to change the drive for the temporaries. Also, if the RAM Disk has been installed, placing the temporary files there will drastically cut the amount of time needed to compile a program.

Examples

PCC blip compiles the file named BLIP.C. The object file will be named BLIP.O.

m:PCC b:blip.ccc tm dm runs the compiler from drive M on the file B:BLIP.CCC. Temporary files are also written on drive M. Note the use of the D option to indicate the location of the other passes of the compiler. The object file will also be named BLIP.O.

PCC blip -ic:\inc\ -a -nNewVersion -nNYear=1985 compiles the file named BLIP.C. Include files are taken from the directory C:\ INC\. An assembly language file is generated named BLIP.A. The N options are equivalent to adding

```
#define NewVersion 1
#define NYear 1985
```

to the start of BLIP.C.

The C language

PCC compiles C programs that conform to the standard definition of the C language as described in the book *The C Programming Language* by Brian W. Kernighan and Dennis M. Ritchie. The following sections describe the implementation.

Preprocessor directives

#define defines a macro with or without parameters.

#undef, #ifdef, and #ifndef test the status of the #defined macros.

#include includes other files into the program. #include's can be nested to a maximum depth of 3. #include "filename" will search the default directory for the file filename. #include <filename> will first search the default directory for filename. If the file was not found, the environment (see DOS 2.X/3.X SET command) is searched for the variable INCLUDE. If the variable is found, it is assumed to contain a set of directory prefixes separated by semi-colons.

For example, if INCLUDE is set as follows,

```
set include=c:\;c:\usr\include\
```

then the line

```
#include <world.h>
```

would cause PCC to search for

```
world.h
c:\world.h
c:\usr\include\world.h
```

#if, #else, #endif—conditionally includes or excludes source statements.

Data types

char	Unsigned byte with a range of 0 to 255.
short int	Signed integer with a range of -32768 to 32767.
unsigned int	Unsigned integer with a range of 0 to 65535.
long int	Signed integer with a range of -2147483648 to 2147483647.
float	Four-byte floating point value. A float number has about 7 digits of precision and has a range of about $1.E-36$ to $1.E+36$. The floating point formats are defined by the IEEE floating-point standard.
double	Eight-byte floating point value. A double number has about 13 digits of precision and a range of about $1.E-303$ to $1.E+303$.
(pointer)	Pointers are two bytes, limiting total data space to 64K.

To take advantage of the 8088/8086 instruction set, expressions involving only char types are not coerced to int before evaluation. The sum of a char equal to 255 and a char equal to 1 is 0 rather than 256. Constants are considered to be int values so that constant plus char is a two-byte integer operation.

Extensions

The UNIX 7 extensions—enumerated types, extended member name-space, and structure assignment—are fully supported.

Enumerated types provide a convenient method of declaring an ordered set of named constants. Values start with zero and can be reassigned with a name=value expression. The same value can be assigned to several names. (See FIG. 6-3 for an example.)

Extended member name-space relaxes the requirement that if a member name appeared in more than one structure or union, then it had

```
enum color {red, blue=4, green} ca, *cp;
enum color cb;
if(ca == red)
        cb = green;
```

is equivalent to

```
#define red   0
#define blue  4
#define green 5
int ca, *cp;
int cb;
if(ca == red)
        cb = green;
```

6-3 Enumerated types furnish a clean way to declare constants.

to have the same data type and offset in every appearance. Now, the only restriction is that the member name must be unique within the structure or union. If a member name is used that is not in the referenced structure, the warning

member not in structure

is issued. As a loophole, a pointer to char can be used as an anonymous pointer to any structure (see FIG. 6-4).

6-4 The same member name in different structures or unions can have different data types and offsets. A pointer to a char can point to any structure anonymously.

```
struct {int i, j, k;} zip;
struct {int j; char i;} zap, *zp;
char *cp;

zip.i = 1;          /* OK */
zap.i = 1;          /* OK */
zap.k = 1;          /* WARNING */
zp->i = 1;          /* OK */
zp->k = 1;          /* WARNING */
cp->k = 1;          /* OK, ANONYMOUS */
```

Structures can be assigned, used as parameters, or returned from a function. *Caution:* This may create problems with existing programs because previous versions of PCC converted the name of a structure in a parameter list to a pointer to that structure, while the current release pushes the entire structure. To highlight this potential problem, PCC will issue the warning

structure assignment

when structures are passed by value, and the warning

returns structure

when a function returns a structure (see FIG. 6-5). These warnings will be removed in a future release.

6-5 Structures passed by value or returned by a function will produce warnings.

```
struct z {int i, j;} zip, zap, zxax();
main(){
        zip = zap;   /* structure assignment */
        zap = zmax(zip, zap);
        }
struct z zmax(a,b) /* func returns struct */
        struct z a, b; {
        if(a.i > b.i)
                return a;
        return b;
        }
```

Note that variable names are significant to 31 characters instead of 8.

An #asm directive has been included to allow in-line assembly language code for time-critical applications. All lines following a line starting with #asm are passed through to the assembler. The next line beginning with the "#" character ends the in-line assembly code (see FIG. 6-6).

```
_move(count, src, tar)
int count; char *src, *tar; {
#asm
            MOV         CX,[BP+4]  ;count
            MOV         SI,[BP+6]  ;src
            MOV         DI,[BP+8]  ;dst
            MOV         AX,DS
            MOV         ES,AX
            CLD
            REP MOVSB
#
            }
```

6-6 Use the #ASM directive to insert assembly language code.

Forward references

PCC is effectively a one-pass compiler, so forward references will not work. This program

```
main() {
   i = 99;
   }
extern int i;
```

will produce a warning that i is undefined and assumed to be a local variable named "i". The global variable i will not be changed.

Structure tags must be defined before being referenced. The only exception is pointers, so that legal structure declarations include structures of the form:

```
struct a {
   struct b *x;
   }

struct b {

   struct a *y;

   }
```

Externs

The rules for "extern" declarations are as follows:

- Statements global to the source file, like intblip;, can be in several different files linked together. PCCL will allocate 2 bytes for the global integer variable `blip`. This is an extension to the standard rule that restricts global declarations to a single file and requires all the other declarations to be external.

- A declaration including the keyword "extern" cannot include initializers and does not allocate any memory. Thus, a variable so declared must be declared somewhere else without the "extern" keyword in order to reserve memory for the variable. For example, if a file contains the declaration `extern int blip`, then some other file must contain the declaration `int blip` to actually allocate storage. If this is not done, the binder will complain about a reference to the unresolved symbol `blip`. You may have both an "extern" and non-"extern" declaration in a single file. For example,

```
extern int blip;
int blip;
```

is valid.

To create include files containing data declarations—if the variable is not initialized (which means it will be initialized with zeros)—either include the declaration:

```
int blip;
```

in every file or include the declaration

```
extern int blip;
```

in every file and add the declaration

```
int blip;
```

to one of the files to actually allocate the storage.

If the variable needs initialization, the second approach must be used. Include the declaration

```
extern int blip;
```

in the include file. However, initialize the value in only one file:

```
int blip = 1985;
```

These rules are about the same as Version 7 UNIX. Extern rules are an area of C that are currently controversial. System V UNIX tried to tighten up the rules, but enough people complained that now 5.2 is back to normal.

Macros

Macro arguments are not replaced within a quoted string. For example, in *The C Puzzle Book* by Alan Feuer, the macros in <defs.h> use the following construct to customize printf( ) calls:

```
#define PR(fmt,v)printf("value=%fmt%t",v);
```

This does not work with the PCC compiler. Instead, add the following defines to <defs.h>:

```
#define D  "value =   %d%t"
#define F  "value =   %f%t"
#define C  "value =   %c%t"
#define G  "value =   %g%t"
```

and change the PR define to

```
#define PR(fmt,v)printf(fmt,(v));
```

Statements of the type

```
PRINT1(d,x);
```

must be changed to

```
PRINT1(D,x);
```

in the programs. Lowercase letters d, f, c, and g would allow the programs to remain unchanged, but variables c and g are used in structure one and variable g is used in structures two and three.

Strings

Literal character strings delimited by quotes (\") cannot contain the NUL character (\0). The compiler terminates the string at the NUL character, even though it checks that the string has a terminating quote character. If you want NUL characters in the string for initialization purposes, use an array assignment:

```
char init1[]="abcdef@xyz@012", *ip=init1;

while(ip = index(ip, '@'))
   *ip = '\0';
```

The PCCA 8088 assembler

PCCA is the 8088/8086 assembler. It reads assembly language source files and produces linkable object files.

Starting PCCA

At the DOS prompt, type the following:

```
PCCA <filename> [ options ]
```

<filename> is the name of the assembly language source file. If it does not include an extension Q, the extension .A is assumed.

Options: The case of the option is not significant. Each option should be separated from other options by blanks. Options may be preceded with the dash (-) character.

L[<filename>]	The assembler will produce a listing from the assembly language input. This listing includes the hex-values generated by the assembler as well as line numbers and pagination. If no name is specified, then the name of the source file with the extension .L is used. If the specified file does not have an extension, .L will be used. Otherwise the listing is written to the specified file. To generate a listing on the printer, use -LPRN:.
O<filename>	The assembler will produce an object file with the specified name. If the name lacks an extension, then the extension .O will be appended to the name. The default object filename is the name of the source file with the extension changed to .O.
T<drive>	The T option specifies the drive where the assembler temporary files will be created. If a RAM Disk is available, redirecting temporary files to that drive will greatly speed development. The assembler normally creates its temporary files on the default drive/directory.
Pnn	Specifies page length, in lines. The default is 66.
Wnn	Specifies page width, in characters, for the list file. The value nn must be a number from 60 to 132. The default is 80.

Example

PCCA blip assembles the file named blip.a and produces an object file named blip.o.

M:PCCA blip.asm -Ob:blip Lblip.lst runs the assembler from drive M: on the file named blip.asm. The output is an object file named blip.o on drive B and a listing file named blip.lst on the default drive.

PCCA blip.a TM -oa:blip.o -lb:blip.lst assembles the file named blip.a. Temporary files are created on drive M. The output of the assembler is placed on drive A in the file blip.o. A listing file is generated and written to drive B in the file blip.lst.

The PCCL object file linker

PCCL is the program that links together object and library modules and forms an executable program. For very long command lines, see the -f option.

Starting PCCL

The DOS command line syntax for PCCL is

```
PCCL <filename> <filename> ... [options]
```

<filename> is a sequence of filenames separated by blanks. The #
filenames should be the names of object (.O) or library (.S) files. If a
filename does not have an extension, .O is assumed. PCCL automatically
looks for the supplied library PCCS.S, so its name should not be included
in the list of filenames.

Options: All options may be in upper/lowercase. Options *must* be separated by blanks and preceded by a hyphen to differentiate them from
<filename>s. Note that this is different from other commands where
the hyphen is optional.

-A
The assembler option keeps PCCL from generating the C initialization code. Instead, execution begins at the beginning of the code
rather than starting at the main_ public
label. ARGC and ARGV are not calculated,
the stack is not set up, and uninitialized variables are not filled with zero. Library functions such as creat( ) and open( ) cannot
be used, as they depend on the zero initialization. The A and S options are useful for a few
cases but caution should be exercised in
their use.

-F<filename>
Identifies a file containing <filename>s
and options to be used by PCCL. This is used
for very long lists of filenames and options.

-L<name>
Specifies the drive/directory containing the
PCCS.S standard library. If this option is not
specified, the PCCS.S file must be on the
default drive. With MS-DOS 2.0 and later versions of the operating system, the PATH system parameter is used to locate the library.

-Mn
Indicates that the object files following this
control should be collected in the memory-
based overlay indicated by the value n (1 to
39). See the description on overlays later for
details on the overlay mechanism.

-O<filename>
Changes the name of the output file to
<filename>.EXE. If this option is not
specified, the name of the first object file in
the list with the .EXE extension will be used.

-P[<filename>]	Generates a sorted list of publics and offsets. C procedures and data declared outside of procedures are automatically public (or extern) unless explicitly declared static. Publics with names starting with an underline are not listed unless the -_option is also specified. The optional name is the destination for the publics list. If omitted, the publics and offsets are listed on the console. The size of # overlays, if any, will also be displayed.
-Shhhh	Specifies the stack size. hhhh is in hex. Normally, PCCL will set the stack size as large as possible. The -S option can be used to limit this size for use with exec( ).
-Vn	Used to create disk-based overlays. All object files following this option, until the end of the list or another overlay option, are collected into the overlay indicated by the value n (1 to 39). See the overlay section later for details.
-_ *(underscore)*	PCCL normally suppresses names that start with an underscore (usually internal names) from the publics list. The underscore option restores these publics to the listing. This option is useful when you need to see all the modules bound to your program.

Examples

PCCL blip binds the file blip.o with PCCS.S and produces the executable file BLIP.EXE.

PCCL proga progb progc lib.s -p binds the files proga.o, progb.o, and progc.o with the user library lib.s and the standard I/O library—PCCS.S—into the application file proga.exe. The map is printed on the screen.

PCCL proga progb -V1 progc -V2 progd -Pmap -_ -Omyprog binds the files PROGA.O, PROGB.O with PCCS.S and creates the executable file MYPROG.EXE and the overlay file MYPROG.OV, which contains two overlays consisting of the object files PROGC.O and PROD.O. The publics map is sent to the file named map and will also list the internal names that begin with the underline character.

Space considerations

A program is restricted to a maximum of 64K of code and 64K of data plus the stack. PCCL calculates the size of code and data and will report the size of each segment (in hex) when the -P option is specified. PCCL cannot calculate the actual stack requirements. If the stack and locals size reported by PCCL seems small, the actual stack requirements should be calculated by hand to make sure there is enough space. The actual requirements are the worst case of four bytes per call plus the size of locals (including parameters) for all active procedures plus about 500 bytes for the Operating System calls. In practice, 2K plus the size of the local arrays simultaneously active should be sufficient.

If PCCL reports that the code limit is exceeded, look in the publics map for the scanf() and printf() routines. These are relatively large routines (around 2K each) and also link in the floating-point routines. Eliminating the use of these routines can result in a large savings. If scanf() and/or printf() are necessary but no floating-point values will be used, try using the PCC7.S instead of the standard PCCS.S library. (Rename the PCCS.S library to something else and rename the PCC7.S library to PCCS.S.) This will assume the availability of the 8087 math chip and will not bring in the software floating-point routines.

Overlays

Another way to solve the space problem is to use overlays. The overlay system provided by this package is very simple. An application is divided into a root portion that is always resident and two or more overlays. Only one overlay is resident (executable) at any given time.

There are two types of overlays: disk-based overlays, and memory-based overlays. The difference between the two types is the location of the overlays. Disk-based overlays, created with the -V option, are stored in a separate file. Memory-based overlays, created with the -M option, are loaded into memory along with the root code. Memory-based overlays should only be used when there is sufficient memory for the root and all of the overlays. The advantage of memory-based overlays over disk-based overlays is in the amount of time needed to make an overlay resident, with memory-based overlays being much faster to load.

The application program is responsible for initializing the overlay subsystem and ensuring that the correct overlay is resident before calling any of the functions in the overlay.

For disk-based overlays, the routine overlay __init() must be called from the root with the name of the overlay file to initialize the overlay system. Overlays are loaded by calling the routine overlay(n), where n is the number of the overlay to be made resident.

For memory-based overlays instead of disk-based overlays, do not call the overlay __init() routine and call the routine moverlay() in place of the routine overlay().

In the example in FIG. 6-7, the root is composed of the file X.C. The first overlay is the file Y.C and the second overlay is in the file Z.C.

```
File X.C:
        main() {
                overlay_init("X.OV"); /* initialize */
                puts("this is the root program\n");
                overlay(1); /* make 1st overlay resident */
                zip();     /* call into 1st overlay */
                overlay(2); /* make the second resident */
                zap();     /* call into second overlay */
                puts("bye\n");
                }

File Y.C:
        zip() {
                puts("  this is ZIP  ");
                }

File Z.C:
        zap() {
                puts("  this is ZAP  ");
                }
```

6-7 An example program using overlays.

The files are compiled in the usual fashion:

PCC x
PCC y
PCC z

Ordinarily, the files would be linked together using this command:

PCCL x y z

Instead, to create the two overlays, use the command

PCCL x -V1 y -V2 z

The -V option is followed by the overlay number, which starts at 1 and runs in ascending order up to 39. All files following the -V or the -M option are included in the overlay. All library modules (from .S files) are included in the root. The result from the execution of the PCCL program with the -V option is the executable root (.EXE) file and the overlay (.OV) file containing the overlays. The result with the -M option is an .EXE file containing both the root and the overlays.

The -P option of PCCL will also display the size of each overlay as well as the overlay for each symbol.

Libraries

Libraries are just concatenated .O files. The .S extension tells PCCL to only include modules that are referenced. If all of the routines in a library are required, rename the .S file to a .O file to force all of the modules in the library to be included.

PCCL includes the entire .O module from a library if any of its public names have been selected by other object modules processed by PCCL. Thus, if a .O file contains several functions, all of them will be bound into a program if any of them are called.

PCCL searches a library once. Thus if you have two modules—A and B—and A calls B, the B must follow A in the library. LIB88 attempts to order the library so that these interlibrary references are ordered so that PCCL will find them. One way around any circular dependencies (e.g., B also calls A) is to include the library twice on the command line.

The PCCS.S standard library

This section describes the standard library, PCCS.S, for the PCC C compiler and PCCA assembler. This library includes routines similar to routines available in UNIX with some inevitable differences due to the MS-DOS Operating System.

All of the routines are in the PCCS.S library file provided on the distribution disk. This file must be on the default drive/directory, in a directory listed in the PATH system parameter, or on the drive/directory referred to by the -L option for PCCL to execute correctly.

There is a PCC7.S library that has the same functions as the PCCS.S library but assumes the availability of the 8087 math chip to perform the floating-point operations. To use the 8087, rename PCC7.S to PCCS.S.

Names

Public names starting with the underline character are reserved for PCC internal routines and should be avoided. Names of this form are also employed for user callable routines such as _move( ) whose names might conflict with user names.

PCC automatically appends the underline character to the end of public names to avoid conflicts with assembly language reserved words. PCCA does not do this so the underline must be manually appended to publics used to link with code generated by PCC. For example, the C puts( ) routine should be referred to as puts_ from assembler. PCCL ignores the case of publics, unlike UNIX, so puts_ matches the name PutS_.

Program initialization

PCCL inserts a jmp _csetup as the first executable instruction in the program. _CSETUP performs the following initialization functions:

- Sets the data/stack segment size to the lower of the following: available memory, 64K, or the size of the static data area plus the PCCL -S option.
- Formats argc and argv[ ] from the Program Segment Prefix.
- Zeros the Uninitialized Data Area.
- Calls main(argc, argv).

Assembly language main programs that require normal initialization should contain the following

```
PUBLIC MAIN_
MAIN_:
```

The initialization code will set the SS, DS, and SP registers so that there is the largest possible stack unless the PCCL -S option is used to restrict the stack size. The stack grows towards the initialized data area. Figure 6-8 shows the memory layout after the initialization code has run.

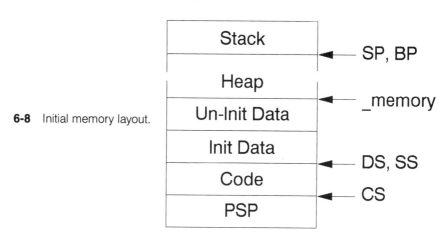

6-8 Initial memory layout.

The memory between the end of the uninitialized area and the stack is not normally used by PCC or the program (unless the program needs an inordinate amount of stack). This area is considered to be free memory. This memory area can be accessed directly by using the _memory( ) and _showsp( ) routines to calculate its extent, or by using the malloc( ) routine. However, do not use both methods; also remember to leave enough space for the stack to grow.

The -A option of PCCL inhibits the call to _csetup. Execution commences with the first instruction of the first filename specified to PCCL. On entry, the registers have the following values:

CS   Address of Code Segment. Execution starts at CS:0.
SS   Address of Data Segment.
ES,DS Address of Program Segment Prefix.
SP   Stack size set by PCCL.

The source code for _csetup is in the file ISETUP.A.

Calling conventions

Arguments to a function are pushed on the stack, rightmost argument first. The calling function is responsible for cleaning up the stack. For example,

```
int i;

zip(i, 6);
```

would generate the following code:

```
mov       ax,6
push      ax
push      word i_
public    zip_
call      zip_
add       sp,4
```

The word modifier is required because PCC allocates two bytes for ints. The add sp,4 removes the two words that were pushed as parameters to zip_. Note the PCC appended "_" on names. If there had been no local variables defined in the function, the clean-up code would have been

```
mov       sp,bp
```

which is faster.

Data is pushed on the stack as follows:

char Pushed as a word, with high-order byte set to zero

```
mov AL,data_
mov AH,0
push AX
```

int Pushed as a word unsigned

```
push WORD data_
```

long Pushed with least-significant word pushed last

```
push WORD data_[2]
push WORD data_[0]
```

float Changed to double and pushed with least-significant word pushed last

```
mov si,offset data_
PUBLIC _FLOADE ; load float
call _FLOADE
PUBLIC _FPUSH ; push double
call _FPUSH
```

double Pushed with least-significant word pushed last

```
push WORD data_[6]
push WORD data_[4]
push WORD data_[2]
push WORD data_[0]
```

struct   Push (sizeof(struct) + 1) >> 1 words, with least
significant word pushed last

```
mov   cx,nn              ; size in words
sub   sp,cx              ; make room on stack
mov   di,sp              ; target
mov   si,offset data_    ; source
mov   ax,ds              ; setup
mov   es,ax              ; es
cld                      ; set direction up
rep   movsw              ; copy to stack
```

Library conventions

Called functions are responsible for preserving CS, DS, SS, SP, and BP
across the function call. All other registers need not be maintained. The
usual preamble for a called function is

```
    PUBLIC fname_
fname_:
    push bp ; save old frame pointer
    mov bp,sp ; establish local frame
```

For functions that don't return structures, parameters begin in the
local frame at [bp+4] and continue upward based on the size of each
parameter. Thus for the fragment

```
blip(x, y, z)
int x;
long y;
double z;
```

the parameters would be referenced in Assembler as

```
mov   cx,WORD [bp+4]  ; x_
mov   ax,WORD [bp+6]  ; lsw of y_
mov   dx,WORD [bp+8]  ; msw of y_
lea   si,[bp+10]      ; addr of z_
```

For functions that do return structures, [bp+4] contains a pointer to
where the structure should be returned. So if the above fragment was

```
struct foo blip(x, y, z)
```

the parameters would be

```
mov   cx,WORD [bp+06]  ; x_
mov   ax,WORD [bp+08]  ; lsw of y_
mov   dx,WORD [bp+10]  ; msw of y_
lea   si,[bp+12]       ; addr of z_
```

Local variables are allocated below the current frame pointer, regardless of what the function returns, so that the fragment

```
{
int aa[2];
long b;
```

would be referenced as

```
sub   sp,8          ; allocate space for locals
mov   ax,[bp-4]     ; aa_[1]
mov   dx,[bp-8]     ; msw b_
```

The standard exit sequence is

```
mov   sp,bp         ; reclaim any local space
pop   bp            ; old frame pointer
ret                 ; caller will clean up stack
```

Values are returned from functions as follows:

`char`	Returned in AX. char values are returned in AL with AH set to zero.
`int unsigned long`	Returned in DX:AX. (AX contains lsw)
`double`	Returned on floating point stack (s/w or 8087)
`float struct`	returned to address in [bp+4]

Disk Input/Output routines

In this implementation of C I/O, procedures like `getc()` are functions rather than macros and a file identifier FILE is simply an integer containing the file number rather than a pointer to a structure. This change means that `read()` and `getc()` calls can be intermingled and little difference exists between `open()` and `fopen()` on a file.

UNIX distinguishes between file and stream I/O. Crudely stated, the functions that have "f" as their first letter—`fopen()`, `fread()`, etc.—deal with streams, and other primitives—`open()`, `read()`, etc.—access files. These two forms of I/O are compatible—`fopen()` can be used to open a file and then `read()` used to read it—but it is best to use either the stream or file primitives only for a particular file for portability. The FILE type is defined in the stdio.h include file and is simply an int type. This int contains the file number, the same number returned by `open()` and `creat()`. To use the stream routines with a file opened with the `open()`, merely pass the file number.

The stream style of I/O primitives are as follows: `fopen()` to open a file; `fread()`, `fgets()`, or `fgetc()` [`getc()`] to read; `fwrite()`, `fputs()`, or `fputc()` [`putc()`] to write; `fseek()` to seek; `fflush()` to write out internal buffers; and `fclose()` to close.

The file type I/O primitives are as follows: open( ), creat( ), read( ), write( ), lseek( ), and close( ).

The maximum number of files that can be open at one time is either 20, or the number specified in CONFIG.SYS, whichever is less. See the earlier sections for details about CONFIG.SYS. New files are creat( )'d and old files are open( )'d.

A closed file may be rename( )'d or unlink( )'d (deleted).

Three predefined file numbers may be used to read from or write to the console. To use them, include the following defines in the program:

```
#define stdin   0
#define stdout  1
#define stderr  2
```

Math routines

If any of the transcendental or sqrt( ) functions are used, include the file math.h or the equivalent declarations to specify them as returning double's.

math.h includes the statement

```
extern int errno;
```

with errno being set to a non-zero value when floating point stack errors occur, if an argument to a math routine is out of range, or if the result of a math routine would under/overflow. Error codes and names (defined in math.h) are as follows:

30 ESTK   F/P stack overflow. The most probable cause is calling a function that returns a double without declaring it as such to the compiler. After eight calls, the f/p stack will be full.

33 EDOM   Invalid argument, i.e., sqrt(-1.0).

34 ERANGE   Invalid arg size, i.e., asin(2.0).

The function rerrno( ) is called by the floating point routines whenever an error is detected. rerrno( ) prints out an appropriate error message and calls exit( ). In order to bypass this effect, install the following function in your program:

```
rerrno( ) {;} /* null function to suppress printing */
```

IBM-PC screen and keyboard interface

A number of functions have been written to simplify the interface between C programs and the IBM-PC and its clones. These routines are not in the standard PCCS.S library but are distributed in source form in the file PCIO.A. To use these routines, they must be assembled and bound in. For example,

```
PCCA b:pcio
PCCL b:blip b:pcio
```

See the comments in the *IBM Technical Reference Manual* for details on the BIOS interface used by PCIO.

Standard library functions

There are 77 standard library functions included with the Personal C Compiler. More complete documentation is included with the PCC disk and is also available in other C language references. The included functions are listed below:

```
abs()      fgets()    open()      scr_ci()       setjmp()
atoi()     floor()    os()        scr_co()       sqrt()
atof()     fopen()    out()       scr_clr()      srand()
atol()     fputc()    peek()      scr_clrl()     sscanf()
ceil()     fputs()    poke()      scr_cls()      strcat()
chain()    frand()    pow()       scr_csts()     strcmp()
close()    fscanf()   putc()      scr_cursoff()  strcpy()
creat()    getc()     putchar()   scr_curson()   strlen()
dates()    getchar()  puts()      scr_rowcol()   strncat()
doint()    gets()     putw()      scr_scdn()     strncmp()
exec()     getw()     qsort()     scr_scrdn()    strncpy()
exit()     in()       rand()      scr_scrup()    times()
exp()      index()    rename()    scr_scup()     ungetc()
fabs()     log()      rindex()    scr_setmode()  unlink()
fclose()   lmove()    scanf()     scr_setup()
fgetc()    longjmp()  scr_aputs() scr_sinp()
```

Registration

When you register, you will receive a disk with several utilities that enhance the compiler:

- **Clist** reads C source files and produces a listing file with a symbol cross-reference.
- **Lib88**, the object code librarian, reads object files and other library files and produces library files.
- **Profile**, C program execution profiler, monitors program execution and shows where time is spent in the program.
- **Xarray** is a library of memory access functions to use the entire 640K RAM space. It comes with source.

Your comments and suggestions on how to improve the product are welcome.

For $30.00, you get

☐ individual registration. This allows you to receive both the utility
  package automatically and a copy of the program if you request so.

The next items are only available to registered users.

☐ Editor (with object code) $15.00
☐ Debugger $15.00
☐ MS-DOS Linker compatibility utility $ 8.00
☐ Special utilities package $ 8.00
☐ Five 5-minute phone support calls $15.00
       (totalling 25 minutes of help time)

Call or write

C Ware Corporation
P. O. Box 428
Paso Robles, CA 94447
(805) 239-4620

Part Three

User interface tools

7
C-Window Toolkit

Program title   C-Window Toolkit   *(Disk 1007)*

Special requirements   Turbo C or Microsoft C.

C-Window Toolkit is designed for both novice and intermediate C programmers who want full screen, color, cursor control, and windowing abilities without programming complex escape sequences or DOS-level interrupts. It's also designed for experienced programmers who need a set of fast I/O windowing and disk access functions. A full set of file access functions are given that trap and handle all usual errors. Access is supported to ASCII, dBASE III+, hashed random, and relative files.

   C-Window Toolkit provides input and output windowing abilities that operate at professional speeds. The output windowing facilities use memory mapping for instant screen display. They take full advantage of color monitors and provide automatic editing of entry and output fields. Pull-down and pop-up menu functions, help screens, and multi-layered windows provide a sophisticated user interface.

The c_wndw and c_ndx libraries

These libraries for Turbo C and Quick C provide windows, menus, formatted entry, file access, indexed file, and relational database functions. The libraries make it easy to write C programs of professional appearance, quality and performance.

Hints and recommendations

Microsoft C

When using the Quick C debugger or Codeview, you might notice that some key entries go astray. This problem occurs with Microsoft C, but you can bypass it by setting SAVEWAIT to 0 during the debugging sessions.

The libraries require Quick C 2.0 or equivalent Microsoft C 5.x. The libraries do not work with Microsoft C 4.x or earlier versions.

If you have Quick C 1.0, the sample programs will probably compile and work, but linker errors will occur. You should upgrade to the vastly superior Quick C 2.0.

The MAK files are very useful, but you probably must modify them before you can use them.

By the way, when you register, you get a Quick C QuickHelp format file.

Turbo C

The libraries require Turbo C 2.0. If you have 1.0 or 1.5, the sample programs will probably work anyway (with linker errors though); still, v2.0 is strongly recommended.

The sample programs

The .PRJ and .MAK files are provided with the sample programs to help you compile and link these programs under the Turbo C and Quick C environments.

The sample programs should be compiled under the medium memory model, to match the MC_WNDW.LIB and MC_NDX.LIB libraries supplied on this shareware software issue.

HELLO.C

The classic understanding of a C language environment is a small program to display the message "hello world" to the screen. The HELLO.C program is this small program. It opens a window on the screen and displays the "hello world" message.

WINDOW.C

The program shows the creation and removal of overlapping windows. If you have a color screen, notice the automatic change of colors between windows.

The c_wndw libraries make and remove windows extremely quickly, and a half-second delay is built into the program between each window.

MENU.C

The program shows the use of the menu( ) function with a simple menu in a floating window. It also shows the use of the flt_wndw( ) function.

MESSAGE.C

The program shows the use of message and query windows with the err_wndw( ) and qry_wndw( ) functions. It also shows the use of the acptint( ) function to enter an integer value from the keyboard.

DATETEST.C

The program shows the use of the date facilities under the c_wndw libraries. The system date is read and can be subsequently modified through the keyboard by the accept( ) function. It also shows the use of the set_keys( ) function to activate the Esc key.

MONY.C

The program shows the use of the mony functions. The *mony* type is a variable with two implied decimal places that can contain any value in the range −9,999,999.99 to 9,999,999.99. This allows most monetary values (e.g., prices, financial computations, etc.) to be figured without the performance and rounding problems of doubles.

Note: Most people probably would have chosen the spelling "money" for this variable type. However, most shareware authors are independent thinkers and tend to do things any way they like. Apparently, the authors of the C-Window Toolkit are no exception.

WRITFILE.C

The program shows the use of file access functions to create a file with a record size of 61 bytes. You are prompted to enter the records, which are written to the end of the field.

READFILE.C

The program reads by record number the file created by the WRITFILE.C program.

DBREAD.C

The program reads sequentially through an indexed dBASE file and displays a field from the file. The data file is opened with the fileopen( ) function, and the index file with the ndxopen( ) function. The records are read with the ndxread( ) function, and the field displayed with the dispdbf( ) function.

DBUPDATE.C

The program opens an indexed dBASE file and allows you to read forward and backward through it to view and modify the records. Further, you can also add new records to the file.

Function summary

The functions included in C_WNDW.H and C_NDX.H libraries are listed here along with short descriptions. See the documentation included with the C-Window Toolkit disks for a more complete description of each function.

```
int accept (byte *field, enum _JUST just, enum ATTRIB
    atb, int len, int dec)
int acptbig (byte *field, enum _JUST just, enum ATTRIB
    atb, int len, int width)
```

accept and acptbig provide for the formatted and validated input of a string from the console. The string is displayed at the current cursor position within the current window while being entered.

```
int acptchar (char *field, enum _JUST just, enum ATTRIB
    atb, unsigned len)
int acptdbl (double *field, enum _JUST just, enum ATTRIB
    atb, unsigned len, unsigned dec)
int acptint (int *field, enum _JUST just, enum ATTRIB
    atb, unsigned len)
int acptlong (long *field, enum _JUST just, enum ATTRIB
    atb, unsigned len)
int acptmony (mony *field, enum _JUST just, enum ATTRIB
    atb, unsigned len)
```

acptchar, acptdbl, acptint, acptlong, and acptmony accept entry of numbers at the current cursor position with justification just, using video attribute atb. The operator interface of these functions are identical to the accept() function.

```
int acptdbf (int fh, unsigned field, enum ATTRIB atb)
```

acptdbf provides for the entry of a field from a dbase3 or hashed-type file with a dBASE-compatible data dictionary. The function behaves like the accept() function, except the field details are taken from the data dictionary (including field size and justification).

`int acptmask (byte *field, byte *mask, enum ATTRIB atb)`

`acptmask` accepts and formats the entry of a string using a character mask to format and control the entry.

`int acptmenu (byte *field, byte *list, enum ATTRIB atb, unsigned len)`

`acptmenu` accepts entry of a string and validates it against a list of options. If the option does not appear on the list, the operator can select an entry from a menu of these options.

`mony atom (byte *text)`

`atom` converts an ASCIIZ string of a number with two decimal places into a mony type field. In keeping with the spirit of `atol()` and `atoi()`, the function does not validate the "text" parameter string and ignores the optional decimal point.

`int cacheoff (int fh)`

`cacheoff` disables c_wndw disk caching for file `fh`. Disk caching can be re-initiated with the `fileinit()` function.

`void clr_keys (void)`

`clr_keys` clears the activated flag of all optional "end of field" function keys. The only permanently activated keys for the `accept()` and its related functions are "ENTER" and "F10—Quit."

`void clr_scrn (char *title)`

`clr_scrn` must be called at the start of the program to initialize the window and file buffers used by the c_wndw software. It also clears the screen and sets up the base window #0. The `title` is displayed centered on the top line.

`void clr_wndw (void)`

`clr_wndw` clears the current window.

`int compress (byte *text)`

compress compresses a string by stripping trailing spaces and replacing any group of TAB_SET number of spaces with a "\t" character.

---

byte* concat (byte *field, int spaces)

concat strips trailing spaces off the string field, optionally adding 1 or 2 depending on the value of spaces.

---

int datecomp (char *d1, char *d2)

datecomp compares two dates held in c_wndw compressed format. The function handles null dates "00/00/00" as dates before any valid date.

---

long datelong (char *d1)

datelong converts the compressed date d1 to a count of the number of days since 1/1/80.

---

void datemath (char *d1, int days)

datemath adds the specified number of days to the compressed date d1. The days variable can be negative for subtraction.

---

void dateread (char *d1)

dateread accesses the system clock to get today's date in compressed c_wndw format.

---

void date_in (char *d1, char *text)
void date_out (char *text, char *d1)

date_in and date_out convert dates in and out of c_wndw compressed 3 char format. date_in( ) converts into compressed format and date_out( ) converts out of compressed format.

---

void dbfdatein (char *d1, char *dbdate)
void dbfdateout (char *dbdate,char *d1)

dbfdatein and dbfdateout convert dates between dBASE format and c_wndw compressed 3 char format. dbfdatein( ) converts into compressed format and `dbfdateout()` converts out of compressed format.

`int dbffield (int fh, char *fldname)`

`dbffield` scans a hashed or dbase3 type file for the field number corresponding to the `fldname` parameter.

`int dbffile (int ndx)`

`dbffile` returns the dbase3 file handle for the index file `ndx`.

`double *dbfgetf (int fh, unsigned field, double *fdest)`
`long *dbfgetl (int fh, unsigned field, long *ldest)`
`mony *dbfgetm (int fh, unsigned field, mony *mdest)`
`char *dbfgets (int fh, unsigned field, char *cdest)`

`*dbfgetf`, `*dbfgetl`, `*dbfgetm`, and `*dbfgets` get a field from the current record of a dbase3 or hashed-type file and format it correctly.

`int dbflist (int fh, char *list, int max, unsigned mask)`

`dbflist` produces a list of field names of a dbase3 or hashed-type file. This list of names is suitable to be passed directly to the `menu()` function.

`int dbfputf (int fh, unsigned field, double d_src)`
`int dbfputl (int fh, unsigned field, long l_src)`
`int dbfputm (int fh, unsigned field, mony m_src)`
`int dbfputs (int fh, unsigned field, char *c_src)`

`dbfputf`, `dbfputl`, `dbfputm`, and `dbfputs` put a field into the current record of a dbase3 or hashed-type file and format it correctly using the information from the data dictionary.

`int dbfread (int fh, enum F_READ mode)`

`dbfread` reads the file `fh` and all related files. The parameter `fh` can be a dbase3 or hashed-type file, or an index file. The relationships to other files are established with the `dbfrelate()` function.

```
int dbfrelate (int fhl, int fh2, int ndx, char *fields)
```

dbfrelate establishes a relationship between files fhl and fh2.
These files can be dbase3 or hashed file types.

```
int dbf_fld (int fh)
```

dbf_fld returns the number of fields in the data dictionary of a
dbase3 or hashed-type file.

```
int dispchar (char field, int rx, int ry, enum ATTRIB atb,
    enum_JUST just, unsigned len);
int dispdbl (double field, int rx, int ry, enum ATTRIB atb,
    enum_JUST just, unsigned len, unsigned dec);
int dispint (int field, int rx, int ry, enum ATTRIB atb,
    enum_JUST just, unsigned len);
int displong (long field, int rx, int ry, enum ATTRIB atb,
    enum_JUST just, unsigned len);
int dispmony (mony field, int rx, int ry, enum ATTRIB atb,
    enum_JUST just, unsigned len)
```

dispchar, dispdbl, dispint, displong, and dispmony display
the numeric value of field with format just at cursor position (rx, ry)
using attribute atb. As a special case, position (0,0) is interpreted to refer
to the current cursor location.

```
int dispdbf (int fh, unsigned field, int rx, int ry,
    enum ATTRIB atb)
```

dispdbf provides for the display to the screen of a field from a dbase3
or hashed-type file with dBASE-compatible data dictionary. The field
details are taken from the data dictionary, including field type, size and
justification.

```
void dispkeys (void)
```

dispkeys redisplays the bottom line of the screen, provided
BOT_LINE is non-zero.

```
void display (byte *field, int rx, int ry, enum ATTRIB
    atb)
```

display displays the string ASCIIZ field at cursor position (rx, ry) within the current window with the color pair attribute atb. The string can contain any of the IBM graphics characters in addition to the ASCII character set. As a special case, position (0,0) is interpreted to refer to the current cursor location.

---

int dispmask (byte *field, int row, int col, enum ATTRIB atb, byte*mask)

dispmask displays a string at the identified location after formatting it through the character mask.

---

int dispwndw (unsigned wndw, byte *field, unsigned rx, unsigned ry, enum ATTRIB atb);

dispwndw displays field at cursor position (rx,ry) within window wndw using attribute atb. field must fit on one line and be entirely visible. The test must not be hidden or partially hidden in the window.

---

int dispwrap (byte *text, int rx, int ry, enum ATTRIB atb, unsigned height, unsigned width);

dispwrap displays a scrollable block of text to the screen. The function supports word-wrap and the \t, \n, \v, and \f control codes. The function ignores the \r and \b codes. If the text is too long for the screen area assigned to it, operator-controlled scrolling is supported.

---

int err_wndw (byte *text, int errcode, int ret)

err_wndw creates a window and displays the message in text. The window is the minimum size needed for the error message. The window is located near the current cursor position, without overwriting it.

---

int fileback (char *fname)

fileback erases any prior file with the .BAK extension and then renames the named file to have the .BAK extension. The file is set to read-only mode.

`int fileclos (int fh)`

`fileclos` closes the file identified with file handle `fh`. If the file has indexes opened with the `ndxcustom( )`, `ndxopen( )`, or `ndxrdex( )` function, these are also closed.

`int fileinit (int fh, unsigned start, unsigned rec_len,`
    `long max_rec)`

`fileinit` sets the record length of the file and the size of the header area at the start of the file. The function is required for binary type files after successful `fileopen( )`.

`int filelist (char *list, char *mask, unsigned max, int`
    `type, char *path)`

`filelist` extracts a set of filenames from a directory. The files are returned as the ASCIIZ string `list` in `menu( )` format.

`int filemenu (char *name)`

`filemenu` uses a menu of filenames to allow the operator to select a filename. The parameter to the function is the directory path and filename mask. The selected filename is returned in the same parameter.

`int fileopen (char *fname, enum F_TYPE type, enum`
    `F_MODE mode)`

`fileopen` opens the file given by `fname` with file-type `type` and under file-mode `mode`.

`int fileread (int fh, enum F_READ mode, long *rec_nbr)`

`fileread` reads a record from the file handle `fh` with read-mode `mode`. This function can be used to read a specific record from a file or to read through a file sequentially. The file can be read sequentially forwards or backwards.

`long filerecno (int fh)`

`filerecno` returns the number of the current record for a binary, dbase3, or hashed-type file.

`int filesave (int fh)`

`filesave` performs cache and file buffer flushing for one or all open files. The function is used to force file changes to disk and out of the c__wndw cache and the DOS file buffers.

`int fileseek (int fh, long loc)`

`fileseek` performs a seek on the file to a specified byte location. The function is rarely used as the `fileread( )` function performs positioning as required. If successful, the new file location is set into component location of FN[ ].

`int filewrit (int fh, long *rec__nbr)`

`filewrit` writes a record from the buffer FN[fh].record to the file. This is a fixed length record unless the file type is ASCII.

`int fld__len (enum __JUST just, unsigned len, unsigned dec)`

`fld__len` returns the required size of a string to hold a field with justification `just` and size `len` with decimal places `dec`. For numeric fields, the `len` parameter refers to the digits before the decimal point.

`int flt__wndw (unsigned h, unsigned w, byte *title)`

`flt__wndw` creates a floating window of h rows and w columns next to the current cursor location.

`byte *ftoascii (byte *text, double field, unsigned len, unsigned dec)`

`*ftoascii` converts a double to an ASCIIZ string in c__number format, with leading sign and a properly located decimal point. The number of decimal places corresponds to the value of the `dec` parameter. The function uses `ecvt( )` to perform fractional rounding. If the value of the double field is too big, the `text` string is filled with "*".

`mony ftom (double dsrc)`

ftom converts a double type field into a mony-type field. The value is rounded nearest.

`void goodbye (short errcode)`

goodbye must be used to end the program. It closes the files and resets the configuration changes made by the clr_scrn( ) function. The function does not return but calls the exit( ) function with errcode to end the program. An errcode of zero is a normal exit, and non-zero is an error exit.

`int grabchar (void)`

grabchar waits for entry of a keystroke from the keyboard, then returns the converted entry character. All key stroke entries, including function keys, are converted into a single value. The key entered is not echoed to the screen.

`int hashmake (char* fname, unsigned fields, unsigned`
`    rec_len, long max_rec, unsigned key_off, unsigned`
`    key_len)`

hashmake creates an empty hashed-type file of name fname, record length rec_len, and with max_rec pre-allocated records. The location of the hash key within the record starts at position key_off with length key_len. The file is in update mode after successful creation.

`long hashread (int fh, byte *key, int access)`

hashread performs a hashed read to a hashed-type file using the field pointed to by key. The key for the file can be a string or a binary code (such as a double).

`void helpmenu (int item)`

helpmenu provides the default help screen for the menu( ) and top _menu( ) functions. The functions pass a parameter identifying the currently highlighted menu item.

---

int helpscrn (byte *field)

hlpscrn provides the default help screen for the accept() and related functions. The parameter is the current entry string contents.

void idleloop (int ticks)

idleloop delays for the number of clock ticks given in the parameter ticks. There are approximately 18.2 ticks per second, 1092 per minute.

int iscache (int fh)

iscache returns whether the c_wndw disk access caching facilities are active on file fh. The file must be of type hashed, dbase3, or binary.

int isendch (byte *field, int c, enum ATTRIB atb)

isendch is primarily used by the accept() and related functions and returns 1 if the parameter c is a valid end-of-field function key code as determined by set_keys(), unset_keys(), and clr_keys(). A zero or negative value means it is not currently an end-of-field key.

int isuniqndx (int ndx)

isuniqndx returns 1 if the index file uses unique keys or 0 if the index allows duplicate keys or is not a valid index file.

byte *justify (enum _JUST just, byte *dest, byte *src,
        unsigned len, unsigned dec)

*justify copies and justifies string src into string dest, using the length parameters len and dec. The function is used to automatically expand and truncate strings, and to format and extract numeric fields.

int lastline (byte *field, unsigned col, enum ATTRIB
        atb)

lastline provides the means to write to the bottom line of the screen. This allows the programmer to customize the display on this pro-tected line of the screen instead of using the dispkeys() function.

```
int ln_ex (byte *dest, byte *src, unsigned len)
```

`ln_ex` extracts a line of text from a string, expanding any `\t` characters into groups of spaces.

```
int maskfield (byte *dest, byte *src, byte *mask)
```

`maskfield` applies a character mask to a field. The `mask` string can contain punctuation and masking characters. The masking characters are A, C, N, S, and X. This is not case-sensitive.

```
int menu (char *menutext, int size, int start, int up)
```

`menu` displays the menu from the string `menutext` within the current window starting from the current cursor position. Each menu item must be terminated with an & or | character.

```
int mk_wndw (int ax1, int ay1, int ax2, int ay2, byte *title)
```

This function creates a window from the coordinates of its top left-hand corner (`ax1`, `ay1`), and bottom right-hand corner (`ax2`, `ay2`). The string `text` is displayed on the top border of the window. All reading and writing to the screen occurs within the bounds of the current window using the `display( )` and `accept( )` and related functions.

```
mony monydisc (mony amount, mony discount)
mony monydiv (mony amount1, mony amount2)
mony monymarkup (mony amount, mony markup)
mony monymult (mony amount1, mony amount2)
mony monypercent (mony amount, mony divisor)
mony monyratio (mony amount, double ratio)
```

`monydisc`, `monydiv`, `monymarkup`, `monymult`, `monypercent`, and `monyratio` perform common arithmetic functions with `mony` type fields as operands. The functions handle overflow situations, rounding and the maintenance of the two implied decimal places.

```
byte *mtoascii (byte *dest, mony msrc)
double mtof (mony msrc)
```

*mtoascii convert mony type fields to double type and ASCIIZ string fields.

`int ndxappend (int ndx)`

ndxappend appends a record to an indexed dbase3 file opened in update or append mode. The parameter to the function is the file handle of an index on the file. This index file must have been previously opened with the ndxcustom( ), ndxopen( ), or ndxrdex( ) function.

`int ndxcustom (int fh, char *xname, int (*makekey)( ), int type)`

ndxcustom opens an index on a dbase3 type file, using a custom index function. The index key entries are calculated with the makekey function passed as a parameter. The custom index function is not supplied with the c_wndw and c_ndx software.

`int ndxdelete (int ndx)`

ndxdelete flags the current record from the dbase3 file as deleted and writes it back out to disk. The file is identified through the index file ndx.

`int ndxfield (int ndx, unsigned fnbr)`
ndxfield returns the data field number of the fnbr index field.

`int ndxopen (int fh, char`

ndxopen opens an index file on a dbase3 file. The details on the index are obtained from the information in the index file. This information includes whether the index is numeric or has unique keys.

`int ndxrdex (int fh, char *xname, char *exprn, int (*make-key)( ), int type)`

ndxrdex creates or recreates an index on a dbase3 file. It supports both dBASE compatible and custom indexes. The function is the only way to create a custom index on a file.

---

int ndxread (int ndx, enum F__READ mode)

ndxread performs a random or sequential read on a dbase3 file via the index file ndx. The parameter mode identifies the type of the read.

int ndxwrite (int ndx)

ndxwrite writes a record to an indexed dbase3 file opened in update or append mode. The parameter to the function is the file handle of an index on the file.

long primenbr (long source)

primenbr returns the first prime number equal to or higher than the number provided. The function is accurate for source values between 8L and 29,999,999. source values under 8L return (11L).

void prn__scrn (void)

prn__scrn prints a copy of the screen onto the main printer. This works with any printer as the IBM graphics characters used by the mk__wndw( ) function are translated to ASCII equivalents, and any other graphics characters are replaced with the # character.

int qry__wndw (byte *text)

qry__wndw creates a window, displays the message in text, and prompts for a yes/no response.

void read__kb (void)

read__kb reads and ignores a keyboard entry. If the Alt-X key is pressed, the function prompts for a controlled termination.

int rm__wndw (void)

rm__wndw removes the current window and redisplays the part of the screen covered by it. All screen activity now takes place in the previous window. The main window, window #0, cannot be removed.

```
void scrnsave (int posn)
```

scrnsave is used by `accept( )`, `read_kb( )`, `err_wndw( )`, and `qry_wndw( )` functions. If the functions have to wait longer than SAVE-WAIT ticks for a keyboard entry, all file buffers are flushed.

```
void scrn_map (byte *field, int ax, int ay)
```

scrn_map writes the `field` string onto the screen starting at the (ax,ay) location using the current color code (set by `set_clr( )`). The function uses absolute screen not relative window coordinates and can be used to write anywhere on the screen without regard to windows.

```
void scroll (int incr, int head)
```

scroll scrolls the window up or down according to the `incr` parameter, leaving a header of `head` lines unscrolled.

```
void set_clr (int clr_nbr, enum ATTRIB atb)
```

set_clr is used to change the color code used by the `scrn_map( )` function. The color code is selected from COLOR[ ] by applying the effect of the attribute `atb`. The function also works to select the display attribute on monochrome screens.

```
void set_crsr (int rx, int ry)
```

set_crsr moves the cursor within the current window to the location given by (rx,ry). The function wraps around from an invalid location to one that fits in the window.

```
void set_keys (unsigned count, unsigned param1, ...)
```

set_keys determines which function keys are recognized by `accept( )` and related functions as end-of-field function keys.

```
int set_wndw (unsigned wnbr, enum _JUST just, enum
      ATTRIB atb, unsigned style)
```

set_wndw sets the window characteristics of border styles and title formats for windows. The set_wndw( ) function must be called before the mk_wndw( ) function in order to properly set up the format.

---

void shortbeep (int tone)

shortbeep produces beep of duration ERR_BEEP clock ticks, with a minimum beep duration of two clock ticks. There are 18.2 clock ticks to the second. The tone of the beep is based on the tone parameter.

---

int sys_wndw (byte *text, int errcode, int ret)

sys_wndw behaves exactly as the err_wndw( ) function except the window is only displayed if ERRORMSG is non-zero. This is used extensively in the c_wndw and c_ndx functions to allow the error displays to be suppressed by setting ERRORMSG to zero after your programs have achieved a stable status.

---

int top_menu (char *menutext, int size, int start)

top_menu displays the menu across the top line of the screen. The items have a maximum size of 27 bytes and the full menu must fit on one line. The returns are as for the menu( ) function. This menu is independent of the window system.

---

void top_spot (int val)

top_spot refreshes the status values on the top line of the screen. These status values are the screen title, available memory, date, and available capacity on the default disk drive.

---

void unset_keys (unsigned count, unsigned param1, ...)

unset_keys deactivates function keys from being used as end-of-field keys by the accept( ) and related functions.

---

int validate (byte *line, enum _JUST just, unsigned len,
    unsigned dec)

validate evaluates the value of line to ensure it is valid. If line is of type date, the month and day are validated. If line is of type c_number, db_number, or decimal, it is checked to see if it has too many digits before the decimal point.

`int v_bool (int c)`

`v_bool` tests the character c against comparison characters stored in BOOL_NO and BOOL_YES. It is not case-sensitive.

`void warble (int tone)`

`warble` turns on the computer's speaker to the tone provided. As a special case, a tone of zero shuts off the speaker.

The enum and struct definitions

`enum ATTRIB {low, high, reverse, blink, blank, alt_low, alt_high, alt_reverse};`

ATTRIB defines the screen attribute code to select which of the 6 color pairs are to be used, plus it supports blink and blank fields. This is used with the `accept( )`, `display( )`, `set_clr( )`, and related functions.

`enum COLOR_OF {Mblack, Mblue, Mgreen, Mcyan, Mred, Mmagenta, Myellow, Mwhite};`

COLOR_OF defines the 8 base colors used by the software, which extend to 16 with the high/low intensity options.

`enum fld_type {alphanum, graphic, flag, boolean, calendar, numeric, value, real, chrono};`

`fld_type` is defined for future use.

`enum F_MODE {append, readonly, recreate, update};`

F_MODE defines the file access mode for the `fileopen( )` function. All access modes are available with all file types except append with hashed, and update with ASCII.

`enum F_READ {firstrec, previous, nextrec, lastrec, random, relative};`

F_READ defines the file read mode for the `dbfread( )`, `fileread( )` and `ndxread( )` functions.

---

enum F_TYPE {ASCII, binary, dbase3, hashed, marietta};

F_TYPE defines the file type for the fileopen( ) function. ASCII-type files have variable length records terminated with \r\n, whereas binary, dbase3, and hashed files have fixed length records that might contain binary information.

---

enum _JUST {left, right, as_typed, center, code, decimal, db_number, c_number, date, _time};

_JUST defines field format (justification) codes used by the accept( ) (and related functions), fld_len( ), and justify( ) functions.

---

struct CLR_TYPE {enum COLOR_OF FORE, BACK; int ALT _CLR}, COLOR[ ], TOP_CLR, ER_COLOR;

CLR_TYPE defines the primary color pair, the number of the alternate color pair for the windows, and the top and bottom lines.

---

struct CURSR {byte X,Y;} _CURSOR;

CURSR contains the current cursor location within current window.

---

struct DBF_DEF {byte dbf_name[11]; int dbf_type, dbf_len, dbf_dec, dbf_set, dbf_dig; enum _JUST just; unsigned posn; ... };

DBF_DEF defines the field format of the dBASE style data dictionary created when a hashed or dbase3 file is opened with the fileopen( ) function.

---

struct F_DEF {long prime, r_count; int key_len, offset, start, ismemo; unsigned rec_len; enum F_TYPE ftype; byte *record; char fname[13], fvol, fpath[61]; void *fnext; ...} *FN;

F_DEF defines the buffers and control variables used by the c_wndw and c_ndx file access software.

```
struct WINDW {int X, Y, H, W, . . . . . . .} *WINDOW;
```

WINDW defines the buffers and sizes used by the c_wndw windowing software. The number of usable columns in the current window is (WIN-DOW[W_NUM].W - 1) and the number of usable rows is (WIN-DOW[W_NUM].H - 1).

```
typedef unsigned char byte;
```

typedef is used in the c_wndw software to contain values in the range (0) to (254). The value (255) by convention is viewed as an error or a null value.

```
typedef long mony;
```

A mony type field is of storage class long, but includes two implied decimal places (e.g., cents in a dollar field). It is the programmer's responsibility, on this type of field, to keep track of these decimal places. The mony field type can contain a signed binary number in the range (-9,999,999.99) to (9,999,999.99). The value LONG_MAX by convention is viewed as an error value.

Configuration constants and variables

ACC_DISP	This enum ATTRIB type field determines the attribute used by the accept( ) function to redisplay the entered field after entry.
A_TRACK	Used by the accept( ) function. If negative, it is ignored; otherwise it becomes the starting cursor position within the display string. At the end of the accept( ) or related function, this is the string location where the function key was pressed.
BANNER_MSG[ ]	The contents of the information window that appears when the clr_scrn( ) function is first called, or when the operator presses the Alt-V key combination.
BOOL_NO	Identifies the uppercase boolean no/false code.
BOOL_YES	Identifies the uppercase boolean yes/true code.
BOT_LINE	This controls the display of the active function keys on the bottom line of the screen.

CLR_TONE	The length of time, in clock ticks, for the display of the initial information window during the clr_scrn() function. The default is 25, about 1.5 seconds.
COMMA	Identifies the thousands separator character.
_COLORS	The maximum number of color pairs.
D_FORMAT	Provides the format of the date. The default is "U". "U" = mm/dd/yy; "E" = dd/mm/yy; "I" = yy/mm/dd.
DISCBLCK	The maximum size of any record accessed by fileread(), filewrit() or related functions. The default is 4100, the minimum is 512, and the maximum 65,000.
D_PUNCT	Identifies the punctuation character for dates.
D_20XX	Identifies the split between the 20th and 21st centuries for 2-digit year fields.
ERR_BEEP	This determines the length of the beep by the shortbeep() function in clock ticks.
ERRORMSG	This is used to suppress the error messages displayed by the c_wndw and c_ndx software.
FLD_FULL	Used by the accept() function. A non-zero value automatically ends field entry when it is full. A zero value requires the Enter key (or an activated function key) to end the field.
GOODBYEMSG	This is used by the goodbye() function. If non-zero, the function issues success or failure messages at the end of the program. If zero, these messages are suppressed.
KEY_DISPLAY[]	This array of seven short strings contains the key names of function keys F3 through F9.
MAXFILES	Maximum number of files open at one time, including the five standard C streams. The default value of 9 actually allows for 4 disk files. The maximum is set by your operating system. 20 is typical, but it can be as high as 99.
MAX_WIND	The maximum heap space to be used by the windowing functions.
MEM_WARN	A warning is issued by the top_spot() function when available heap space falls below this

	value. The default is 1024, with a range of 0 to 9999.
MENULINE	This determines if an information line for menus is displayed on the bottom line of the screen while the menu( ) and top_menu( ) functions are active.
PERIOD	Identifies the decimal point character that must be different from COMMA.
SAVEWAIT	The scrnsave( ) function waits this time (in clockticks) before flushing the file buffers. Setting to zero suppresses this facility.
SCRN_LEN	The number of lines on the screen. This is normally the default of 25. It allows utilization of 43 and 50 line per screen systems.
SCRN_WID	The number of columns on the screen. This should remain 80.
TOP_LINE	The number of lines dedicated for status line and the top_menu( ) function at the top of the screen.
_WINDW	The maximum allowed number of windows.

Registration

If you like and use the c_wndw and c_ndx libraries, you should subscribe and get the full benefits of being a registered user. When you subscribe to the Marietta Systems' c_wndw and c_ndx software, you are entitled to the following:

☐ A copy on 360K 5.25″ diskette(s) of the latest version of the software for Borland and Microsoft C compilers with
  ~ both medium and large memory models
  ~ enhanced facilities of the c_wndw and c_ndx software
  ~ additional sample programs including programs to create index files, modify the dBASE data dictionary, and edit indexed files
  ~ the software includes disk caching facilities
  ~ removal of the shareware banner appearing at the start of each program

☐ Free phone support for the first 90 days for up to 1 hour of connect time

☐ A non-exclusive, non-transferable license to use the full version of the c_wndw and c_ndx software on a single computer system

☐ Periodic newsletters

The normal retail price of the c_wndw and c_ndx object libraries is $95.00, but shareware users can register for $79.00 plus shipping and handling. Source code licenses are available for $179.00 (normal retail price is $195.00).

Mail to

Marietta Systems, Inc
C_wndw and c_ndx libraries
P.O. Box 71506
Marietta, GA 30007
(404) 565-1560

8
Window Boss

Program title   Window Boss   *(Disks 873 and 1113)*

Special requirements   See "Technical Considerations" in this chapter.

The Window Boss is one of the most powerful and cost-effective products available to enhance and accelerate the development of system and applications programs in the C language. The Boss will let you create programs that have the same look and feel as top sellers like Lotus 1-2-3, Sidekick, dBASE III, and Framework. You can easily implement such devices as pop-up windows, pull-down menus, status lines, and in-context on-line help functions. Your applications can drag windows around the screen and automatically sense the video card installed (and all of this without snow, flicker, or delay).

The Boss's assistant, the Data Clerk, is always on call to handle the tasks associated with data entry. Whether they be as simple as fetching a line of text or as complicated as the coordination of filling out a form, the Data Clerk will be there to assist and, if necessary, validate precious information as it is entered.

Also, registered users can take advantage of the "Source Plus" policy that provides meticulously commented source code, technical support, and minimal fee updates.

Technical consideration

The Window Boss supports PC/MSDOS for the IBM PC/XT/AT, PS/2, and compatibles. However, you'll need one of the following compilers in order to take advantage of the state-of-the-art techniques available from the Boss:

Lattice C	Microsoft C
Microsoft Quick C	Borland Turbo C
Computer Innovations CI86	Datalight
Watcom and Watcom Express C	Zortech
Aztec C	Mix Power C

The Boss is written in C and assembly language. You'll need the Microsoft Assembler, MASM, to assemble any local changes to the assembler source.

Boss has the following limits:

Maximum windows	Limited only by compiler and memory
Maximum window	Full screen (25×80, 43×80, 50×80)
Minimum window	1 row 1 column (borderless)
	3 rows 3 columns (framed)
Minimum fields	None
Maximum fields	Limited only by compiler and memory

To operate Boss, simply include the library at link time and invoke the desired function.

The basics

The Window Boss is an extensive library of C functions for the creation, management, and manipulation of text windows. It takes care of all the housekeeping and lets you, the programmer, continue with developing your application with a minimum of fuss.

Both the Window Boss and the Data Clerk are based on a layered software design in which powerful, easy-to-use functions are created from a series of lower-level primitives. As a programmer, you will quickly appreciate the clean and uncluttered approach to getting the job done.

Windows are created and defined by opening them. Once created, you can write to them, move them around, change their attributes, use them as the basis for data entry, or "kill" them by closing them. Windows are nothing more than a subdisplay of a larger display—the physical screen. They are defined to have size, location, and attributes such as foreground color, background color, border colors, and so on. The Boss includes a whole host of functions for defining and manipulating your windows.

Windows can also serve as the backdrop for data entry. Once a window is created, you can use it to convey or retrieve information. The Data Clerk will assist you, whether you are dealing with something as simple as a single line of text or as complex as a complete form.

Forms are an ordered collection of input requests (fields) occurring within a specific window. Fields have size, location (relative to the window in which they will be displayed), and attributes (foreground color, background color, mask values, fill characters, type integer, float, long, text, validation ranges, and so on). Like windows, forms are created by your opening them. Their contents must then be defined by using the provided field definition functions or with your own custom field definition functions. Once created and defined, a form becomes part of the window and moves with it. Forms are "killed" by closing them (incidentally, killing a form has no effect on the window to which it was anchored or to the information displayed in it, form or otherwise). The same functions used to input single data items are used to build forms. This consistency, coupled with an uncluttered approach and flexibility, gives the Window Boss its power.

Window basics

Figure 8-1 is a variation of the famous "hello" program that seems to be the standard C Language example. As you can see, it's pretty simple to put windows into your applications with the Window Boss.

```
#include "windows.h"              /* REQUIRED */
main()
{
WINDOWPTR w1;                     /* window handle */
int batrib;                       /* border atrib */
int watrib;                       /* window atrib */

/*
 * Set attributes:
 *
 *       border - blue/white box
 *       window - white background/black letters
 *
 */

   batrib = (BLUE << 4) | WHITE; /* border atrib */
   watrib = (WHITE <<4) | BLACK; /* window atrib */

/*
 * Open window at 0,0 - 25 cells wide and 10 cells high
 */

   w1 = wn_open(0,0,0,25,10,watrib,batrib);
   if(!w1) exit();

/*
 * Print the famous string and wait for key to be struck.
 * Close window on key strike.. exit.
 */

   wn_printf(w1,"Hello World...");
   v_getch();                        /* wait for key */
   wn_close(w1);                     /* close the window */
   exit(0);                          /* and exit */
}

/* End */
```

8-1 The Hello program demonstrates the use of BOSS windows.

Data entry basics

Let's expand our "hello" program to prompt and fetch a name. See FIG. 8-2.

```
#include "windows.h"          /* REQUIRED */
main()
{
WINDOWPTR w1;                 /* window handle */
int batrib;                   /* border atrib */
int watrib;                   /* window atrib */
char name[15];                /* name */

/*
 * Set attributes:
 *
 *       border - blue/white box
 *       window - white background/black letters
 *
 */

  batrib = (BLUE << 4) | WHITE; /* border atrib */
  watrib = (WHITE <<4) | BLACK; /* window atrib */

/*
 * Open window at 0,0 - 25 cells wide and 10 cells high
 */

  w1 = wn_open(0,0,0,25,10,watrib,batrib);
  if(!w1) exit();

/*
 * Print the famous string, prompt and fetch a name,
 * wait for key to be struck.
 * Close window on key strike.. exit.
 */

  wn_printf(w1,"Hello World...");

  *name = NUL;                 /* init buffer for name */
  wn_gtext(XEQ,NFRM,NFLD,w1,2,1,"Name: ",watrib,'_',15,name,NSTR,NSTR);

  v_getch();                   /* wait for key */
  wn_close(w1);                /* close the window */
  exit(0);                     /* and exit */
}

/* End */
```

8-2 This expanded Hello program prompts for and fetches a name.

Form basics

Now we will expand a bit further to read a 2 field form. See FIG. 8-3.

```
#include "windows.h"          /* REQUIRED */
main()
{
WINDOWPTR w1;                 /* window handle */
WIFORM f1;                    /* form handle */
int batrib;                   /* border atrib */
int watrib;                   /* window atrib */
char name[15];                /* name */
char city[15];                /* city */

/*
 * Set attributes:
 *
 *       border - blue/white box
 *       window - white background/black letters
 *
 */

  batrib = (BLUE << 4) | WHITE; /* border atrib */
  watrib = (WHITE <<4) | BLACK; /* window atrib */
```

8-3 Use of a two-field form.

```
/*
 * Open window at 0,0 - 25 cells wide and 10 cells high
 */

    w1 = wn_open(0,0,0,25,10,watrib,batrib);
    if(!w1) exit();

/*
 * Print the famous string, create, define, and fetch form
 * wait for key to be struck.
 * Close window on key strike.. exit.
 */

    wn_printf(w1,"Hello World...");

    *name = NUL;                        /* init buffer for name */
    *city = NUL;                        /* init buffer for city */
    f1 = wn_frmopn(3);                  /* open form 2 + 1 Fields */
    wn_gtext(SET,f1,0,w1,2,1,"Name: ",watrib,'_',15,name,NSTR,NSTR);
    wn_gtext(SET,f1,1,w1,3,1,"City: ",watrib,'_',15,city,NSTR,NSTR);
    wn_frmget(f1);                      /* read the form */

    v_getch();                          /* wait for key */
    wn_frmcls(f1);                      /* first close the form */
    wn_close(w1);                       /* then close the window */
    exit(0);                            /* and exit */
```

Popup menu basics

Popup and pull-down menus add that extra sparkle to your applications. The Window Boss includes a simple popup menu system that is fast and easy to use. The system consists of two functions; wn_popup( ) and wn_qpopup( ). wn_popup( ) is an interactive version of wn_qpop-up( ) (i.e., wn_popup( ) can be used to solicit user input, while wn_qpopup is an *information-only* popup). The "q" in qpopup stands for "quick." Both functions have function parameters and require the menu structure pmenu to be initialized. Pmenu is defined in windows.h.

Popup menus, like windows, have size (height and width), an origin (row and column), and attributes (text and border). These are passed as parameters to both wn_popup and wn_qpopup in the same fashion as they would be for a call to wn_open. In addition to the normal window stuff, popup menus also have information that must be displayed and, in some cases, information that must be returned to the calling function. This additional information is passed to popup via the pmenu structure. The pmenu structure allows us to tell wn_popup what text is to be displayed where, and what value (return code), if any, is to be provided back to the calling function.

Both wn_popup and wn_qpopup call wn_open to open a window defined by the calling parameters. Calls to wn_putsa are then made to display the text defined in pmenu within the window just opened at the location in the window specified by the values defined in pmenu. A menu item is highlighted by moving either the cursor keys, space bar, or by pressing the first character of the menu item desired. Control is passed back to the calling function when the Enter or Escape key is pressed. Figure 8-4 is a typical call to wn_popup.

```
wat = (WHITE<<4|BLACK);
bat = (BLUE<<4|WHITE);
rv = wn_popup(0, 0, 0, 33, 14, wat, bat, &intelc, FALSE);
```

Normal wn_open parms ———

pmenu structure ———

window close flag ———

8-4 Example of a call to the wn __popup function.

The normal wn_open parameters define the popup menu's location,
size, and color. The pmenu structure address allows wn_popup and
wn_qpopup to access the contents of the intelc pmenu structure. The
window close flag is used to tell wn_popup whether or not to close the
popup menu when returning to the calling function. Telling wn_popup to
not close the menu when returning to the calling function allows you to
create nested popups.

The pmenu structure definition from WINDOWS.H is shown in FIG.
8-5.

```
struct mitem {                    /* POPUP menu item template */
    int r;                        /* row */
    int c;                        /* col */
    char *t;                      /* text */
    int rv;                       /* return value */
};

struct pmenu {                    /* POPUP menu structure */
    WINDOWPTR wpsave;             /* place to hold window id */
    int winopn;                   /* leave window open flag */
    int lndx;                     /* last index */
    int fm;                       /* first menu item index */
    int lm;                       /* last menu item index */
    struct mitem scrn[WN_MXROWS*4]; /* a bunch of menu items */
};                                /* NOTE RELATIVE LIMIT */
```

8-5 Definition of the pmenu structure.

mitem Popup menus contain a number of menu items. Each menu
item has a location (within the window), text (to be displayed in the window), and an integer return code that is passed back to the calling function
to let the caller know which menu item was selected. r and c define the
row and column, t is a pointer to the text, and rv is integer return code.

pmenu In addition to the information needed about each menu item,
we need to do some internal housekeeping on the popup menu itself.
wpsave is used to store the WINDOWPTR that was returned from the call
to wn_open made by popup. winopn is used internally by popup as an
indicator of whether or not the window referenced by wpsave is currently

open. lndx is used internally to hold the index of the menu item last referenced or selected. The combination of wpsave, winopn, and lndx provide wn_popup with the ability to correctly handle both nested and non-nested popups. The structure members wpsave, winopn, and lndx should not be modified but only initialized.

The Window Boss's popup menus allow you to have informational headers and trailers, which is handy for providing multiple line titles and/or trailing instructional messages. For example, consider FIG. 8-6.

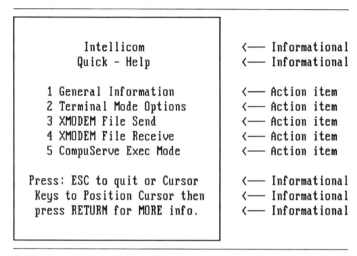

Intellicom	<— Informational
Quick - Help	<— Informational
1 General Information	<— Action item
2 Terminal Mode Options	<— Action item
3 XMODEM File Send	<— Action item
4 XMODEM File Receive	<— Action item
5 CompuServe Exec Mode	<— Action item
Press: ESC to quit or Cursor	<— Informational
Keys to Position Cursor then	<— Informational
press RETURN for MORE info.	<— Informational

8-6 Construction of a pop-up menu.

Figure 8-6 contains 10 menu items: 5 are action-oriented, and 5 are informational. They are numbered 0 through 9 and correspond to the scrn array of pointers in the pmenu structure. fm and lm are the indexes of the first and last action items in scrn array. In the case of the above popup, fm and lm would be initialized to 2 and 6 respectively. fm and lm, like the other housekeeping structure members, should not be modified but only initialized. The pmenu structure for this popup is shown in FIG. 8-7.

The end of the pmenu structure is designated by defining a menu item at row 99, column 99, with null text and a return code of 99. You must always do this. Figure 8-8 shows the code for creating the menu.

To make the popup menu disappear upon return, change the call to wn_popup to this:

```
rv = wn_popup( 0, 0, 0, 33, 14, wat, bat, &intelc, TRUE );
```

The calling sequence and setup of wn_qpopup is similar to wn_popup, but the functions significantly differ operationally. The parameter list differs in that wn_qpopup has no window close flag parameter. More significantly, concerning operations, wn_qpopup places the popup window

```
static struct pmenu intelc = {
    0, FALSE, 0,                             /* wpsave, winopn, lndx */
    2, 6, {                                  /* fm, lm */
    1,  2, "         Intellicom", 0,              /** ----- **/
    2,  2, "        Quick - Help", 0,             /*         */
    4,  5, "1 General Information  ", 1,          /*    |    */
    5,  5, "2 Terminal Mode Options", 2,          /*    |    */
    6,  5, "3 XMODEM File Send      ", 3,         /* 10 menu */
    7,  5, "4 XMODEM File Receive  ", 4,          /*  items  */
    8,  5, "5 CompuServe Exec Mode ", 5,          /*         */
   10,  2, "Press: ESC to quit or Cursor", 0,     /*         */
   11,  2, " Keys to Position Cursor then", 0,    /*         */
   12,  2, " press RETURN for MORE info.", 0,     /** ----- **/
   99, 99, "",99 }                          /* ALWAYS ADD THIS LINE */
};
```

8-7 The pmenu structure for Fig. 8-6.

```
#include "windows.h"

static struct pmenu intelc = {
    0, FALSE, 0,
    2, 6, {
    1,  2, "         Intellicom", 0,
    2,  2, "        Quick - Help", 0,
    4,  5, "1 General Information  ", 1,
    5,  5, "2 Terminal Mode Options", 2,
    6,  5, "3 XMODEM File Send      ", 3,
    7,  5, "4 XMODEM File Receive  ", 4,
    8,  5, "5 CompuServe Exec Mode ", 5,
   10,  2, "Press: ESC to quit or Cursor", 0,
   11,  2, " Keys to Position Cursor then", 0,
   12,  2, " press RETURN for MORE info.", 0,
   99, 99, "",99 }
};

main()
{
WINDOWPTR w1;
int wat, bat, rv;

    wn_init();
    w1 = wn_open(0,11,1,31,2,NORMAL,NORMAL);
    if(!w1) exit(1);
    wat = (WHITE<<4|BLACK);
    bat = (BLUE<<4|WHITE);
    rv = wn_popup(0, 0, 0, 33, 14, wat, bat, &intelc, FALSE);
    wn_printf(w1, "wn_popup returned: %d\n",rv);
    wn_printf(w1, "Press any key to continue..");
    v_getch();
    wn_close(w1);
    wn_exit();
    exit(0);
}
/* End */
```

8-8 Example code for making a pop-up menu.

on the screen and then immediately returns a WINDOWPTR to the open and active popup window. The calling function assumes full responsibility for the window from then on (i.e., moving, closing, etc.).

Quick popups are used to display information only and do not contain action menu items (see FIG. 8-9).

Notes on popup menus Popup menu items are highlighted by moving the cursor bar with the arrow keys, space bar, or by pressing the first letter/digit of the menu item. wn_popup will return as soon as the Enter or

```
#include "windows.h"

static struct pmenu m1 = {
  0, FALSE, 0,
  0, 0, {
  1, 2, "Presenting", 0,
  99, 99, "",99 }
};

main()
{
int wat, bat;
WINDOWPTR w2;

  wat = (WHITE<<4|BLACK);
  bat = (BLUE<<4|WHITE);
  w2 = wn_qpopup(0,0,0,16,3,wat,bat,&m1);
  v_getch();
  wn_close(w2);
  wn_exit();
  exit();
}
/* End */
```

8-9 Example of a quick pop up for displaying information.

Escape key is struck. The return code specified in the pmenu structure is returned when the Enter key is pressed, while Escape causes return code of 99 to be passed back to the calling function.

Menu navigation is from the current to next or current to previous menu item when using the cursor keys or space bar. Item skipping can only be accomplished by using the "first-character" selection method. Skip selection will only work as anticipated, if the first character of each action menu item is unique.

Source code is provided (through WN_HELP.C) to allow you to customize and/or enhance the popup menu system to meet your needs.

The BossDEMO program contains coding samples showing the use of wn_popup, wn_qpopup, and how to implement pull-down menus using wn_popup.

Help system basics

The Window Boss includes a file-based help system that can be used to provide your applications with context-sensitive help.

It would be helpful for you to print out a few pages of INTELC.HLP (if you have a copy of the software) that you could refer to during the following discussion. You should also run the BossDEMO program and exercise the Intellicom Quick Help popup menu. This code uses the help system to produce the displays when menu selections are made.

The system uses plain ASCII text files you create with your favorite editor. A special, but easy to follow, file layout is used. The file layout allows the plain ASCII text files to be indexed using the supplied index generation utility GENINDEX. The indexing provides the system with the ability to rapidly locate and display help messages when called upon to do so. Since the source (WN_HELP.C and GENINDEX.C) to the entire help system is provided, you can modify it to meet your own needs.

In order to use the help system in your application, you must prepare the ASCII text file in the specified format and run the GENINDEX program. For example, you first create a text file called TAXES.HLP using Brief, Vedit, Edlin, or your favorite word processor in non-document (ASCII) mode and then run the GENINDEX program by typing

```
GENINDEX TAXES.HLP
```

The GENINDEX program reads TAXES.HLP and produces TAXES.NDX. Both TAXES.HLP and TAXES.NDX must be available to the application program at run time.

To actually use the help system in your application, you must first initialize the help system by calling wn_hlinit. This must be done before any attempt is made to display help messages. The help system must only be initialized once and is done through the call of form

```
. . . . .                                              /* code */
rv = wn_hlinit(row, col, width, height, atrib, batrib, file)
. . . .                                                /* code */
```

The parameters define the location, size, and attributes of the window in which the help messages will be displayed along with the name of the help file to be used. wn_hlinit returns TRUE if all is well and FALSE otherwise.

Initialization does not cause a window to be displayed but merely sets the system up for later use by opening and reading the index file into memory.

To initialize the system for full screen help messages in a window with white letters on blue background and a similar border using the file INTELC.HLP, the call to wn_hlinit would be

```
wn_hlinit( 0, 0, 78, 23, ( BLUE << 4 | WHITE ), ( BLUE
  << 4 | WHITE ), "intelc" );
```

The help system is now initialized to display full screen help messages using INTELC.HLP and INTELC.NDX as the help message database. (The BossDEMO program uses the above code.)

Important: Unless you intend to modify the help system, the above call to wn_hlinit should always be used, modified only to reflect the name of your help file.

Obtaining help at run time is accomplished by calling the wn_help function with a subject key word, such as

```
rv = wn_help( "%general information%" );
```

Subject key words are located in the ASCII help file you prepare and are processed by the GENINDEX program. The usage of wn_help() should be clear once we complete the discussion of the file layout.

The text file you prepare consists of help system commands, subject key words, and the actual text to be displayed which is formatted to fit inside the window defined by wn_hlinit.

Commands Here are the help system commands:

.cp Signals end of page
END Signals end of page and end of help for this subject

Text is sequentially displayed a screen at a time from the subject key-word through any number of .cp delimited screens through and including the screen delimited by *END*. The system allows for forward and reverse display via the PgDn and PgUp keys. The .cp signals the end of a single screen in a series of 2 or more screens. When .cp is detected, the message "Esc to quit help, PgUp for previous screen, any other key to continue . . ." is displayed. When *END* is detected, the message "End of help, PgUp for previous screen, any other key to continue . . ." is displayed.

Keywords Keywords are always enclosed within percent signs (%) and signal the beginning of text on a particular subject. They are used by the GENINDEX program to create the index (NDX) file and are used by you as parameters to the wn_help( ) function.

In the case of INTELC.HLP, you will find the following keywords:

```
%ksend%, %ksend1%, %krecv%, %krecv1%, %checksum xmit1%,
%checksum recv1%, %terminal/c1%, %cistty1%, %terminal%,
%terminal/c%, %cistty%, %status%, %dos window%, %exit to
    dos%,
%close capture%, %autodial%, %ascii xmit%, %checksum
    xmit%,
%checksum recv%, %general information%, %bossinfo%,
%end-of-file%
```

Text Each screen of text is delimited by either a keyword, the .cp command, or the *END* command. Text is always formatted to fit inside the help window. In the case of INTELC.HLP, there are two leading spaces and the text is right justified to end at column 76. The two leading and trailing spaces center the text between the borders. Blank lines at the top of each screen (page full) can be used to vertically center the text. Spaces on the left can be used to horizontally center text.

Important: Unless you intend to modify the help system, the format defined by INTELC.HLP should always be followed for any help files you create for your own use.

Notes on help menus The help system is configured to provide a full-screen text message, subject keys are limited to 25 characters, and there is a limit of 255 subject keys per file. This can be changed by modifying the functions found in WN_HELP.C.

Note: There is a direct correlation between the parameters used to initialize the help system and the layout of the ascii text file read by the genindex program. If you modify the code, be sure to also modify the location and text of the messages to be displayed when .cp and/or *END* are detected.

The GENINDEX program is provided in source form. An EXEcutable must be created locally. You might also have to adjust the logic to account for the way the various compilers treat <CR> <LF> sequences. This usually amounts to nothing more than changing the "rb" to "r" in the fopen statement. To best determine if you have built a properly functioning GENINDEX program, run your newly created GENINDEX program against INTELC.HLP to create a new INTELC.NDX. Then rebuild the BossDEMO program and test to see if the Intellicom Quick Help popup is functioning properly. If it is, you are all set. If you receive a "Sorry - No info on . . ." message, then you must edit GENINDEX to make the "rb" to "r" change.

This help system has nothing in common with the way in which the data entry help and error messages get displayed.

Help files always have a filename extension of .HLP. Index files always have a filename extension of .NDX.

Figure 8-10 is a sample program that uses INTELC.HLP.

```
#include "windows.h"
main()
{
WINDOWPTR w1;                        /* window handle */
int batrib;                          /* border atrib */
int watrib;                          /* window atrib */

    wn_init();
    batrib = BLUE<<4 | WHITE;
    watrib = WHITE<<4 | BLACK;
    w1 = wn_open(0,0,0,25,10,watrib,batrib);
    if(!w1) exit(1);

    wn_hlinit(0,0,78,23,(BLUE<<4|WHITE),(BLUE<<4|WHITE),"intelc");

    wn_printf(w1, "Press any key\n"); v_getch();
    wn_help("%ksend%");
    wn_printf(w1, "Press any key\n"); v_getch();
    wn_help("%ksend1%");
    wn_printf(w1, "Press any key\n"); v_getch();
    wn_help("%krecv%");
    wn_printf(w1, "Press any key\n"); v_getch();
    wn_help("%krecv1%");
    wn_printf(w1, "Press any key\n"); v_getch();
    wn_help("%checksum xmit1%");

    wn_printf(w1, "Press any key\n"); v_getch();
    wn_close(w1);
    wn_exit();
    exit(0);
}

/* End */
```

8-10 Use of the help system.

Mouse basics

The Window Boss includes a collection of routines that provide the building blocks for developing applications incorporating mouse support. As a programmer, you will need following:

- The mouse and its associated hardware
- The mouse driver software
- C and/or Assembly level functions to communicate with the mouse

The first two are provided by the mouse manufacturer and must be installed as outlined in the manufacturer's literature. The last item is provided as part of the Window Boss. The Window Boss's mouse functions adhere to the de facto Microsoft standard. However, all of the routines have been extensively tested with both Microsoft and Logitech mice.

Mouse communication The only practical method of communicating with the mouse is through the mouse device driver, which is accessible via software interrupt 33H. This interrupt is not used by DOS and is claimed by the mouse device driver at its invocation. Information is exchanged between the mouse device driver and calling software via the standard 8086/88 registers. As a Window Boss user, you will be pleased to know that the burden of having to deal with the mouse at this level has been replaced by a collection of C level routines that handle all of the aforementioned setup, software interrupts, and register loading/unloading.

Mouse usage Once the mouse has been initialized (reset), you can show it, hide it, move it, ask it where it is, check to see if its buttons have been pressed or released, make it emulate a light pen, put a cage around it (set its region), define its shape and associated attribute, or ask it how many buttons it has.

Mouse functions The standard Microsoft mouse supports 16 functions. Logitech's are the same, although some are tweaked a tad to handle the third button. The Window Boss provides an easy to use interface to the low-level mouse functions and several higher level functions to ease your applications level programming.

TABLE 8-1 summarizes the 16 Microsoft mouse functions.

In addition to the low-level interface routines in Table 8-1, the following application's level functions have been implemented to ease the mouse's natural display adapter sensitivity. Without these routines, mouse applications would have to deal with the mouse in a 640×200-pixel plane, even in text mode.

```
mo_rcpos( )      Return current mouse position (row, col)
mo_locate( )     Locate mouse (row, col)
mo_press( )      Get button pressed info (button, location..)
mo_release( )    Get button released info (" " " " " " " ")
mo_region( )     Set mouse hot area (row, col, width, height)
mo_setptr( )     Set mouse pointer (style, attributes)
mo_wait( )       Wait for mouse to settle (de-bouncing logic)
mo_nbut( )       Return # of buttons on mouse
```

Most mouse applications will use and generally only need to use: mo_reset( ), mo_show( ), mo_hide( ), and most or all of the application-level functions.

Table 8-1   The Microsoft mouse functions.

Function	Description	Window BOSS function
0	Initialize mouse	mo_reset ( )
1	Show mouse	mo_show ( )
2	Hide mouse cursor	mo_hide ( )
3	Get position & status	mo_pos ( )
4	Set mouse position	mo_move ( )
5	Get button press info	mo_pbinfo ( )
6	Get button release info	mo_rbinfo ( )
7	Set min/max columns	mo_clim ( )
8	Set min/max rows	mo_rlim ( )
9*	Define graphics pointer	mo_sgcursor ( )
10	Define text pointer	mo_scursor ( )
11	Read motion counters	mo_motion ( )
12*	Define event handler	mo_task ( )
13	Light pen emulation on	mo_lpon ( )
14	Light pen emulation off	mo_lpoff ( )
15*	Set motion pixel ratio	mo_ratio ( )

*Interfaces to these functions are provided but not supported by Star Guidance.

The low-level functions are provided for those who prefer to deal with the mouse on its 640 × 200 pixel plane. See FIG. 8-11 for a mouse programming example.

Important concepts

The preceding programming examples serve as the foundation for some fundamental but very important concepts:

WINDOWS.H   The Window Boss requires the file windows.h to be included in any source code files that are going to reference any of the windowing, data entry, or form-control functions. Take time to peruse this file, as it contains all of the constants and structures used by both The Window Boss and Data Clerk. Also, please note that WINDOWS.H includes other standard compiler header files.

Window handles   All windowing functions (any function beginning with wn_) either explicitly require an associated window pointer to work or assume that one already is (or will be) created.

Mouse handles   All mouse functions (any function beginning with mo_) either explicitly require an associated mouse pointer to work or assume one already is (or will be) created.

Window origin   Windows have an origin relative to the upper left-hand corner of the screen, which is row 0, and column 0.

Text and data field origins   Text and data fields have an origin relative to the upper left-hand corner of the window, which is always row 0, column 0.

```
#include "windows.h"                        /* ALWAYS */

main()
{
MOUSEPTR m1;                                 /* my mouse ptr */
int mstat, mclik, mrow, mcol;                /* mouse stuff */
int i;                                       /* scratch */

  v_cls(NORMAL);                             /* clear the screen */
  v_locate(0,0,0);                           /* locate the cursor */

  m1 = mo_reset();                           /* init mouse */

  if(m1) {                                   /* mouse exists */
    printf("Mouse exists with %d buttons.\n", mo_nbutt(m1));
    mo_setptr(m1, 0x1E, NORMAL);             /* set mouse pointer style */
    mo_reigon(m1, 0, 0, 80, 25);             /* set mouse "window" */
    mo_show(m1);                             /* show the critter */

    v_locate(0,5,0);
    printf("Roll test... move mouse, click left or right to end.\n");
    do {                                     /* rolling test */
      mo_rcpos(m1, &mstat, &mrow, &mcol);
      v_locate(0,6,0);
      printf("Mouse @ %03d,%03d", mrow, mcol);
    } while (!mstat);

    v_cls(NORMAL);                           /* clear screen */
    v_locate(0,0,0);                         /* home cursor */
    mo_hide(m1);                             /* hide mouse */
    m1 = mo_reset();                         /* reset mouse */
    exit(0);                                 /* finito */
  }
  else {
    printf("NO MICE HERE!!\n");              /* tell of woe... */
    exit(0);                                 /* exit */
  }
}

/* End */
```

8-11 Using the mouse functions in a program.

Attributes Attributes (foreground/background colors) must be specified for windows, borders, and data entry fields. Prompts for data entry
fields always have the same attributes as the window. The fields themselves can have but do not require a different attribute set.

Fields and forms Fields are defined by calling the field definition functions (wn_gdate, wn_gtime, wn_gphone, ...) with "SET" as the function code (1st arg), a valid form handle (2nd arg), a field sequence number
(3rd arg), and the window handle (4th arg) belonging to the window in
which the form is to be displayed. The same functions used to retrieve dis-
crete information can be combined to create a form when used in conjunction with wn_frmopn() and wn_frmget(). Note the use of XEQ vs.
SET, NFRM vs. f1, and NFLD in the preceding two program examples.
XEQ stands for "execute now," while SET stands for "set up for later execution under wn_frmget()."

Forms are anchored to a particular window and must be created by
wn_frmopn() and defined with field definition functions.

Data entry fields can be edited, be prefilled, have validation ranges,
and have both help and error messages associated with them.

Return values Some functions return an indication of success or failure that you either can foolishly ignore or check to determine what action to take.

Closing forms and windows Both forms and windows should be closed when no longer needed. Although you can close them in any order, it makes sense to close all forms associated with a window before closing the window itself. As a side note, attempting to reference either forms or windows that have been closed can lead to unpredictable results.

Overlapping windows The Window Boss fully supports the concept of overlapping windows (i.e., you can have several windows on the screen at the same time and freely access any one of them without having to be concerned with the order in which they were opened or whether or not any other windows overlap the one you want to access). The Window Boss employs the "most recently used is active" concept. This concept is based on the following:

- The last window referenced is the current active window
- The current active window is always the top window

Let's assume that you have opened three overlapping windows in the following order; Window 1, Window 2, and Window 3 (as shown in FIG. 8-12). Window 3 is considered to be the top window because it was the last window referenced. If you now reference or explicitly activate Window 2, the Window Boss will automatically adjust the screen image to ensure that Window 2 is now the top window with Window 3 and Window 1 being partially hidden by Window 2 (see FIG. 8-13).

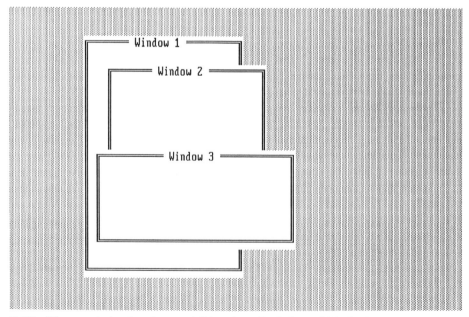

8-12 When a window is referenced, it is automatically brought to the top.

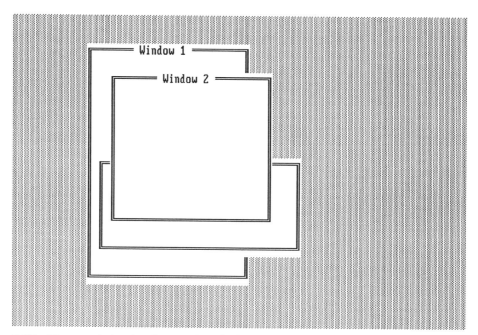

8-13 When a window is referenced again, it comes back up to the top.

You must keep in mind that the Window Boss will automatically activate (i.e., bring to the top) the window being referenced. By keeping your screen layouts attractive and uncluttered, only a minimum of window thrashing (which is both annoying and time-consuming) will occur.

Functions The Window Boss's functions fall into four major groups: those that manipulate windows, those that deal with data entry, those that deal with the mouse, and those that deal with the video or keyboard interface at a relatively low level. All window and data manipulation functions begin with the prefix wn_ (e.g., wn_open). All mouse functions begin with mo_ (e.g., mo_reset). All video and keyboard based functions begin with v_ or _ (e.g., v_getch or _putch). This convention makes it easy to remember where to look when you want to do something. Additionally, several global functions begin with wns_. These functions, although visible to the outside world, are used internally by the Window Boss.

So ends the tale of the basics. You are now ready to add sizzle, bright lights, and artistic touches to all your applications.

Included Files

The disks contain the files listed here, stored in compressed form.

LHARC.EXE	Archive utility
LHAR_DOC.LZH	Archive utility document archive

BOSS_DOC.LZH	Window Boss documentation archive
BOSS_SUP.LZH	Support archive (code, etc.)
BOSS_LB2.LZH	Library archive (Watcom, Zortech)
BOSS_LB1.LZH	Library archive (Microsoft)
BOSS_LB3.LZH	Library archive (Mix, Aztec, C86)
BOSS_LB4.LZH	Library archive (Datalight, Lattice, Borland Turbo C)
READ.ME	Important notes

Contents of BOSS_SUP

AZCS.BAT	Compiler driver—Aztec
C86.BAT	Compiler driver—CI86
DLCS.BAT	Compiler driver—Datalight
LCS3.BAT	Compiler driver—Lattice 3.4
LCS6.BAT	Compiler driver—Lattice 6.0
MSC5.BAT	Compiler driver—Microsoft C 5.X
MSC6.BAT	Compiler driver—Microsoft C 6.X
MSQC20.BAT	Compiler driver—Quick C 2.0
MSQC25.BAT	Compiler driver—Quick C 2.5
PCCM.BAT	Compiler driver—Mix Power C
TCS.BAT	Compiler driver—Turbo C
WECS.BAT	Compiler driver—EXPRESS C
WOCS.BAT	Compiler driver—Watcom C
ZTCS.BAT	Compiler driver—Zortech C
LOADAZ.BAT	Link batch file—Aztec
LOADC86.BAT	Link batch file—CI86
LOADDLC.BAT	Link batch file—Datalight
LOADLC3.BAT	Link batch file—Lattice 3.4
LOADLC6.BAT	Link batch file—Lattice 6.0
LOADMS5.BAT	Link batch file—Microsoft C 5.X
LOADMS6.BAT	Link batch file—Microsoft C 6.X
LOADQC20.BAT	Link batch file—Quick C 2.0
LOADQC25.BAT	Link batch file—Quick C 2.5
LOADPC.BAT	Link batch file—Mix Power C
LOADTC.BAT	Link batch file—Turbo C
LOADWAT.BAT	Link batch file—Watcom C
LOADWEC.BAT	Link batch file—EXPRESS C
LOADZTC.BAT	Link batch file—Zortech C
BOSSDEMO.C	Source to BossDEMO
BOSSDEMO.EXE	DEMO program
GENINDEX.C	Source to GENINDEX
HELLO.C	The classic . . .
INTELC.HLP	Demo DATA file
INTELC.NDX	Index for demo DATA file

REV.HST	Revision history
REV.LEV	Revision level
SAMPLE.C	Data entry sample program
WINDOWS.FN5	Type checking INCLUDE file
WINDOWS.FN6	Type checking INCLUDE file
WINDOWS.FNZ	Type checking INCLUDE file
WINDOWS.EXT	External definition INCLUDE file
WINDOWS.H	Boss INCLUDE file
WN_FRMGE.C	Data entry form reader
WN_GDATE.C	Data entry function (dates)
WN_GFLOA.C	Data entry function (floats)
WN_GPHON.C	Data entry function (phone)
WN_GTIME.C	Data entry function (time)
WN_GULON.C	Data entry function (unsigned long)
WN_GBOOL.C	Data entry function (logical)
WN_GDOUB.C	Data entry function (double)
WN_GINT.C	Data entry function (integer)
WN_GLONG.C	Data entry function (long)
WN_GPWOR.C	Data entry function (password)
WN_GTEXT.C	Data entry function (various text)
WN_GUINT.C	Data entry function (unsigned int)
WN_IEMSG.C	Data entry error message handler
WN_IHMSG.C	Data entry help message handler
WN_HELP.C	Help function source
WN_POPUP.C	Popup function source
WN_PUTS.C	Source to wn_puts( )

Contents of BOSS_LB1

SMSC5.LIB	Boss library—Microsoft C 5.X
SMSC6.LIB	Boss library—Microsoft C 6.X
SMSQC20.LIB	Boss library—Quick C 2.0 (QCL)
SMSQC25.LIB	Boss library—Quick C 2.5 (QCL)

Contents of BOSS_LB2

WATEC.LIB	Boss library—EXPRESS C
WATOC.LIB	Boss library—Watcom C
ZTECH.LIB	Boss library—Zortech C

Contents of BOSS_LB3

MWIN.MIX	Boss library—Mix Power C
SAZTEC.LIB	Boss library—Aztec C
SC86.LIB	Boss library—CI86

Contents of BOSS_LB4

SDLC.LIB	Boss library—Datalight
SLAT3.LIB	Boss library—Lattice C 3.4
SLAT6.LIB	Boss library—Lattice C 6.0
STC.LIB	Boss library—Turbo C

Installation

Follow the steps below to install your copy of the Window Boss:

1. First make backup copies of your disks. This, of course, goes without saying.

2. Use LHARC to unarchive the various LZH files. You will need more than 1200K of free disk space for all of the files. Alternatively, you can extract only those files you need for use with a specific compiler. Simply use LHARC to extract all the files from Boss_SUP .LZH then the library(s) you need from Boss_LB?.LZH. For example,

   ```
   A:LHARC E A:Boss_SUP
   A:LHARC E A:Boss_LB1 SMSC5.LIB
   ```

3. Copy the LIBrary corresponds to the compiler you are using onto the disk(s) and/or subdirectories containing your C compiler's run-time libraries. Be sure that the small model library is named SWIN.LIB (see later notes). The large model library should be named LWIN.LIB. The Mix Power C library is MWIN.MIX, while the EXPRESS C library is XMWIN.LIB.

   Note: The examples used in the documentation assume the library's name to be SWIN.LIB (small memory model). You might want to rename the library you extracted to conform to this naming convention to eliminate any possible confusion. For example,

   ```
   RENAME SMSC5.LIB SWIN.LIB
   ```

   Note: Large model libraries are not provided as part of the shareware disk set.

4. Copy (or rename) the compiler driver batch file that corresponds to the compiler you are using to CSM.BAT

5. If WINDOWS.FNS is not contained in the archive for your compiler or is not present after you unarchive the required files, copy (or rename) WINDOWS.FN5, WINDOWS.FN6, or WINDOWS.FNZ to WINDOWS.FNS as shown below:

Compiler	File
LC3 & LC6	WINDOWS.FN5
Power C	WINDOWS.FN5

WATCOM, EXPRESS C	WINDOWS.FN5
MSC5, Quick C 2.0	WINDOWS.FN5
MSC6, Quick C 2.5	WINDOWS.FN6
Turbo C	WINDOWS.FN5
CI86	————————
AZTEC	WINDOWS.FNZ
DLC	WINDOWS.FNZ
ZORTECH	WINDOWS.FNZ

6. Read the "Compiling," "Linking," and "General Notes" sections in this book. The "General Notes" section has across the board information that everyone should review and compiler specific tips that are very important.

7. Suggestion: After installing the Window Boss, build the HELLO program using the command line compiler and command line linker to confirm that you have installed everything correctly. To do this you will need the following:

YOUR COMPILER	Check PATH and ENVIRONMENT setup
CSM.BAT	Compiler driver batch file
SWIN.LIB	Small memory model library
WINDOWS.H	Window Boss INCLUDE file
WINDOWS.FNS	Window Boss INCLUDE file
WINDOWS.EXT	Window Boss INCLUDE file
HELLO.C	C Program

8. Remember, you don't need magic to use the Window Boss. It's simple.

Compiling

Compile your source code in the following manner:

```
csm hello
```

Notes

ALL compilers should be invoked with the compiler driver batch files supplied with the Window Boss. Some compilers require ".c" to be added to the name of the source file (e.g. "csm hello.c"). The examples in this manual assume you are creating small memory model programs.

The Window Boss includes windows.h, windows.fns, and windows .ext. These files can be placed with your compiler's other INCLUDE files, or they can remain in the same directory as your C programs. Depending upon your installation, you might have to edit HELLO.C and/or WINDOWS.H to follow the .vs. < > include file convention. All of Boss's includes are of the form:

```
#include "include_file_name"
```

If you examine CSM.BAT you will notice some command-line parameters that are passed to your compiler. These command-line parameters are an absolute requirement and must always be present. They are used by windows.h to set various conditions required by your specific compiler.

Linking

Simply specify the ?WIN.LIB file corresponding to the compiler/memory model you are using. Don't forget to include your compilers runtime library as well. The following examples demonstrate basic linking using the small model library (medium for MIX Power C):

Lattice
```
link c+hello,hello,,swin+lcm+lc+
  lapi+lcr                             ( v3.41 )
lmb hello,hello,,swin+lcr;             ( v6.XX )
```

Computer Innovations
```
link hello,hello,,swin+c86s2s
```

Datalight
```
link c+hello,hello,hello,swin+nl
```

Microsoft C
```
link hello,hello,,swin                 ( v5.X )
link hello,hello,,swin;                ( v6.X )
```

Microsoft Quick C
```
link hello,hello,,swin                 ( v2.0 )
qlink hello,hello,,swin                ( v2.5 )
```

Borland
```
tlink /c c0s hello,hello,hello,swin emu maths cs
```

Mix Power C
```
pcl hello;mwin [5k,40k,0]
```

Aztec
```
ln hello swin.lib m.lib c.lib
```

Watcom
```
link file hello library swin,maths,clibs
```

EXPRESS C
```
wlink file hello library xmwin,wcexpl
```

ZORTECH
```
blink hello,hello,,swin
```

Linking notes

The linking examples might have to be modified to include the complete path specifiers for each library. For example,

```
link hello,hello,,c:\msc5\lib\swin
```

Fixup offset errors are always the result attempting to link code compiled under one memory model with libraries created for use with another memory model.

Unresolved externals can be caused by missing user functions, missing library functions, linking command errors, missing project files, missing MAKE files, or attempted linkings of a nonconforming library. Misplaced commas on the command line and C code typing errors are the most common problems. In the case of integrated environment fans (Quick C, MSC 6.0 PWB, Turbo C), errors are almost always due to forgetting to *set the program list* to include the Window Boss library or (in the case of Turbo C) forgetting to create a project file including an entry for the Window Boss library.

General notes

Source code is provided for all of the high-level data entry functions, the help system, and the popup menu functions. This is done so that you have a wide variety of templates to base any local data entry functions on and so that you have the source to the code for those functions (help and popup) commonly changed to suit individual taste.

WN_BIOS.C and the various assembler files (*.ASM) contain all of the BIOS interface functions. Only `v_kstat()`, `v_border()`, `_vidblt()`, and `xferdata()` are written in assembly language.

A really important note is that both the C and assembly functions make very heavy use of pointers. The code contains numerous checks to ensure that memory (outside of that being used by the program) is not corrupted. If you attempt to do something that would cause memory to be corrupted, an error message will appear and your program will exit. This message will usually say that a bad handle was passed to some function and is usually triggered by a stray pointer in the application code. Check all your pointer operations. Doing strcpy's to arrays with insufficient space will always cause this type of problem.

Generally speaking, the members of the window control block (refer to windows.h) should not be modified unless you are familiar with how they are used by the various functions. You should obtain a hard copy of windows.h and review it even if you don't have any intentions of modifying the code. A great deal of information contained in windows.h might be helpful to you when you write your application.

Although the routines appear to support the multi-page capabilities of the IBM Color Card, actual support of this feature has not been implemented. Invoking the functions with references to video pages other than those documented might produce interesting, but undesired, results.

Programs such as Wordstar and Lotus change the video mode when they run. If your system is equipped with a color monitor and your windows are appearing in black and white, issue a call to v_smode to set the video mode to 3. Alternatively, you can use the MODE CO80 command at DOS level before you run your application.

The best way to manipulate the method by which windows are updated is via the wn_dmode( ) function. Calling wn_dmode(PAINT) causes the image to be painted, while wn_dmode(FLASH) causes the image to be flash updated. Flash updating is the preferred (default) method. Please keep in mind that windows are always flash updated on monochrome systems.

Upgrading: impact on existing applications

If you are upgrading from a previous version of the Window Boss, be sure to recompile and relink your application. This will eliminate the possibility of any "unusual" problems.

Current compilers and libraries

The distribution libraries were created on an IBMPC/AT under DOS 3.3 using Lattice 3.41, Lattice 6.02, Microsoft 5.1, Microsoft 6.0, Microsoft Quick C 2.0, Microsoft Quick C 2.5, Borland Turbo C 2.0, Datalight 3.10, Aztec 4.2b-1, Watcom C 7.0, Mix Power C 1.3.0, Zortech 2.06, and Computer Innovations CI86 2.30A. Marion was used to create the LIB files for CI86. Microsoft's LIB was used for the Microsoft variants, Datalight and Zortech. Lattice, Aztec, Watcom and the Mix Power C libraries were created with the library managers shipped with the respective compilers. The test hardware was IBMPC/XT/AT, PS/2, with IBM Monochrome, CGA, EGA, and VGA video adapters. Additionally, a wide variety of clones (8088, 8086, 80186, 80286, 80386) with brand name and noname components were also tested.

Several of the compilers support a compile-time command-line parameter that results in structures being byte-aligned instead of word-aligned. In all cases, the default (i.e., no command-line parameter) option was used to compile the modules in the various libraries.

EGA and VGA Expanded Line and Column modes

The Window Boss supports the Expanded Line and Column modes of both the EGA and VGA video adapters. However, in order to preserve the Window Boss's device independence, you must do a little extra work if you intend to write an application to take advantage of one of these expanded modes. The rules are quite simple. Your application must remain in one mode and can be (25 × 80), (80 × 132), (80 × 43), (80 × 50), or whatever size your adapter supports. The adapter must be in the mode you chose prior to calling ANY of the Window Boss functions. `wn_psinit()` must be called first, called only once, and called with parameters that reflect the physical screen size that your application is going to use. That's all there is to it.

Terminate and Stay Resident (TSR) programming

The Window Boss has been successfully incorporated in TSR programs. Due to the complexities involved in writing and resolving conflicts associated with TSR(s) and the lack of any real standards for TSR(s), Star Guidance Consulting, Inc., cannot provide any form of support or assistance for TSR-related problems. However, they will work with you in resolving any problem you can replicate when the program is not resident.

Important globals

Several global symbols are used by the various functions. All are defined in windows.c and referenced in windows.ext. A few are worthy of special mention:

```
int wn_dmaflg;
int wn_sbit;
int wns_escape;
    wns_dmaflg
```

When TRUE, `wn_dmaflg` enables direct writes into video ram. This is the default setting and should work in all cases. Setting `wn_dmaflg` to FALSE will disable these direct writes. When `wn_dmaflg` is FALSE, the BIOS video routines are used, resulting in slower screen updates. However, this method does have the advantage of being considered "well-behaved" by IBM's Topview, Microsoft's Windows, and DESQ.

```
wn_sbit
```

`wn_sbit` controls the window refresh rate on systems with color cards. When set to SLOW (defined in windows.h), window displays will appear to be painted on the screen rather than flash displayed. (This is the default value.) Setting `wn_sbit` to FAST enables flash displays. Artistic use of `wn_sbit` can give your application that extra visual touch. Experiment!

From a performance standpoint, the fastest (flicker and snow-free) screen updates will occur when `wn_dmaflg`=TRUE (default) and `wn_s-bit`=FAST (default). The key words here are flicker and snow-free. Scrolling speed can be increased, with a proportional increase in flicker (perhaps), by using wn_scroll() function to set the scrolling method for the window to BIOS. This technique will provide the fastest screen updates and scrolling on color systems.

    wns_escape

wns_escape is set to TRUE whenever wn_input detects that the escape key has been pressed. Because wn_input is the underlying logic for the entire data entry package, knowledge of this global might help you manage your data entry activities better. For example, you might want to follow one logic path if data entry completed normally and another if data entry was terminated through use of the Escape key.

Microsoft C

Some large programs might require a stack greater than 4096 bytes.

PWB and Integrated Development Environment fans take note—if program and/or data space is at a premium, disabling debugging can sometimes restore significant program and/or data space.

Microsoft 5.XX libraries were generated using the /Z1 command-line parameter. This should ensure compatibility with previous versions of the compiler.

Microsoft 6.XX Programmer Workbench fans must define MSCV6 = 1 in the defines dialogue box. Do this by selecting OPTIONS and then C COMPILER OPTIONS.

The same rules that apply to the creation of MAKE files for Quick C (Setting the Program List) also apply. The program list can be set by selecting the MAKE dialogue box and then SET PROGRAM LIST. Be sure to include an explicit entry for the Window Boss library.

Microsoft Quick C

All Integrated Development Environment users MUST create MAK files in order to be able to create EXEcutable programs from within the Developmental Environment. The MAK file must contain the names of all of the programs that comprise the application along with specific entries for all third-party libraries being used. In the case of third-party libraries, the complete path specification for the library must be provided (e.g., C:\ MSC\LIB\SWIN.LIB). The MAK file is created when you set the program list. Select the MAKE dialogue box and then SET PROGRAM LIST. Follow the standard rules for the creation of MAK files.

Quick C 2.0 Integrated Development Environment

MSCV4 = 1 must be defined in COMPILER FLAGS's DEFINES dialogue box (select OPTIONS, MAKE, COMPILER FLAGS, and then fill in DEFINES with MSCV4 = 1).

Quick C 2.5 Integrated Development Environment

MSCV6 = 1 must be defined in COMPILER FLAGS's DEFINES dialogue box (select OPTIONS, MAKE, COMPILER FLAGS, and then fill in DEFINES with MSCV6 = 1).

Borland Turbo C

Borland Turbo C pre-v1.5 users who prefer the Integrated Environment over the Command-line Version MUST define the symbol BORLAND = 1. (Select Options, Compiler, Defines, and enter BORLAND = 1 in the dialogue box without quotes and in uppercase.)

Integrated Environment users MUST create PROJECT files in order to be able to create EXEcutable programs from within the Integrated Environment. The PROJECT file must contain the names of all of the programs that comprise the application along with specific entries for all 3rd party libraries being used. In the case of 3rd party libraries, the complete path specification for the library must be provided (e.g., c: \ turboc \ lib \ swin.lib).

MIX Power C

- Merge files must be created and edited with text editors that do not insert ^Z for end-of-file.
- PCO.EXE should be in the default directory (the same directory that your C files are in).
- The linker should always be told the amount of memory to be assigned to the stack, heap, and far heap. Because the Window Boss uses both heap and far memory outside of your program, it is imperative that PCL be invoked with reasonable parameters. Typical values are [5k,40k,0] or [5k,40k,100k]. Refer to the chapter on the Mix Linker in the Power C manual.

Datalight C

BossDEMO.C and WN_FRMGE.C must be compiled with the BIG compiler.

Zortech C

ZORLIB (as distributed with Zortech C 2.0) cannot produce a correctly formatted library of the Window Boss functions. Microsoft's library manager LIB was used to create the libraries distributed with the Window Boss. Please do not attempt to recreate or update any of the Window Boss libraries with ZORLIB. Zortech has been notified of the problem.

BossDEMO.C must be compiled with the BIG compiler.

Watcom C

Express C: has a difficult time with the BossDEMO program unless you edit BossDEMO.C and set MAXWIN to around 50. You must also play with the OPTION STACK when linking (2k seems to work).

Lattice C

Lattice large model programs sometimes require the heap to be set to a minimum value. This can be accomplished by setting __MNEED or by specifying the stack and heap size at run time. A minimum heap size of 32K will usually satisfy most applications. Remember, this is for the *large* model only. Refer to the Lattice reference manuals for further information on setting the stack and heapsize.

Aztec C

Use the following command when recompiling BossDEMO.C:

```
csm -Z6000 bossdemo
```

The Aztec C linker (LN) sometimes requires that the Window Boss library be included as part of the command line twice to eliminate unresolved externals. For example, to link the HELLO program, the command line would be

```
ln hello swin.lib swin.lib m.lib c.lib
```

Hints on resolving common problems

In case you have some problems, here's a few hints.

Unresolved externals   These are most common with the programming environments of Turbo C and Quick C. Both of these programming environments require "program lists" or "make files." This type of error can also be caused by not explicitly specifying a Window Boss library on the link command line. All linkers must have explicit knowledge of what third-party libraries are to be linked with the compiler libraries and your applications object files. This problem is usually resolved by creating a program list or make file that includes an explicit reference to one of the Window Boss libraries, or explicitly specifying the correct Window Boss library as part of the link command line. Refer to your compiler documentation for further information.

Fixup offset errors   These are always the result of attempting to link code compiled under one memory model with libraries created for use with another memory model.

Bad handle exits   Both the C and assembly functions make very heavy use of pointers. The code contains numerous checks to ensure that memory does not get corrupted or randomly written over. This error is normally caused by a stray pointer in the application code. Check and recheck all your pointer operations. Doing strcpy's to arrays with insufficient space will always cause this type of problem.

Often, switching from the small memory model to large memory model will initially produce these errors in programs that worked fine in the small model. In nearly every case, the problem was traced to a stray pointer or improper pointer usage.

Fatal compilation errors All command-line compilers should be invoked with the compiler driver batch files provided as part of the Window Boss. This ensures that the compiler specific compile time parameters are specified correctly. If you elect to use your own method, be sure to include ALL of the command-line parameters specified in the provided batch files.

Linking errors See "Unresolved Externals." Most linking errors are the result of forgetting to specify the library to link, specifying the wrong library, or creating command-line syntax errors. Double check your compiler documentation for the proper way to link "other libraries" or "third party libraries."

Making changes

Incorporating local modifications or enhancements is, in part, why you would want to acquire the source code. Incorporating your modifications or enhancements should be a relatively straightforward task, provided you follow the basic guidelines outlined in the subsequent sections.

General considerations

First, be sure that you are familiar with the existing conventions and compiler specific feature test switches. Refer to the various BATch files for specific examples of compiler-specific defines etc.

Please note that I assume that you have installed your compiler exactly as suggested in the compiler's manual. This includes suggested subdirectories, PATH specifiers, and environment setup. Check and double check the "include" file requirements—make sure you have the required files and that they have been edited to correspond to the memory model for which you are writing code. Creating code that compiles under numerous compilers is not an easy task. If you run into problems, review your compiler's documentation and browse through the batch files provided. If you still have problems, call.

Carefully review the area of code you want to modify or enhance—be sure to get a complete understanding of what's currently going on before you add your own code. With the exception of the ASM files, compiler and memory model specific feature test switches are specified on the command line.

Depending upon the compiler being used, several warning errors will be generated. Warnings created by the unmodified distribution code can be safely ignored—all others should be investigated.

A note of caution: PC/MS-DOS 2.XX's LINK can complain if you build a new library that takes advantage of later LINK enhancements. If this occurs, you can upgrade to DOS 3.1 or above.

Specific changes to consider

Both the Shareware and Source versions of the Window Boss and Data Clerk are supplied with the numerous common source code files.

The source code was provided to serve as the basis upon which you could develop your own enhancements to the product and to provide you with those modules that might need to be modified for your particular application. The latter is true of wn_frmget, wn_iemsg, and wn_ihmsg. You should consider modifying these routines if you want to change the way in which data entry forms are handled when completed (wn_frmget), the way in which data entry field help messages are displayed (wn_ihmsg), or the way in which data entry field error messages are displayed (wn_iemsg).

In the case of wn_frmget, the code needing modification is at the tail end of the file and is clearly labeled. Data entry Help messages are displayed by wn_ihmsg whenever the HELP key is depressed. Data entry error messages are displayed by wn_iemsg whenever validation for a particular field fails. Refer to the source code files and the descriptions of these functions in the full documentation.

The changing procedure

To make changes, modifications, and enhancements, follow these steps:

1. If applicable, edit the assembler level modules as needed. Be sure to set LPROG and LDATA (if they apply). *Assemble.*

2. If Applicable, edit the C level modules. *Compile.*

3. Test your changes by linking the new/modified code with the existing libraries. For example, to link your modified WN_MOVE.C and v_getch, do this (Microsoft example):

   ```
   link myapp+wn_move+msvlib,,,swin
   ```

   If required, refer to your compiler documentation for explicit instructions on linking.

4. Update the existing Window Boss libraries with the new OBJ files. This is done with the librarian provided with your compiler. Alternatively, you can use the batch files provided with the source code to recompile the entire library and rebuild, rather than update, the Window Boss libraries.

If necessary, refer to your compiler documentation for explicit instructions on how to use their librarians to update libraries.

Remember, the memory model of the assembly OBJ file must correspond to the memory model of the C OBJ files and the memory model of any existing libraries.

Assembly language object files

The Source Media Kit includes the object files of the assembly language functions used by The Window Boss. This will free you from having to acquire, or use, an assembler unless you intend to make changes to those functions written in assembly language. Now, all you have to do is copy and/or rename the appropriate object file before running the MAKELIB batch file. An object file matrix is provided to assist you in determining which object file should be used with which compiler and memory model.

Assembly language object file matrix   The matrix that follows identifies the relationship between the object filename, compiler memory model, and the filename used as part of the MAKELIB batch utility provided as part of the Window Boss. Use this matrix to determine what file to rename (or copy) when recreating Window Boss libraries that *do not* include any changes or additions to existing assembly language functions.

Compiler	Small	Medium	Compact	Large	Makelib name
QuickC 2.0	SMSVLIB	MMSVLIB	CMSVLIB	LMSVLIB	MSVLIB.OBJ
QuickC 2.5	SMSVLIB	MMSVLIB	CMSVLIB	LMSVLIB	MSVLIB.OBJ
MSC 5.X		SMSVLIB	MMSVLIB	CMSVLIB	LMSVLIB MSVLIB.OBJ
MSC 6.X		SMSVLIB	MMSVLIB	CMSVLIB	LMSVLIB MSVLIB.OBJ
Turbo C		SMSVLIB	MMSVLIB	CMSVLIB	LMSVLIB MSVLIB.OBJ
Watcom		SWCVLIB	MWCVLIB	CWCVLIB	LWCVLIB WCVLIB.OBJ
Express C	———	MWCVLIB	———	———	WCVLIB.OBJ
Datalight	SDLVLIB	PDLVLIB	DDLVLIB	LDLVLIB	DLVLIB.OBJ
Lattice 3	SVLIB	PVLIB	DVLIB	LVLIB	VLIB.OBJ
Lattice 6	SVLIB	PVLIB	DVLIB	LVLIB	VLIB.OBJ
Zortech		SMSVLIB	MMSVLIB	CMSVLIB	LMSVLIB MSVLIB.OBJ
CI86		SVLIB	———	———	LVLIB VLIB.OBJ
MIX		———	PCVLIB	———	——— PCVLIB.MIX
AZTEC		SAZVLIB	MAZVLIB	CAZVLIB	LAZVLIB AZVLIB.O

For example, to rebuild the Large model library for Microsoft C 5.X, 6.X, or Quick C, you would

1. Use LCOMPILE to compile all C functions:
   ```
   LCOMPILE
   ```

2. Copy LMSVLIB.OBJ to MSVLIB.OBJ:
   ```
   COPY LMSVLIB.OBJ MSVLIB.OBJ
   ```

3. Rebuild the LARGE model library:
   ```
   MAKELIB LWIN
   ```

Notes: The HUGE memory model requires the same object file as the LARGE. Naturally, this only applies to those compilers that support the HUGE memory model.

Assembler code

Computer Innovations and Lattice

- VLIB.ASM   Edit—Set LATTICE to 1 for Lattice
  DOS.MAC determines the memory model.

  Set LATTICE to 0 for Computer Innovations.
  MODEL.H determines the memory model.

- MODEL.H   CI86 only—Set "SMALL" and "LARGE"
  See MODEL.H for discussion.

Microsoft C, Quick C, Borland Turbo C, Watcom C, and Zortech

- MSVLIB.ASM   Set LDATA and LPROG to TRUE or FALSE
  WCVLIB.ASM   LDATA is TRUE for LARGE DATA
  LPROG is TRUE for LARGE CODE
  Assemble using

  ```
  MASM /MX MSVLIB;    <- All but WATCOM
  MASM /MX WCVLIB;    <- WATCOM only
  ```

Datalight

- DOS.MAC   Edit to reflect memory model.
  Additionally, MACROS.ASM must be present.
  Assemble using

  ```
  MASM /MX dlvlib;
  ```

MIX Power C

- PCVLIB.ASM   Set LDATA to FALSE, LPROG to TRUE
  Assemble using
  > MASM /ML PCVLIB;

  Run the MIX utility on PCVLIB.OBJ

Aztec C

- AZVLIB.ASM   Set LDATA and LPROG to TRUE or FALSE
  LDATA is TRUE for LARGE DATA
  LPROG is TRUE for LARGE CODE
  Assemble using
  > AS AZVLIB;

C Code

Pattern your enhancements after existing code. The most common mistakes are failing to call wn_activate, failing to check for error returns, and failing to rebuild the libraries correctly.

Incorporating custom data entry functions is a straightforward task if you follow these guidelines:

- Pattern your data entry routine after wn_gfloat.

- Study the relationship between wn_gfloat and wn_frmget.

- Study the way in which arguments are loaded using the unions v1 through v8.

- Edit windows.h and expand the table of data entry function codes to include a new code above 100, such as

  > #define GCUSTOM 101

  The table of data entry function codes is located towards the tail end of WINDOWS.H and begins with

  > #define GDONE 0

- Edit WN_FRMGET.C, expanding the large case statement to include a case for your custom data entry function. Pattern the code you are adding after the existing code.

- Rebuild the libraries adding your custom function and replacing wn_frmget with the new version.

The general logic is to call the data entry function with the argument list corresponding to this occurrence of this type of field. The data entry function tests the value of fun. If it is "XEQ", then control immediately passes to the logic that handles data entry. If fun is "SET", then the data entry function loads the form control block (indexed by fld) with the arguments being passed. This sets the stage for subsequent calls (in a predetermined order) from wn_frmget! When called, wn_frmget first displays all the prompt fields and then calls the data entry functions in the order determined by the form control block.

Library rebuilding

Support for Microsoft C 5.1, Quick C 2.0, and Lattice 3.41 will eventually cease. At this time, Star Guidance Consulting is not distributing preconfigured libraries for these compilers with registered versions of the Window Boss. They are, however, providing all the tools required to rebuild the libraries on the end user's machine. They have also certified these compilers to work with the current version of the Window Boss. The steps to follow are outlined next and should not take longer than 20 minutes to run.

1. Unarchive CFILES.LZH:

   ```
   lharc e cfiles
   ```

2. Unarchive MS5.LZH or MSQC20.LZH or LC3.LZH with *one* of these commands:

   ```
   lharc e MS5
   lharc e MSQC20
   lharc e LC3
   ```

3. Based on the memory of the library you want to create, use one of the ?COMPILE.BAT batch files to compile all of the C files. The first character of the batch file corresponds to the memory module you wish to create. For example, to compile for the Large memory model you would:

   ```
   LCOMPILE
   ```

4. Using the previously discussed "Assembly language object file matrix" copy the memory model specific .OBJ file to either MSVLIB.OBJ or VLIB.OBJ. For the large memory model you would

   ```
   COPY LMSVLIB.OBJ MSVLIB.OBJ     (Microsoft)
   ```
   or
   ```
   COPY LVLIB.OBJ VLIB.OBJ          (Lattice)
   ```

5. Create the library using the MAKELIB batch file. Name the library ?WIN where ? corresponds to the memory model you are creating. For example, to build the Large library you would:

   ```
   MAKELIB LWIN
   ```

That's all there is to it.

List of function calls

Below is a list of all of the Window Boss function calls, along with short descriptions of each. This is only intended to give you an idea of what is available. The documentation you receive when you purchase the Window Boss completely describes each of these functions.

wn_init	Initialize window system
n_exit	Exit window system
wn_psinit()	Initialize window system—physical size
wn_dmode	Set window display mode
wn_open	Open window
wn_title	Title window
wn_titla	Title window with attribute
wn_stitle	Super title window
wn_stitla	Super title window with attribute
wn_close	Close window
wn_save	Save screen image
wn_restore	Restore saved screen image
wn_move	Move window
wn_locate	Locate cursor in window
wn_printf	Window printf
wn_puts	Put string (high speed)
wn_putc	Put character
wn_gets	Get string with validation
wn_putsa	Put string and attribute (high speed)
wn_putca	Put character and attribute
wn_insrow	Insert row in window
wn_delrow	Delete row from window
wn_clr	Clear window
wn_activate	Activate window
wn_color	Set window and border attribute
wn_wrap	Set/clear line wrap flag
wn_sync	Set/clear cursor synchronization flag
wn_scroll	Set scrolling method for window
wn_dma	Set/clear write RAM directly flag
wn_fixcsr	Update window cursor position
wn_boxset	Set box drawing character set
wn_natrib	Set new attribute in window NOW
wn_dborder	Draw (replace) border on window
wn_input	General purpose window input
wn_frmopn	Open data entry form
wn_frmget	Get (read) data entry form
wn_frmcls	Close data entry form
wn_gdate	Input date in window
wn_gtime	Input time in window

wn_gphone	Input phone number in window
wn_gtext	Input text in window
wn_gutext	Input uppercase text in window
wn_gltext	Input lowercase text in window
wn_gatext	Input text and graphics characters
wn_gpword	Input password in window
wn_gint	Input integer in window
wn_guint	Input unsigned integer in window
wn_glong	Input long integer in window
wn_gulong	Input unsigned long integer in window
wn_gfloat	Input float in window
wn_gdoubl	Input double in window
wn_gbool	Input logical in window
wn_dtext	Display text on input form
wn_iemsg	Display input error message
wn_ihmsg	Display input help message
wn_shkey	Set HELP key code
wn_popup	Display and act on popup menu
wn_qpopup	Display quick popup window
wh_hlinit	Initialize help system
wn_help	Display help message
wn_sleftj	Left justify string
wn_srightj	Right justify string
wn_scenter	Center string
wn_sdelspc	Delete leading/trailing spaces
wn_strndx	Return index of s2 in s1
mo_reset	Reset/init mouse
mo_show	Show mouse
mo_hide	Hide mouse
mo_pos	Get mouse pixel position & status
mo_move	Move mouse pixel cursor
mo_pbinfo	Get pressed mouse button status
mo_rbinfo	Get released mouse button status
mo_clim	Set mouse min/max pixel column limits
mo_rlim	Set mouse min/max pixel row limits
mo_sgcursor	Set mouse graphics cursor
mo_scursor	Set mouse cursor
mo_motion	Get mouse motion counters
mo_task	Define mouse event handler
mo_lpon	Mouse lightpen emulation on
mo_lpoff	Mouse lightpen emulation off
mo_ratio	Set motion to pixel ratio
mo_rcpos	Return current position of mouse
mo_locate	Locate (position) mouse cursor
mo_press	Get mouse button press status

mo_release	Get mouse button release status
mo_region	Set mouse region
mo_setptr	Set mouse pointer and attributes
mo_wait	Wait for mouse to settle
mo_nbutt	Get mouse button count
_getca	Get character and attribute
_putca	Put character and attribute
_vidblt	Video block transfer
v_spage	Set active display page
v_cls	Clear entire video screen
v_smode	Set video mode
v_wca	Write character and attribute
v_wtty	Write character TTY mode
v_locate	Locate (position) cursor
v_hidec	Hide cursor
v_sctype	Set cursor type (style)
v_sapu	Scroll active display page up
v_sapd	Scroll active display page down
v_rcpos	Return current cursor position
v_rcvs	Return current video state
v_getch	Get keyboard character and scan code
v_kstat	Get keyboard status
v_kflush	Flush keyboard buffer
v_border	Set border color

Registration

You are encouraged to register your copy of the Window Boss for $55.00.
Registration grants you the following benefits:

- ☐ Serialized diskette containing all source code for all supported compilers
- ☐ Telephone Support and minimal fee updates. Minimal fees cover the cost of media, packaging materials, shipping, handling, and update preparation

To register, send to

Star Guidance Consulting
273 Windy Dr.
Waterbury, CT 06705
(203) 574-2449

9
FlashPac C Library

Program title   FlashPac C Library   *(Disks 1872 and 2306)*

Special requirements   None.

FlashPac C Library was created to provide programmers with low-level routines that access the video display, keyboard, printer, disk, and mouse devices. The library routines are not intended to replace the standard features of C but greatly extend the C programming environment for MS-DOS and PC-DOS operating systems.

To simplify using the routines, the number of global variables needed for this library has been kept to an absolute minimum. All of the functions in the library were written in assembly language using the Pascal parameter passing conventions.

The library contains routines for the disk, keyboard, mouse, printer, and video display devices, as well as a couple of DOS functions. The header file FPCLIB.H contains all of the function and variable declarations needed for this library:

DISK	Supports several DOS function calls that use byte streams when accessing disk files.
GETKEY	Required for EditSt.
KBD	Supports BIOS and DOS keyboard function calls.
MOUSE	Supports basic mouse functions, including a mouse event handler. Support BIOS printer functions.
VIDEO	Several video routines that provide direct access to the video display. Routines include saving and restoring the screen,

framing windows, setting the absolute position of the cursor, etc.

Installation

The FlashPac C library consists of two files:

FPCLIB.H
FPCLIB.LIB

Place the header file FPCLIB.H in the same subdirectory that contains your other header files, and place FPCLIB.LIB into the same subdirectory that your other library files are in. You are now ready to use the FlashPac C library.

Compiling and linking a test program

To compile and link DEMO.C and GETKEY.C modules, use the following instructions appropriate for your compiler.

Turbo C

In the Turbo C integrated environment, follow these steps:

1. Select the large memory model under the Options, compiler menu.
2. Create a project file with the following three lines:
   ```
   demo (DEMO.C)
   getkey (GETKEY.C)
   fpclib.lib
   ```
3. Select the project file under the compile menu option select build all to create an executable file called DEMO.EXE.
   If you are working from the command line, enter the following:

   ```
   tcc  -IC:\INC  -LC:\lib  -ml  demo.c  getkey.c
        \lib\fpclib.lib
   ```

where the parameters are

-IC:\INC	C:\INC is the include subdirectory for header files
-LC:\LIB	C:\LIB is the library subdirectory for Turbo C libraries
-ml	Selects large memory model
\lib	The subdirectory where FPCLIB.LIB is located

Microsoft C

For Microsoft C, type the following at the DOS prompt

```
cl /AL /F 4000 demo.c getkey.c \lib\fpclib.lib
```

where the parameters are

/AL   Selects large memory model.
/F 4000   Create a 16K stack area.
\lib   The subdirectory where FPCLIB.LIB is located.

The FlashPac C functions

The functions included in the FlashPac C Library are listed below with short descriptions of their various uses. Complete instructions on how to use each function are included on disk with the library.

BorderColor	Sets the color for the border screen.
ClrWin	Clears window area with the specified color.
ColorMsg	Displays string on the screen using the color attribute specified.
DspMsg	Displays string on the screen without changing the color attribute that is currently on the display screen.
EditSt	Edits an existing or null string from the keyboard.
FillColAttr	Displays a column of attribute bytes on the screen.
FillColCell	Fills a column on the screen with a character.
FillColChar	Fills a column on the screen with a character.
FillFrameAttr	Fills the frame area defined by x1, y1, x2,y2 coordinates with the attribute byte defined.
FillFrameCell	Fills the frame area defined by x1, y1, x2,y2 coordinates with the cell defined.
FillFrameChar	Fills the frame area defined by x1, y1, x2,y2 coordinates with the character byte defined.
FillRowAttr	Writes N copies of the attribute byte on the screen starting at the specified x,y coordinates.
FillRowCell	Writes N copies of the character and attribute byte on the screen starting at the specified x,y coordinates.
FillRowChar	Writes N copies of the character byte on the screen starting at the specified x,y coordinates.
FrameWin	Frames the window currently defined by

	the global variables WindMax and Wind-Min with the specified characters.
GetCursorSize	Reports the starting and ending scan lines of the current cursor.
GetFrameAttr	Reads the attribute bytes for the specified area on the screen into the buffer area.
GetFrameCell	Reads the character and attributes bytes for the specified area on the screen into the buffer area.
GetFrameChar	Reads the character bytes for the specified area on the screen into the buffer area.
GetScrn	Reads the character and attribute bytes starting from specified position on the screen into the buffer.
GetVideoCols	Gets the number of columns per line for the current display mode.
GetVideoInfo	Gets general video display information.
GetVideoMode	Gets the current video mode.
GetVideoPage	Gets the active display page currently in use.
GotoxyAbs	Positions the cursor at the specified position on the screen without regards to the global variables WindMin and WindMax.
HideCursor	Hides the cursor from view of the video display.
InitVideo	Initializes the video mode.
PutFrameAttr	Writes the data in the buffer to the attribute byte in the specified area on the screen.
PutFrameCell	Writes the data in the buffer to the character and attribute bytes in the specified area on the screen.
PutFrameChar	Writes the data in the buffer to the character byte in the specified area on the screen.
PutScrn	Displays the data in the buffer to the specified screen position in character attribute byte form.
RvsAttr	Reverses the video attribute byte passed.
ScrollDown	Scrolls the specified portion of the screen down N lines filling in new lines with spaces and the specified attribute.
ScrollLeft	Scrolls the specified portion of the screen left N columns filling in new columns with spaces and the specified attribute.
ScrollRight	Scrolls the specified portion of the screen

	right N columns filling in new columns With spaces and the specified attribute.
ScrollUp	Scrolls the specified portion of the screen up N lines filling in new lines with spaces and the specified attribute.
SetCursorSize	Sets the size of the cursor.
SetVideoPage	Sets the active display page.
ShowCursor	Shows the cursor on the video display.
VioInit	Initializes the Video units global variables.
WhereXAbs	Returns the column the cursor is in.
WhereYAbs	Returns the row the cursor is on.
WindowFP	Sets the window coordinate variables WindMin and WindMax.
WriteSt	Displays a string on the screen.
WriteStln	Displays a string on the screen.
BiosKbdClr	Clears the keyboard buffer.
BiosKbdGetElmt	Returns an integer value for the key pressed on the keyboard.
BiosKbdHit	Reports if a keystroke is waiting to be read from the keyboard buffer.
BiosKbdRead	Reads a character from the keyboard.
BiosKbdStat	Gets the keyboard status byte.
DosKbdClr	Clears the keyboard buffer.
DosKbdGetElmt	Returns an integer value for the key pressed on the keyboard.
DosKbdHit	Reports if a keystroke is waiting to be read from the keyboard buffer.
DosKbdRead	Reads a character from the keyboard.
GetKey	Returns a keystroke and maps it into a keyboard element number for EditSt.
BiosPrtChar	Sends a character to the printer.
BiosPrtInit	Initializes the printer
BiosPrtStatus	Returns the current status of the printer.
DosPrtChar	Sends a character to the printer.
CloseFile	Closes a file and flushes all file buffers for a file.
CreateFile	Opens an existing file or creates a new file if it does not exist.
DosFindFirst	Finds the first file that matches the given filespec and attributes.
DosFindNext	Returns the next file entry that matches the filespec and attributes used in a previous call to DosFindFirst.
FSeek	Changes the logical read/write position of the file pointer.

GetDrive	Reports the current default disk drive.
GetDTA	Returns the current disk transfer area.
GetFileSize	Reports the number of bytes in a disk file.
GetNDrvs	Reports the number of disk drives.
OpenFile	Opens the file given in the string passed.
ReadFile	Reads a file or device for a specified number of bytes.
ResetDisk	Resets the disk and flushes all file buffers.
ResetErrCodes	Resets global variables that indicate device errors to their initial settings.
RestInt24	Uninstalls or restores the programs critical interrupt error handler.
SetDTA	Sets the file attribute for the file specified.
SetInt24	Initializes the critical error handler routine and its global variables for use with your system.
WriteFile	Writes to a file or device for a specified number of bytes.
MButtonPress	Returns the current button status information.
MButtonRel	Returns the current button status information.
MGetPos	Returns the current button status and the location of the mouse cursor.
MGetSpeed	Returns the distance the mouse has moved since the last call to this routine.
MGraphCursor	Defines the shape and color of the mouse cursor when in graphics mode.
MHideCursor	Removes the mouse cursor from the screen.
MInitEventHandler	Initializes the mouse interrupt event handler.
MPollQue	Returns a copy of the oldest event in the mouse event queue. The event queue is left unchanged.
MResetMouse	Determines if the mouse hardware and software are installed.
MRetQue	Returns the oldest event in the mouse event queue and removes the event from the queue.
MSetEvent	Simulates a mouse event.
MSetPos	Sets the position of the mouse cursor.
MSetSpeed	Sets mouse motion to screen pixel ratio.
MSetXRange	Sets the column boundaries the mouse cursor will be allowed to move within.

`MSetYRange`	Sets the row boundaries the mouse cursor will be allowed to move within.
`MShowCursor`	Displays the mouse cursor on the screen.
`MTextCursor`	Defines the mouse text cursor.

Registration

The registration fee is $50. When you register, you will receive the following:

☐ A new distribution diskette with your registration number
☐ One free major update
☐ Documented source code

Write to

SimpleSoft Inc
1209 Poplar St.
La Crescent, MN 55947
(507) 895-8237

10
MPLUS
Graphic Interface Library

Program title   MPLUS Graphic Interface Library   *(Disk 2032)*

Special requirements
- CGA, EGA, or VGA graphic display (EGA or VGA recommended).
- Microsoft C 5.0, 5.1, or 6.0 (with GRAPHICS.LIB).
- Microsoft or compatible mouse (optional).

MPLUS is a graphic interface library for Microsoft C. If your programs include business or scientific charts, fractal images, or just sets one pixel, MPLUS might be of use. By providing menus, windows, dialogue boxes, and mouse support, MPLUS gets your program up to speed quickly and easily.

Is MPLUS for you? When designing your application, remember these things:

- *Remember your software's needs.* If your program deals only with characters, a text-based windowing system might be what you need. If your program requires graphing, multi-tasking, dynamic data exchange between applications, and a real-time feed to a stock quotation system, you might need Microsoft Windows or OS/2. MPLUS is best suited for single-tasking, graphical applications.

- *Remember your audience.* Will your end-user have a fast 386 machine with 4 megabytes? Or will your end-user own IBM's new 286-based PS/1 for home and school? Requiring relatively little memory, MPLUS will fit comfortably in both extremes.

- *Remember your timetable.* If you have five or more years to develop your project, then a long term outlook is necessary. By then, fast 386 machines with 4 megabytes should be commonplace and OS/2, UNIX, or Windows may be the proper choice for a platform. Projects due out in less than five years might benefit from MPLUS. The venerable 286-AT class machine with 640K is today's and tomorrow's most popular machine. And it won't disappear anytime soon (it's been rumored that there are still some 8088 PCs around).

It's evident that the application's requirements, audience, and timetable are all critical in choosing an interface and environment. From a programmer's view, MPLUS' major strengths are low memory requirements, a low learning curve, and an uncluttered look. These qualities make MPLUS effective for prototyping as well as producing a finished product. Clearly, MPLUS' simplicity doesn't allow it to do as much as the "big GUIs," and for some of you, that will be a drawback. For others, simplicity is a virtue.

The documentation supplied here is for your evaluation. The complete functional documentation is included with the MPLUS software.

Using MPLUS

To best install MPLUS, copy the desired MPLUS library into your Microsoft C library subdirectory \MSC\LIB and the headers into Microsoft's \MSC\INCLUDE.

Virtually every MPLUS function requires that you include Microsoft's GRAPH.H header file, and it must be placed before any of MPLUS' own header files.

For example,

```
#include <graph.h>   /* Microsoft's */
#include <gplus.h>   /* MPLUS' */
```

The application program should be linked with Microsoft's GRAPHICS.LIB and with the correct memory model of the MPLUS library. If you have a mouse, remember to load the driver. The MPLUS mouse functions will check for the presence of a mouse and use it if found.

This next line builds the graphic window demo, GWDEMO.EXE, in the large memory model:

```
cl -AL gwddemo.c -link graphics lmplus
```

If you have built a combined Microsoft library, one already containing GRAPHICS.LIB, then just omit the `graphics` specification from the command line.

Note: There is no huge model library of MPLUS. Huge model programs might be linked with the large model MPLUS library.

Graphic support

Two routines here are named after Microsoft's functions and are distinguished by an mp prefix instead of an underscore: mpouttext() and mpsetvideomode(). They behave similarly to the originals but have additional features. While it is optional to use mpouttext() (although preferred), using mpsetvideomode() is essential. mpsetvideomode() maintains external variables that other MPLUS functions must reference. The programmer can also reference these variables by setting up the appropriate declarations. The functions are summarized here:

mpouttext()	Outputs text with a specified foreground color on the specified background color.
mpsetvideomode()	Sets the screen's video mode.
mpwordwrap()	Enables/disables word wrap when using mpouttext().

Graphic windows

In GRAPHICS.LIB, text output could only appear in a "text window" while graphic output was restricted to the "graphic viewport." The MPLUS graphic window, also known as GWDW, is a hybrid object that can present both text and graphic output. In addition, a graphic window can be opened and closed, respectively saving and restoring the background area.

The graphic window is achieved by overlaying a text window with a graphic viewport. Note that a text window, being character-oriented, must be byte-aligned, whereas a graphic viewport can be pixel-aligned. Because precise overlaying is not always possible, the text window is always placed "inside" the graphic viewport.

A graphic window is typically positioned and opened by specifying pixel coordinates (X,Y); gwdwopen() performs this task. Sometimes it may be more convenient to think and program in terms of text coordinates—rows and columns—especially when opening a window primarily to display text. Use gwdwtopen() for those occasions; it accepts text coordinates. Regardless of the way a graphic window is opened, a GWDW will accept both text and graphic output.

The number of graphic windows that can be opened at once depends upon available memory. Graphic windows can overlap, but the programmer should not write to the one underneath. Output—text or graphic—won't be clipped properly and will overwrite the contents of the upper window. Problems also occur when closing the lower graphic window prior to closing the upper one: the lower one's background will be restored over the upper graphic window. The management of overlapping windows can be avoided if graphic windows are arranged as tiles.

One special form of graphic window is known as the *root window*. This root window behaves similarly to the standard graphic window, the difference being that it conserves memory by not saving the background area. In effect the root window serves as the background screen. Consequently, there should be only one root window in any given program and it must be opened before any graphic window is opened and closed after all graphic windows are closed. Use of the root window is optional. For more details, refer to the function descriptions of `grootopen( )`, `groottopen( )`, and `grootclose( )`.

No matter how a graphic window is opened—whether with `gwdwopen( )`, `gwdwtopen( )`, `grootopen( )`, or `groottopen( )`—you have the option of giving it one of four basic appearances: with a border, without a border, raised, or sunken. While all four looks are fine for displaying information, the last two (because of their depth) are particularly useful for simulating push buttons.

The graphic window's appearance is governed by three arguments:

border   Border type
fg   Foreground and border color
bg   Background or "fill" color

The border constants control the appearance of borders:

_GFILLINTERIOR   The graphic window is opened without a border. The interior is filled with the color specified in bg.

_GBORDER   The graphic window is opened with a border. The border is displayed with the color specified in fg and the interior is filled with the color specified in bg.

_GRAISE   The graphic window opened appears raised. The borders along the left and top sides are WHITE, and the borders along the right and bottom sides are BLACK. The interior is filled with the color specified in bg.

_GSINK   The graphic window opened appears sunken. The borders along the left and top sides are BLACK, and the borders along the right and bottom side are WHITE. The interior is filled with the color specified in bg.

Concerning _GRAISE and _GSINK, if you specify the background color as WHITE or BLACK, the border colors automatically change to BRIGHTWHITE and GREY to ensure contrast. Recommended background colors are GREY, WHITE, or BLUE. Bright colors tend to wash out the 3-D effect.

A demo program and its source resides on the distribution disk as GWDWDEMO.EXE and GWDWDEMO.C, respectively. It opens three windows, plots a sine and cosine wave, and finally closes all windows and exits. The window functions are listed here:

`grootclose()`	Closes the root window.
`grootopen()`	Opens the root window using graphic coordinates.
`groottopen()`	Opens the root window using text coordinates.
`gwdwclose()`	Closes a graphic window.
`gwdwclr()`	Clears the graphic window.
`gwdwgetactv()`	Gets the active graphic window.
`gwdwgetorg()`	Gets the logical origin of a graphic window.
`gwdwopen()`	Opens a graphic window using graphic coordinates.
`gwdwsetactv()`	Makes a graphic window active.
`gwdwsetorg()`	Sets the logical origin of a graphic window.
`gwdwtopen()`	Opens a graphic window using text coordinates.

Graphic dialogue

A dialogue box presents information in a graphic window and solicits a response from the user. The user response can be from either the mouse or keyboard. There are three classes of dialogue boxes: information, warning, and error. Any can be presented with the predefined prompts "Okay," "Okay/Cancel," and "Yes/No."

The location of the box on screen is defined by the following relationships:

```
row1 = _videoconfig.numtextrows / 4;
row2 = row1 + 6;
col1 = _videoconfig.numtextcols / 4;
col2 = col1 * 3;
```

Warning and error boxes are displayed with a title and have room for three rows of text. The information box, having no title, can present four rows of text. As for characters per line, high resolution graphics allows 40, while medium resolution graphics provides 20. When writing to the dialogue box, text will wrap. Scrolling is not supported in a dialogue box; thus it is important not to exceed three rows of text in a warning or error box and four rows of text in an information box.

A demo program and its source resides on the distribution disk as GDDEMO.EXE and GDDEMO.C, respectively. They illustrate the calls to all three classes of dialogue box.

Dialogue functions are prefixed with gd.

`gdclose()`	Closes a dialogue box.
`gdialog()`	Opens a dialogue box.
`gdprompt()`	Solicits a response from the user.
`gdwrite()`	Outputs text to dialogue box.

Graphic image

The functions provided here deal with images—picking them up, sliding them across the screen, and putting them down. Of course, functions dealing with the screen correctly must make sure that the mouse cursor does not interfere with the image; these functions hide the mouse cursor before reading or updating the screen, and restores the mouse cursor when done. You will have to manage the mouse cursor yourself when using any of Microsoft's output or drawing functions.

Also, there are two functions used for rubberbanding: `xorpt()` and `xorline()`. Consider a line where one end point is anchored and the other end point is variable and designated by the mouse cursor. As the user slides the mouse around, the old line is erased and a new line is drawn to the new end point; all this happens without the destruction of the background screen. The effect is a line that moves, stretches, compresses, and pretty much behaves like a rubber band. Rubberbanding is common in paint programs and computer-aided design applications.

For Microsoft C 6.0 users, a faster alternative to `xorline()` would be to use `_setwritemode(_GXOR)` with `_moveto()` and `_lineto()`.

Moving objects and rubberbanding are made possible with the "exclusive or," also known as XOR. A wonderful little operator, XOR behaves as shown in TABLE 10-1.

Table 10-1   Behavior of the XOR operator.

Bit A	Bit B	A XOR B
1	1	0
1	0	1
0	1	1
0	0	0

When an image is XORed onto the screen, it appears on the screen and gets combined with the background. When the image is XORed onto the screen twice, the image disappears and the background is restored.

The graphic image functions are listed below.

`gpickup()`	Allocates memory and saves a rectangular screen image to it.
`gputdown()`	Restores an image to the screen and frees allocated memory.
`loghighlite()`	Highlights an image specified by logical coordinates.
`mpgetimage()`	Saves a rectangular screen image.
`mpputimage()`	Restores an image to screen.

`physhighlite()`	Highlights an image specified by physical coordinates.
`xorline()`	Draws a line using the XOR operator.
`xorpt()`	Draws a point using the XOR operator.

The menu bar

The functions described in this section create a horizontal bar menu with pull down windows. Depending upon available memo screen space, up to five levels of submenus are supported, although two levels should be sufficient for most applications. The menu also supports *greyout*, a technique used to disable a menu choice. Menu functions are prefixed with an mb__.

The mouse and keyboard are supported input devices. To make a menu selection with a mouse, position the cursor in the bar over a menu title. Pressing the left button will highlight the menu title and open a pull-down menu. The button must be held down to keep pull-down menu open. To close the pull-down menu and open others, keep the left button down and slide the cursor over to other titles along the bar.

To select one of the options in the pull-down menu, drag the cursor over one of the choices and release the left button. If no selection is desired, slide the cursor out of the pull-down menu and release the left button.

Using a keyboard to select from the menu bar requires an Alt key combined with the first character of the desired menu title (this opens a pull-down menu). The Left and Right cursor keys can be used to enter submenus (if present) or to close the current pull-down menu and open adjacent menus. Tab and Shift-Tab behave similarly but bypass all submenus.

Use the Up and Down cursor keys to point to titles within the pull-down menu. These selections can also be made by pressing the first character of the titles (no Alt this time). If more than one title begins with the same character, pressing that character again will point to the next matching selection. Pressing Return makes the decision final, while pressing Escape just closes the pull-down menu with no further action.

Setting up your menus requires plugging in titles and pointers to functions into two structures shown in FIG. 10-1 and FIG. 10-2.

```
struct MENU_INFO
{
    int    exitkey;          /* quit key */
    int    (*exitfun)();     /* ptr to quit function */
    word   fg0, bg0;         /* color of menu bar */
    word   keycolor0;        /* color of ALT KEY */
    word   greyout0;         /* color of disabled bar title */
    word   border;           /* border flag */
    word   fg, bg;           /* color of pull-down menu */
    word   keycolor;         /* color of title's first char */
    word   greyout;          /* color of disabled title */
};
```

10-1   The MENU__INFO structure.

```
struct MENU_ITEM
{
    char *title;                    /* title string */
    int (*function)();             /* ptr to function */
    struct MENU_ITEM *menu_item;   /* titles for submenu */
    unsigned submenu: 1            /* bit indicates submenu */
    unsigned greyout: 1            /* bit disables title */

    /* Remaining six bits reserved for future */
};
```

10-2   The MENU__ITEM structure.

The structure MENU__INFO is used to define various attributes of the menu, including its colors, an exit key, and an exit function. Regarding colors, you may initialize them to a default set with the function mb__std-colors( )—see the function description for details.

Defining an exit key and an exit function would save the user from hunting through an array of menus to find that "quit" function. The exit key can be any key that has a scan and ASCII code but typically would be Esc, Ctrl-Q, or Alt-X. The function mb__run( ) will watch for the assigned key and, if detected, return a pointer to your exit function.

Suggested exit keys	Scan and ASCII code
Esc	0x011B
Ctrl-Q	0x1011
Alt-X	0x2D00

The structure MENU__ITEM is used to store your menu titles, pointers to functions, submenu titles, and other menu attributes. Examples of initializing this structure can be found in the function description for mb__open( ) and in the file MENUDEMO.C supplied with the distribution disk.

Mouse support

The mouse routines support a Microsoft or compatible mouse and provide a range of services from resetting the mouse to retrieving input from either the mouse or keyboard. If no mouse is present, calling these functions will have no effect.

Note that these functions are valid only in graphic video modes; text modes are not supported. When using Microsoft's graphics output routines, remember to hide the mouse before updating or reading the screen. Otherwise, the mouse will interfere with the screen image. Except where indicated, all MPLUS functions handle the mouse automatically.

A few routines reference a structure named ms__status; it is defined in mouser.h and has the elements shown in FIG. 10-3.

Mouse activity is returned in this structure for easy reference. Note that the element condmask, currently used only by dev__ready( ), is a mask defining the type of mouse activity the user applied. It can have one or a combination of the values listed in TABLE 10-2.

```
struct ms_status
{
      unsigned int condmask;     event mask or type of activity
      int lbtn;                  left button: 0 = up, 1 = down
      int lbpress;               the number of left button presses
      int lbrelease;             the number of left button releases
      int rbtn;                  right button: 0 = up, 1 = down
      int rbpress;               the number of right button presses
      int rbrelease;             the number of right button releases
      short x, y;                mouse cursor position
}
```

10-3 The ms_status structure is used by some of the mouse routines.

**Table 10-2   Values
returned by the** condmask **element.**

Constant	Hex value	Meaning
_CSRMOVED	0x01	Cursor moved
_LBPRESSED	0x02	Left button pressed
_LBRELEASED	0x04	Left button released
_RBPRESSED	0x08	Right button pressed
_RBRELEASED	0x10	Right button released

The mouse functions are listed below.

dev_ready( )	Checks the keyboard and mouse for input.
ginrectangle( )	Determines if point (X,Y) lies in a rectangle or not.
ginwindow( )	Determines if point (X,Y) lies in a graphic window or not.
ms_cursor( )	Returns the cursor status—on or off.
ms_getposition( )	Gets the cursor position and the status of the mouse buttons.
ms_getpress( )	Retrieves the status of the specified button and the number of times it was pressed since this function was last called.
ms_getrelease( )	Retrieves the status of the specified button and the number of times it was released since this function was last called.
ms_hidecursor( )	Hides the cursor.
ms_poll( )	Polls the mouse for input.
ms_ready( )	Determines if the mouse has input.
ms_reset( )	Resets the mouse driver.
ms_setevent( )	Enables/disables mouse event checking.
ms_setposition( )	Positions the cursor at specified coordinates.
ms_showcursor( )	Displays the cursor on the screen.
ms_window( )	Defines the screen region where the cursor may roam.

Library incompatibilities

Certain calls to Microsoft's GRAPHICS library can confuse MPLUS. The side effects of using Microsoft's _outtext( ) and _setvideomode( ) functions have already been mentioned in the section on Graphic Support. Presented here are other Microsoft functions you should use carefully, if at all.

The _getimage( ) and _putimage( ) functions

These functions do not recognize the presence of a mouse. A visible cursor will interfere with the "putting" and "getting" of the screen image.

If your application uses a mouse, then MPLUS' mpputimage( ) and mpgetimage( ) is recommended.

The _remapallpalette( ), _remappalette( ), and _setbkcolor( ) functions

The #defines in GSCREEN.H are not universal and are valid only for the default palette and background. Remapping the palette or setting the background color will render the #defines incorrect. Consequently, you will need to write your own #defines that map to your new colors.

These Microsoft functions will also alter the colors used by the dialogue boxes. For now, the only way to preserve the colors is to avoid remapping BLUE, WHITE, BRIGHTWHITE, BLACK, RED, and YELLOW.

If you simply desire a new background color instead of an entirely new palette, see grootopen( ) or use the following code fragment:

```
_setcolor( background );
_rectangle( _GFILLINTERIOR, 0, 0,
    _videoconfig.numxpixels-1,
    _videoconfig.numypixels-1 );
```

This paints the entire screen with the color of your choice.

The _settextwindow( ) and _setviewport( ) functions

These functions generally shouldn't be needed because MPLUS provides graphic windows (see the gwdwopen( ) graphic function). If you open a graphic window and then call _setviewport( ) or _settextwindow( ), you will lose the graphic window because you've altered the output region.

The graphic window can be recovered by setting it active again with

```
gwdwsetactv( gwptr );
```

Note to MSC 6.0 users

If you are using Microsoft C 6.0, you'll discover an unresolved external when linking with the MPLUS library. MSC 6.0 renamed a couple of its functions, replacing 5.x's _getlogcoord( ) and _setlogorg( ) with _getviewcoord( ) and _setvieworg( ), respectively. If you are a registered user, you have access to the MPLUS source code and can rebuild the entire system using MSC 6.0. A make file for NMAKE is provided: MPLUS.NMK. Refer to the section about source code for more details.

If you don't have access to source or don't want to rebuild the system, compile MPORIGIN.C (using MSC 6.0) in the model of your choice and add it to the appropriate MPLUS library. This example does this for the small memory model:

```
cl -c -AS -Ox -Zl MPORIGIN.C
lib SMPLUS.LIB + MPORIGIN,;
```

Please note that while the MPORIGIN solution is quick and easy, rebuilding the MPLUS system with MSC 6.0 yields optimal code.

About source code

This section is for those interested in working with the source code.

The Make files

There are two make files.

MPLUS.MAK   For MSC 5.x MAKE utility.
MPLUS.NMK   For MSC 6.0 NMAKE utility. Rename to "makefile" if you prefer.

To build a model of the MPLUS Graphic Interface Library, you'll need the following:

Microsoft C Compiler 5.x or 6.0.
Microsoft Macro Assembler 4.x or Turbo Assembler 1.x.

For simplicity, the make files provided assume that all MPLUS header and source files are in the current directory, and that all output goes to the current directory. It also assumes you will be using MASM. Customize as needed.

The default library created will be the small model. To specify other models, use the following line for MSC 5.x:

```
make model = X mplus.mak
```

For MSC 6.0, use

```
nmake model = X /f mplus.nmk
```

where X can be S, M, C, or L.

MPLUS will not run properly as a huge model library. Applications compiled in the huge model can be linked with the large model MPLUS library.

MSC 6.0 users should note that while NMAKE is smarter than MAKE, NMAKE requires more memory. If the compiler complains about running out of heap space, you can use MAKE on MPLUS.MAK:

```
make model=X compiler=MSC6 mplus.mak
```

The C compile flags are the same for both MSC 5.x and 6.0:

-Ox   Maximum optimization.
-Zl   Don't include library-search records in object file.

For MASM, there is only one required switch:

/MX   Mixed case.

Likewise for TASM:

/ml   Mixed case, all symbols.

Common header files

These are the same header files distributed with the Shareware version of MPLUS.

MPMENU.H   For menu functions.
GPLUS.H   For MPLUS graphics functions.
GSCREEN.H   Contains color constants.
MOUSER.H   For mouse support.

Special header files

These headers are for the internal development of MPLUS:

MPABORT.H   For abnormal exits.
MPKEYS.H   Scan and ASCII codes for keyboard.
MPMEM.H   For memory routines.

C source

MPLUS is split into 14 C modules:

MPABORT.C   Abort routine—resets the screen to the default, prints out the DOS errno, and calls abort( ).
MPMENU.C   Menu system.
MPDIAL.C   Dialogue boxes.
MPIMAGE.C   Graphic images.
MPLUS0.C   mpsetvideomode( ) and related routines.
MPLUS1.C   mpouttext( ) and related routines.
MPLUS2.C   Other "core" graphics routines.
MPGWDW0.C   Graphic windows.
MPGWDW1.C   Code for the graphic root window.

MPXORL.C	xorline( ) and xorpt( ).
MPMEM.C	malloc( ) calls are routed here.
MPMOUSE0.C	Mouse interrupt 33H.
MPMOUSE1.C	Simple mouse routines.
MPMOUSE2.C	Complex mouse routines.

Asm source

MPLUS has one assembler module:

MS_EVENT.ASM   Interrupt routine for mouse event handler.

Expanded memory support

If your application requires expanded memory support, MPMEM.C is the place to build it because all MPLUS malloc( ) calls are routed to this file. If you don't have expanded memory routines yet, don't reinvent the wheel. Contact Intel for a free copy of their EMS Toolkit:

Intel Corporation
Development Tools Operation
5200 NE Elam Young Parkway
Hillsboro, OR 97124
(800) 538-3373

Ask for *The EMS TOOLKIT for C Developers.*

Registration

MPLUS is available in two flavors:

- Small model with documentation on disk
- Registered version (includes source code)

For personal, non-commercial use, the small model MPLUS library is available for $12.00. This fee covers the cost of materials, shipping, and handling.

The full registered version costs fifty dollars ($50.00) per copy and provides the following:

☐ All source code
☐ Small, medium, compact, and large model libraries
☐ Laser printed manual (Times Roman font)
☐ Support via U.S. mail, CompuServe email, and voice mail
☐ Upgrades at a discount

A registered copy of MPLUS licenses you to use the product on a regular basis and to distribute your programs created with the MPLUS library.

The license is good for only one user, and is royalty-free.
Send to

Michael Yam
230 East 88th St., Apt 6B
New York, NY 10128

11
Turbo Designer

Program title   Turbo Designer   *(Disk 1353)*

Special requirements   512K RAM, hard drive, and Turbo Pascal 4.0 or higher.

In today's programming world, your application programs cannot be considered top quality if they are not easy to use. Users should not be forced to learn cryptic keystroke commands because better methods are now available (e.g., windowing systems with pop-up and pull-down menus). Windowing systems, however, can take weeks and even months to design, debug, and implement properly. However, with Turbo Designer, a complete environment—windows and all—can be created in a matter of minutes.

Any non-trivial program can be broken into three parts: input, processing, and output. In theory, each part should be emphasized equally. In practice, however, usually only functionality is emphasized. Too often, the other parts are simply afterthoughts. Sometimes, when functionality is the only requirement, this works out OK; many programmers ignore the user interface and still get along fine. However, in today's market, selling software without a top quality user interface is getting harder. A poor user interface severely hampers the marketability and appeal of a software product and severely limits the scope of its potential users. Should the programmer concentrate his/her allotted time on producing an elaborate user interface or instead produce programs that can perform sophisticated tasks?

In today's software industry, companies generally hire large teams of programmers to make both sophisticated and marketable programs.

"Lone-wolf" programmers are rare today simply because individuals cannot compete with large companies due to the difficulty of producing sophisticated and user-friendly programs.

The majority of applications programs produced have failed not because they lack functionality but because either the user interface was clumsy or the programs were not adequately upgraded. Turbo Designer mainly should provide the applications programmer with an easy-to-use interface so that he/she can concentrate on producing highly functional programs without worrying about the interface details.

Turbo Designer is capable of editing and generating vertical and horizontal pop-up menus, pull-down menus, context-sensitive status lines, and context-sensitive interactive pop-up help screens. Furthermore, Turbo Designer lets you completely customize the environment's appearance.

The environment in which Turbo Designer operates is the same user-friendly environment that it generates, which means that Turbo Designer users can experience the environment while also programming applications using this environment.

Specifically, Turbo Designer's windowing environment consists of three precompiled units: TD1VARS, TD1VIDEO, and TD1UTILS. The files included with Turbo Designer are listed here:

TD1.EXE	The main program file
TD1.HIN	Help screens for TD1.EXE
TD1.HLI	
TD1.HTE	
TD1.PIF	Specification to run under Microsoft Windows 2.03
T50VARS.TPU	Library code for Turbo Pascal 5.0
T50VIDEO.TPU	
T50UTILS.TPU	
T55VARS.TPU	Library code for Turbo Pascal 5.5
T55VIDEO.TPU	
T55UTILS.TPU	
TP50INST.BAT	Installs Turbo Designer for Turbo Pascal 5.0
TP55INST.BAT	Installs Turbo Designer for Turbo Pascal 5.5
FLPYINST.BAT	Installs Turbo Designer onto floppy disks
SHOWMAN.EXE	Use this to view TD1.DOC
SHOWMAN.DOC	Documentation for ShowMan

Some important user interface terms

Pull-down menus

A *pull-down* menu is a menuing system where a horizontal menu bar (usually located on the top of the screen) presents the menu headers.

When the pull-down menu system is activated, one menu header on the menu bar is highlighted. The user sequentially cycles through the menu headers by pressing the arrow keys to move the selection bar in the direction indicated on the arrow key. When the user arrives on the topic of choice, the user selects the menu header by pressing Enter, and a submenu appears.

Alternately, the user can type the hot key associated with the menu header of choice. Basically, a menu bar is comprised of a group of menu headers, each menu header containing exactly one letter both highlighted and unique to the set of highlighted letters on the menu bar. This highlighted letter is called a *hot key*.

While the pull-down system is active and the submenus are not activated, pressing a key on the keyboard corresponding to a hot key on the menu bar will move the selection bar to the corresponding menu header if necessary and activate the submenus. A *submenu* is a box that pops up under the corresponding menu header. A submenu box displays 0 through 22 selections. Each selection is similar to a menu header in that it might contain a hot key, and this hot key is operated on in the same fashion as described with menu header hot keys above. A selection can differ from being active in one of two ways: it could be *dead*—displayed in a neutral color and unable to be accessed through both hot keys and the selection bar; or it could be defined as a *partition*, displayed as a vertical bar composed of multiple copies of a single character across the width of the submenu, and unable to be accessed through both hot keys and the selection bar. *Entry* is a term synonymous to selection. Selecting an entry causes the action associated with that entry's label to occur.

Esc is the complement to Enter. Pressing Esc will cause the system to jump back one step. If the submenus are active and the user presses Esc, the submenus will deactivate and the user will be prompted to select a menu header from the menu bar. One case in which this doesn't occur is when a submenu contains 0 entries: pressing ESC here will deactivate the entire pull-down menu system. Likewise, if the submenus are deactivated and the user presses Esc, the entire pull-down system will deactivate and the flow of control will return to the main program.

Horizontal pop-up menus

A *horizontal pop-up menu* is a pop-up menu with a prompt. The *prompt* is usually a statement or a question. Under the prompt are between 1 and 10 (inclusive) *entries* (or *selections*). The entries are set up in a grid-like formation. Horizontal pop-up menus currently do not support hot keys, allowing entry selection only through use of the arrow keys. To move the selection bar, the user moves the arrow key associated with the direction he/she wants to travel. An entry is selected by pressing the Enter key. Abandoning the horizontal pop-up menu and returning to the application program is accomplished through the Esc key.

Vertical pop-up menus

A *vertical pop-up menu* is a "normal" pop-up menu. The menu contains between 1 and 22 (inclusive) entries. The user can select an entry by using the arrow keys and Enter—or (as a shortcut), the user can elect to use hot keys instead. The method for selection is identical to that of submenus (described previously).

When a menu is referred to as a *pop-up* menu, without indication of its alignment, the reader can correctly assume that a *vertical pop-up menu* is being referenced.

Pop-up help screens

A *pop-up help screen* is a window that, when activated, appears on the screen and contains the help text. The bottom of the help screens might or might not contain selections. When there are selections, the user uses the arrow keys to sequentially move the selection bar around the list of selections. If the user presses Enter, the selection highlighted by the selection bar will be processed, and another help menu described by that selection will appear. If the user presses F1 in a help screen, a *help index* (if one exists) will appear. A help index is a normal help screen usually containing access to most or all of the other help screens. Some help screens are independent of the rest of the help system and have no selections. The user can escape the help system and return to the program at any time by pressing Esc.

Pop-up directory

A *pop-up directory* is a window that, when activated, shows a directory listing inside the window. First, the user enters a *mask* definition. The directory will pop up with a listing of all files in that mask. The mask is the same type of mask that DOS uses, so that the mask can, and usually will, contain wildcard characters—(e.g., * and ?). (See the DOS manual for further reference on masks.)

If no files match with the mask definition, an error message will be displayed and the directory listing subroutine will be terminated. When filenames match with the mask, they will be displayed in a grid-like format with the top left entry selected. The user can move the selection bar through the grid horizontally or vertically using all four arrow keys. The selection bar will "wrap around" to the other side if the user tries to move it beyond the defined boundaries.

If the entry begins with a back slash character (\ ), that entry is actually a name of a subdirectory. If the selection bar is on a subdirectory and the user presses Enter, the mask will concatenate the current directory path with the new path, and display a new listing. If the subdirectory name is " \ ..", then the parent directory is displayed. (See the DOS reference book for complete definitions of the terms defined above.)

If the mask matches more than 112 filenames, only the first 112 filenames will be displayed on the screen. If the user attempts to access the filenames below the bottom of the displayed names, the selection bar will disappear but will be logically where it is supposed to be. The selection bar will reappear when moved back up onto the visible portion of the screen. The user can escape from the directory listing at any time by pressing Esc.

Trash Can

The *trash can* is a process of deleting files more sophisticated than the DOS DELETE (or ERASE) command.

Using the trash is a three-step process. First, the user puts a filename in the trash can. Then the user can examine the trash can and remove accidentally thrown-out filenames. Finally, the trash can is emptied and the filenames are deleted from the disk.

In more detail, first the user will be prompted for a file mask, and a directory listing will be displayed. The user operates the directory listing in the exact method described above in "Pop-up directory," with one exception : any filename selected with the Enter key will cause an action to take place. If the filename is a subdirectory, a new directory listing will appear. If the filename is an actual file, the filename will be put in the trash can list. A filename in the trash can list still exists in actuality and will show up in any directory listing. To throw out more than one filename at a time, a *trash group* facility was established. The trash group facility prompts the user for a mask definition and will put all filenames matching the mask in the trash can.

Secondly, the user can look at the contents of the trash can, which are displayed in a list. The user can move up and down the list with the appropriate arrow keys. The list on the screen will scroll if the user moves the selection bar outside the set boundaries. If the user presses Enter, the filename under the selection bar will be removed from the trash can. If the user presses Esc, the trash can is de-selected and the program returns to normal execution.

Finally, the files are removed both from the trash can and from the disk. The user is asked to confirm this option (similar to the DOS DELETE "Are you sure? (Y/N)" message). If the user proceeds, the files are deleted and the trash can list is left empty. If any disk errors during this process, the filename is removed from the trash can but might not necessarily be removed from the disk.

The trash icon is at the bottom right of the screen; it appears as a trash can with the caption "TRASH."

Access System Clock

In this option, a vertical pop-up menu appears containing two entries. The first entry shows the current date, while the second entry is continually updated to show the current time. If the user selects either of these entries, another window appears prompting the user to change the time or date. If the user makes any changes, the system time and/or date changes also. The icon for this option resembles a clock and bears the caption "Access System Clock."

Turbo Designer's pull-down menu system

This section will describe the pull-down menu system inside TD1. The first menu header is drawn as a tiny box on the menu bar and has a hot key of "A." Its submenu contains two entries.

System control

Selecting this entry will call up a pop-up window containing a great deal of technical information. Press Enter to leave.

About Turbo Designer

Selecting this entry calls up a pop-up window containing compiler release information. Press Enter to leave.
    The second menu header is the File submenu and has a hot key of "F."

Load Work File

Selecting this entry will load a previously edited file into Turbo Designer. First, you will be asked if you want to save the current work file; you can respond either with "Yes," "No," and "Cancel." If you want to abandon the Load Work File option, this is your last chance; select "Cancel" to return to the pull-down system. If you choose "Yes" or "No," the appropriate save action will take place. You will then be prompted for a load filename in the same fashion as described previously in "Pop-up directory." After you select a filename, the file will be loaded. If you press Esc in the directory listing, the current file will be erased from memory and the filename will be set back to "NONAME."

Create Work File

Selecting this entry will set up a new work file. First, you will be asked if you want to save the current work file. The responses are "Yes," "No," and "Cancel." If you want to abandon Create Work File, select "Cancel" and return to the pull-down system. If you choose "Yes" or "No," the appropriate save action will take place. You will then be prompted for a new work filename. This work filename can be up to eight characters in length and may be anything legal in DOS, with the following exception: the filename cannot end with "UNT1" or "UNT2," or the code generated for your program will be incomplete. All the necessary files will be created at this time.

Save Work File

Selecting this entry will unconditionally save the current work file. Make sure you have enough space on your disk to save the work file.

Rename Work File

Selecting this entry will allow you to rename your work file. You will first be prompted for a new work filename. This filename can be up to eight characters in length and may be anything legal in DOS, with the following exception: the filename may not end with "UNT1" or "UNT2," or the code generated for your program will be incomplete. This entry uses the RENAME function from DOS.

Show Directory

Selecting this entry will call up a pop-up directory. For more information, see "Pop-up directory."

Change Directory

Selecting this entry will call up a pop-up edit window. Type in the new directory name and then press Enter. This command will use DOS's CHDIR command and report any errors that DOS returns.

Trash Filename

Selecting this entry will cause the first step of the process described previously in the "Trash Can" section to take place. For more information, see "Trash Can."

Trash Group

Selecting this entry will cause the "Trash group" process described previously in the "Trash can" section to take place. For more information, see "Trash can."

OS Shell

Selecting this entry will load and run COMMAND.COM. To return to Turbo Designer, type EXIT at the DOS prompt.

Quit

Selecting this entry will end TD1 and return to DOS. Before leaving, however, you will be asked if you want to save the current work file. Your choices are "Yes," "No," and "Cancel." If you want to abandon the Quit option, select "Cancel" and return to the pull-down system. If you choose "Yes" or "No," the appropriate save action will take place. TD1 will then halt and return to DOS.

The third menu header is Edit, with a hot key of "E." Selecting Edit (which has no submenus) will return you to editing your work file.

The fourth menu header is View, with a hot key of "V."

View Clock

Selecting this entry will cause the access clock function to activate. For more information, see "Access System Clock."

View Trash Can

Selecting this entry will cause the second step of the process described previously in the "Trash Can" section to take place. For more information, see "Trash Can."

The fifth menu header is Special, with a hot key of "S."

Reshadow

Selecting this entry will cause TD1's pull down system to toggle the pull down shadow. Select this a few times to see what it does. To call this in your generated program call Procedure ReShadow;.

Empty Trash Can

Selecting this entry will cause the third step of the process described previously in the "TRASH CAN" section to take place. For more information, see "TRASH CAN." Because files will be erased, be careful with this selection.

Toggle Print Screen

Selecting this entry will toggle the ability to use print screen on and off. This entry uses `Procedure SetPrtSc(Switch : Boolean);` from TD1VARS. To set Print screen on, use `SetPrtSc(TRUE);`, and to turn print screen off, use `SetPrtSc(FALSE);`.

Select Me! and Choose Me!

These entries demonstrate the use of dead entries. Selecting one of these will kill the entry, and revive the other. The procedures used are `Procedure KillEntry(X,Y : Byte);` and `Procedure ReviveEntry(X,Y : Byte);` from TD1VIDEO. X is the coordinate of the submenu in the pull-down system, while Y is the coordinate of the entry in that submenu. (In calculating the Y coordinate, partitions should be included). You can also use page 4 of designing pull-down menus. See "Designing pull-down menus."

Directories

This entry lets you select Turbo Designer's home directory and the Generated code's destination directory. Turbo Designer's home directory has the same syntax as the PATH command in DOS. An example would be C:\ TD1;C:\;C:\TP. TD1 looks in each of those paths for its help screens.

For more information, see your DOS manual. The generated code's destination directory is a drive letter and a directory path. (An example would be C:\TP\TD1CODE\ ; note that the path should end with a backslash (\)). Choosing Save Pick File will save the names to the disk and load them back every time TD1 is loaded from that directory.

The sixth menu header is Generate, with a hot key of "G."

Generate Turbo Pascal code

This entry, when selected, generates the Turbo Pascal code defined by your work file. Once the code has been generated, press a key to return to the pull-down system.

Getting started

Installing TD1

Copy all files onto an empty, formatted disk or an empty directory. Place the precompiled units TD1*.TPU in your Turbo Pascal unit directory. Place TD1.EXE and TD1.H* in your Turbo Designer directory.

Loading TD1

Load TD1 at the DOS prompt by typing TD1. Make sure TD1.EXE, TD1.HLI, TD1.HTE, and TD1.HIN are in the current directory and drive.

If your monitor is a black and white (or black and green, or black and amber, etc.) type TD1 -m.

Once TD1 is loaded, read the registration screen and press Enter when done. You will then see the screen in FIG. 11-1. You can then proceed to edit your system. If you need help right away, press Enter or F1. You would most likely need to use the pull-down menus to load or create a file. After activating them with F10, press "F" to activate the File submenu. Using the arrow keys if needed, select either Load or Create, and you will be on your way. For a sample session, see "A sample session" later on in this chapter.

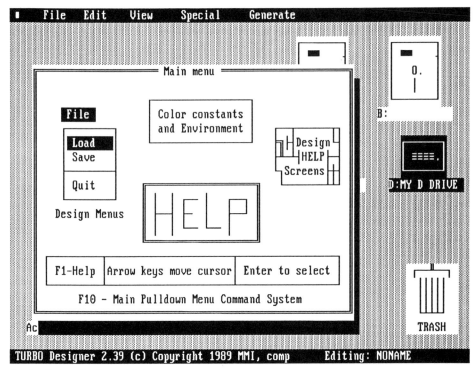

11-1 Turbo Designer Main menu.

To make sure you're familiar with the environment, you should design a few test files before actually doing serious work.

Designing pull-down menus

Here's a page-by-page description of the pull-down menu creation process.

Page 1 In this page, the menu bar is designed. The text is entered as it would be through a word processor. Displayed at the top of the screen is the number of menu headers on the line being edited. If you should want help, press F1. If you want to go back to the Design Menus icon menu, press PgUp. When you want to proceed to page 2, press PgDn. This triggers a syntax error check that confirms (or not) that 1 to 15 menu headers exist, that each menu header has a hot key, and that each hot key is unique.

Page 2 In this page, the entries in the submenu are defined. Move the selection bar to the selection you want to choose. Now press the Backspace key, and the selection bar will turn into a cursor. Type in the entry name using the same method described for entering the menu bar from page 1. Do not use the underscore as the first character in the entry name. Pressing Enter will make the selection bar reappear. Move the selection bar to edit more entries, using the help menus on the side and bottom as a guide.

Press PgUp to go back to page 1, or press PgDn to go to page 3. Another syntax check will take place, confirming (or not) that a blank line exists between two non-blank entries, that each menu has a unique hot key, and that each non-blank entry has a hot key.

Page 3   In this page, the context-sensitive help lines are entered for the pull-down system. To enter a help line for an entry, move the selection bar to the entry you want to put help in. Pressing Enter will make a pop-up edit window appear. Type in the text of the help line in the same fashion as entering the menu bar, and press Enter to return to the pull-down system. To enter a help line for a menu header, move the selection bar to the sub-menu you want to put help in. Pressing F5 will cause a pop-up edit window to appear. Type in the text of the help line in the same fashion as entering the menu bar, and press Enter to return to the pull-down system. If you want to change the status of the pull-down shadow, pressing F2 will toggle the shadow on and off. Pressing PgUp will go back to page 2, while pressing PgDn will go to Page 4. No syntax error checks take place.

Page 4   This page allows you to "kill" entries if necessary so that the generated program will start off with "dead" entries. Dead entries are entries displayed in a neutral color and cannot be accessed. The Special menu in TD1 contains an example of a dead entry.

To kill an entry, move the selection bar to the entry you want to kill and press F5. If nothing happens, press F2 and then F5 again. Pressing F2 toggles the Kill mode between Kill and Revive. To Revive an entry, put the system in Revive mode if necessary, move the selection bar to the dead entry you want to revive, and press F5. If you want to know which mode you are in, just look on the help screen displayed at the F5 section. If you need more help than provided, press F1. To go to page 3, press PgUp; and to go on, press PgDn. This will take you back to the Design Menus icon and also save the pull-downs as you have defined them. The help definitions you entered in page 3 will be shown at the bottom of the screen.

Due to a persistent bug, the bottom line might not be correct. Do not worry; the generated code does not have this problem.

The process can be repeated many times if you must go back to change some aspect.

Note: If you go back and edit the menu bar and the number of menu headers change, the entry definitions in the previous set of pull-down menus will *not* change, and will be inaccurate.

Designing horizontal pop-up menus

Here's a page-by-page description of the horizontal pop-up menu creation process.

Page 1   This page can come in two forms, depending on whether or not you already have previously defined horizontal pop-up menus.

Form 1: If there are no horizontal pop-up menus to enter, a pop-up edit box will appear. If you want to leave, press Enter without typing anything; otherwise, type in the name of the *key*. The *key* is TD1's method of organizing the menus. To simplify using the generated menus, please do not use any characters other than "A" . . . "Z" and "0" . . . "9." Press Enter when you have typed in the key name.

Form 2: If there are previous horizontal pop-up menus loaded, a list of the key names will appear. Among these names is "<New Menu Name>." Move the Up and Down arrow keys to move the selection bar and press Enter to select an entry name.

Page 2   On this page, you will be asked to supply the prompt to your pop-up menu, after which a pop-up edit window will appear. Edit the prompt as you would edit a document in a word processor and press Enter when done.

Page 3   On this page, you select the colors you want to use in the pop-up menu. To select the colors, use the Up and Down arrow keys to select which set of colors to change: Normal, Highlighted, or Inverse. Press Enter, and a color change screen will appear. To change the background color, use the Left and Right arrow keys to move through the list of background colors. To change the foreground color, use the Up and Down arrow keys to move through the list of foreground colors. Press Enter when you decide on the color to use.

To go to page 4, press PgDn.

Page 4   On page 4, you can reconfigure the border style used by your pop-up menu. Use the arrow keys to move the selection bar and the Enter key to change the character associated with that selection.

Press F1 if you need help. Press PgDn to go to page 5.

Page 5   Page 5 lets you enter the entries to be used in the pop-up menu. Up to 10 entries can be defined. To edit an entry, move the selection bar to the entry you want to edit and press Backspace. Then type in that entry using the keys you would use in a word processor. Press Enter to bring the selection bar back. Press PgDn to go to page 6. Before proceeding to page 6, a syntax error check occurs, looking for a blank line between two non-blank entries. Hot keys are not implemented for horizontal pop-up menus.

Page 6   Page 6 is a pop-up menu that asks you whether or not you want a shadow with your pop-up menu. Type in "Y" or "N" to go to page 7. The "Cancel" operation is not defined for this window.

Page 7   With page 7, you can set the coordinates for the pop-up menu. The pop-up menu you have just specified will appear on the screen, but none of the selections will be highlighted. Move this menu around using the arrow keys. When you have placed it where you want it, press PgDn to exit editing the pop-up menus. You will then return to the Design Menus icon menu. The pop-up menu you just designed will be saved.

Designing vertical pop-up menus

Here's a page-by-page description of the vertical pop-up menu creation process.

Page 1 This page can come in two forms, depending on whether or not you already have previously defined vertical pop-up menus.

Form 1: If there are no vertical pop-up menus to enter, a pop-up edit box will appear. If you want to leave, press Enter without typing anything; otherwise, type in the name of the *key*. The key is TD1's method of organizing the menus. To simplify using the generated menus, please do not use any characters other than "A" . . . "Z" and "0" . . . "9." Press Enter when you have typed in the key name.

Form 2: If there are previous vertical pop-up menus loaded, a list of the key names will appear. Among these names is "<New Menu Name>." Move the Up and Down arrow keys to move the selection bar. Press Enter to select an entry name.

Page 2 On this page you select the colors you want to use in the pop-up menu. To select the colors, use the Up and Down arrow keys to select which set of colors to change: Normal, Highlighted, or Inverse. Press Enter and a color change screen will appear. To change the background color, use the Left and Right arrow keys to move through the list of background colors. To change the foreground color, use the Up and Down arrow keys to move through the list of foreground colors. Press Enter when you decide on the color to use. To go to page 3, press PgDn.

Page 3 On page 3, you can reconfigure the border style used by your pop-up menu. Use the arrow keys to move the selection bar and the Enter key to change the character associated with that selection.

Press F1 if you need help. Press PgDn to go to page 4.

Page 4 Page 4 lets you enter the entries to be used in the pop-up menu. Up to 10 entries can be defined. To edit an entry, move the selection bar to the entry you want to edit and press Backspace. Then type in that entry using the keys you would use in a word processor. Press Enter to bring the selection bar back. Press PgDn to go to page 5. Before proceeding to page 6, a syntax error check occurs, looking for a blank line between two non-blank entries, confirming that each entry has a hot key, and confirming that each hot key is unique.

Page 5 Page 5 is a pop-up menu that asks you whether or not you want a shadow with your pop-up menu. Type in "Y" or "N" to go to page 6. The "Cancel" operation is not defined for this window.

Page 6 With page 6, you can set the coordinates for the pop-up menu. The pop-up menu you have just specified will appear on the screen, but none of the selections will be highlighted. Move this menu around using the arrow keys. When you have placed it where you want it, press PgDn to exit editing the pop-up menus. You will then return to the Design Menus icon menu. The pop-up menu you just designed will be saved.

Color constants and your program's environment

Setting your program's colors

On this icon menu, you select the default colors you want to use in your program. There are four sets of colors used in the program: Background colors, Standard colors, Directory colors, and Icon colors. In order to change the colors, use the arrow keys to move the selection box to the set of colors you want to change and then press Enter. To change the set of colors, use the Up and Down arrow keys to select which type of colors to change: (where appropriate) Normal, Highlighted, Inverse, or Dead. Press Enter, and a color change screen will appear. To change the background color, use the Left and Right arrow keys to move through the list of background colors. To change the foreground color, use the Up and Down arrow keys to move through the list of foreground colors. Press Enter when you decide on the color to use. Press PgDn to go back to the icon menu. Press Esc to leave the icon menu.

Setting your program's environment

Here's a page-by-page description of how to manipulate your environment.

Page 1 This page lets you define your program's *background character*. The background character is used in the beginning of your program to make a background. In this screen, you can either choose "Select" to choose another background character, "Use Default" to keep the current background character, or "Cancel" to return to the previous icon menu. If you choose "Select," a selection screen appears, and you choose a new background character by moving the cursor with the arrow keys until it points to the character you want and then press Enter. Another screen will appear with the background drawn. If you like it, press Enter; if it's not what you imagined, press Esc.

Page 2 This page lets you edit the *permanent status bar*. Just type in the status bar as you would with a word processor. If you need more help than provided, press F1. To return to page 1, press PgUp; and to go on to page 3, press PgDn.

Page 3 On page 3, you can reconfigure the border style that your pull-down menu uses. Use the arrow keys to move the selection bar and Enter to change the character associated with that selection. Press PgUp to go to page 2, and press PgDn to go back to the icon menu.

Help screen definitions

Edit help screen definition

Here's a page-by-page description of the help screen creation process.

Page 1 This page can come in two forms, depending on whether or not you already have previously defined help screens.

If you have not defined help screens previously, a pop-up edit box will appear. If you want to leave, press Enter without typing anything; otherwise, type in the name of the *key*. The key is TD1's method of organizing the menus. To simplify using the generated menus, please do not use any characters other than "A" . . ' Z" and "0" . . . "9." Press Enter when you have typed in the key name.

If you have defined previous help screens, a list of the key names will appear. Among these names is " < Enter New Name >." Move the Up and Down arrow keys to move the selection bar. Press Enter to select an entry name.

Note: Naming your help screen key as Help_Index makes that definition the help index. In your generated program, pressing F1 after loading a help screen will load the help index.

Page 2   On this page you will be prompted for a title to your help menu. A pop-up edit window will appear. Edit the title as you would edit a document in a word processor and press Enter when done.

Page 3   With this page, you define the coordinates of the help screen you want to design. You first use the arrow keys to move the top left corner to the coordinate you want to use and press Enter when you reach that coordinate. You then will move the bottom right corner to the coordinate you want to use and press Enter when you reach the coordinates you want. Then, either press Enter to accept this definition and go on to page 4, or press Esc to redo the definition. Press F1 at any point to receive help.

Note: A shortcut to moving the cursor around: holding the Shift key down while moving the arrow keys on the numeric keypad causes the cursor to jump 5 units in each direction.

Page 4   On this page, you select the colors you want to use in the help screen. To select the colors, use the Up and Down arrow keys to select which set of colors to change: Normal, Highlighted, or Inverse. Press Enter, and a color change screen will appear. To change the background color, use the Left and Right arrow keys to move through the list of background colors. To change the foreground color, use the Up and Down arrow keys to move through the list of foreground colors. Press Enter when you decide on the color to use. To go to page 5, press PgDn.

Page 5   On page 5, you can configure the border style used by your help screen: either *single* or *double* border. Press Enter to go to page 6.

Page 6   Page 6 is a pop-up menu that asks you whether or not you want a shadow with your pop-up menu. Type in "Y" or "N" to go to page 7. The "Cancel" operation is not defined for this window.

Page 7   The help definition you defined is displayed on the screen. If you are satisfied with it, press Enter; otherwise, press Esc to go to page 2.

Edit help screen text

Here's a page-by-page description of how to edit help screen text.

Page 1   If previous help screens are defined, a list of the key names will appear. Move the Up and Down arrow keys to move the selection bar, and press Enter to select an entry name.

Page 2 A help window with the definition described by the help screen definition you selected in page 1. This screen is a full-screen editor. Use the arrow keys to move the cursor around. Press Enter to go to the next line. Pressing Backspace will move the cursor back one character and is non-destructive. Type in the text of the help screen like you would with a word processor. This editor is permanently stuck in Typeover (or Overwrite) mode, meaning that if you are typing along a line, the words to the right of the cursor are not moved. Pressing the Insert key will insert a space at the current cursor position. Pressing Delete will delete a character at the current cursor position.

Pressing F1 will call up a help screen.

Pressing F8 will abort this help screen and return to the last icon menu.

Pressing the End key will save this screen and return to the last icon menu.

Pressing the F3 key will toggle the link mode on and off.

To use the link mode, move the cursor to the position you want to start to link at and press F3. You will be able to move the cursor to the right only (and left, just as long as you don't move beyond the start of the link). Move the cursor right until you reach the ending position and press F3 again. A pop-up menu with all the help screens will appear; choose one of these. The area you defined as the link area will now be displayed in the inverse color of that help screen. You can move the cursor through the link area but you cannot type anything in it. If your cursor is on a link area and you press Enter, the help screen you are working on will be saved and the help screen linked to the link area will be loaded and edited.

Note: After starting or finishing a link, the change is permanent. Please sit down and map out your help screens on paper before using TD1.

A sample session

Now that TD1 is installed on your system, load TD1 using the method described in "Getting started."

Press Enter after reading the registration screen.
Press F10 to activate the pull-down menus.
Press "F" to activate the File submenu as shown in FIG. 11-2.
Press "W" to select the "create Work file" entry.
Press "N" to tell the system "NO! I don't want to save NONAME!"
Type TEST1 when you are prompted for a filename.
Press Esc to deactivate the File submenu.
Press "E" to select Edit submenu.
Press the Left arrow key once, so that the icon menu cursor lies on the Design Menus option.

Press Enter to select the Icon. Another set of icons will appear.

Press the Left arrow key once so that the icon menu cursor lies on the Pull-down Menus option.

Press Enter to select the Icon. A line editor will appear as shown in FIG. 11-3.

On the line, type (exactly as shown) the four words, "This Is A tEst," keeping the capital letters capitalized. You may put as many spaces between the words as you want, however. Press F1 if you need any help. Notice that, at the top of the window, the Number of Headers equals 4.

Before you press Enter, use the arrow keys to edit the line so that it reads "This Is Some how A tEst," with only one space between "Some" and "how." Notice that the Number of Headers equals 6.

Move the arrow keys between "Some" and "how" and press the Delete key on your keyboard. The line should read "This Is Somehow A tEst." The Number of Headers equals 5.

Without moving the cursor, press the F3 key. A hard space was added between "Some" and "how," so the line reads "This Is Some how A tEst" and the Number of Headers equals 5.

Press the F2 key. Notice that the hard space has become a flashing "*." Press Esc to leave that mode.

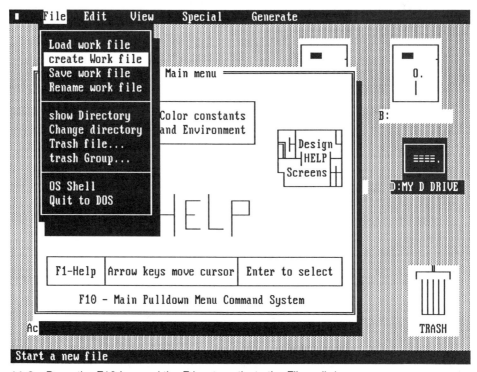

11-2 Press the F10 key and the F key to activate the File pull-down menu.

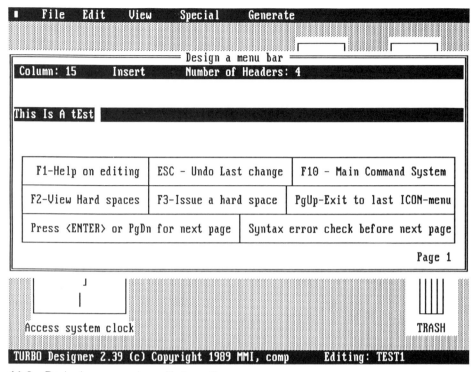

11-3 Designing a menubar with the editor.

Move the cursor to the "S" in "Some how" and press the Delete key until "Some how" no longer exists.

Now press Enter to go to page 2.

Using the help menus on the side as a guide, type in the following entries under the "This" menu header:

```
This
Is
One
Menu
```

Press the Right arrow key to move the selection header to "Is." Notice that the previous entries have disappeared. Press the Left arrow key. Notice that the entries have reappeared. Press the Right arrow key. (See FIG. 11-4.)

Type in the following entries:

```
This
Is
```

Now, without moving the cursor, press the F5 key. A "partition" will appear. Do not edit this partition. If you accidentally edit it, press F5, and another partition will be generated. (See FIG. 11-5.)

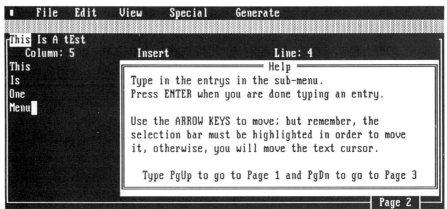

11-4 Use Page 2 to design the pull-down menu.

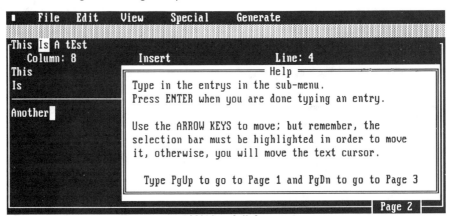

11-5 Press F5 to place a partition in the pull-down menu.

Press the Down arrow key to leave the partition and type

Another

Press the Right arrow key to move the header selection to "A."
Press the Right arrow key again to move the header selection to "tEst."
Type in the following entries:

One
smAll
Pull
Down
Menu

When you are done typing those entries in, press PgDn to go to page 3. (See FIG. 11-6.)

Press Enter to enter the status help line for the entry "This."

Type "This is nonsense" in the box that appears, as shown in FIG. 11-7, and press Enter.

Press F5 to enter the status help line for the submenu "This." Type "This is ludicrous" in the box that appears, and press Enter.

Move the selection bar around, and enter other status help lines for other entries and menu headers. Notice how you can't enter a status help line for the partition.

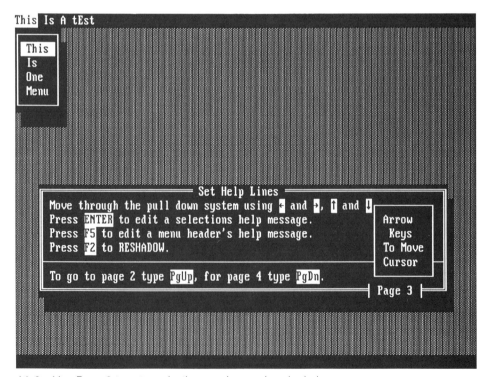

11-6 Use Page 3 to enter selections and menu header help messages.

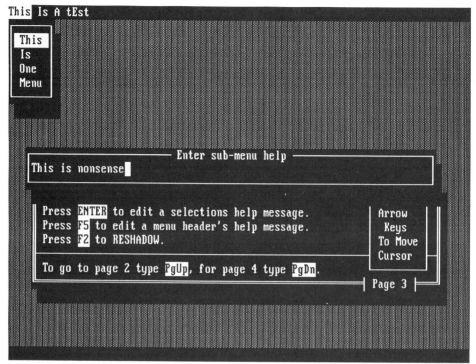

11-7 Entering a submenu help line.

Move to the "tEst" submenu. Press F2 a few times, and watch the underlying shadow disappear and reappear.

Also notice that there are no entries under the "A" submenu.

Press PgDn to go to page 4.

On page 4 move the cursor around, and observe the submenus as they change from one to another. Move the cursor to the "This" submenu. (See FIG. 11-8.)

Move the cursor to the "One" entry in that submenu and press F5. You have just killed that entry. The entry will change into a neutral color. Press F5 again. Oops, you have just killed "Menu," and let's suppose you actually didn't want to kill it. Press F2, and F5 will change from "Kill" to "Revive." Move the selection bar to the dead entry "Menu," and press F5. "Menu" has just come back to life and is displayed in its original color. If you have not grasped this concept yet, feel free to use the above methods to kill and revive other entries. *Note:* Make sure that F5 is in the right mode (either "Kill" or "Revive").

Press PgDn to return to the Design Menus icon menu.

Move the selection box to Design Horizontal Pop-up Menus and press Enter.

For the key name, type TESTING. Press Enter to go to page 2.

For the prompt, type Are you sure?. Press Enter to go to page 3.

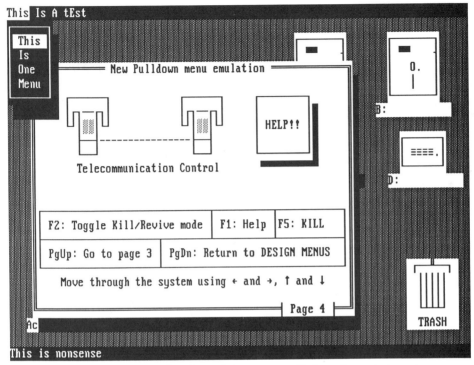

11-8 Page 4 allows you to review the pull-down menus that you have designed.

For the colors, set the colors to your liking (see FIG. 11-9). If you need help, refer to the section on setting the colors. Press PgDn to go to page 4.

On page 4, shown in FIG. 11-10, you set the border style. At this time, just accept the default border style by pressing PgDn. Once you have experience with Turbo Designer, you should experiment with setting the border style.

On page 5, you type in the entries for the pop-up menu as shown in FIG. 11-11. Type in these entries:

```
Yes
No
Cancel
```

Press PgDn to go to page 6.

Page 6 asks you whether or not you want a shadow. Press Enter because you want a shadow.

Page 7 shows you the pop-up menu (see FIG. 11-12). Move it around by pressing the arrow keys. Press PgDn after you move it to a location that you feel is good. (For example, try to put it in the center of the screen.)

You will return to the Design Menus icon menu.

Move the selection box to Design Pop-up Menus and press Enter.

For the key name, type TEST2. Press Enter to go to page 2.

Background
Black Blue Green Cyan Red Magenta Brown LightGray

Foreground: Black
Blue
Green
Cyan
Red
Magenta
Brown
LightGray
DarkGray
LightBlue
LightGreen
LightCyan
LightRed
LightMagenta
Yellow
White

This is an example

Press Enter when done, or ESC to abort

11-9 Choosing colors.

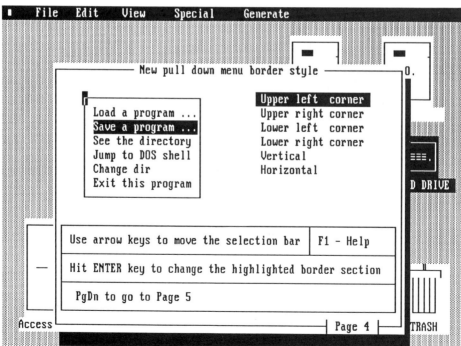

Page 4   Choose the new border style

11-10 Change the border style with this screen.

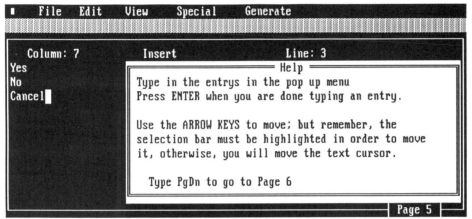

Page 5   Enter the entries for the horizontal pop up menu

11-11   Create the entries for the pop-up menu with Page 5.

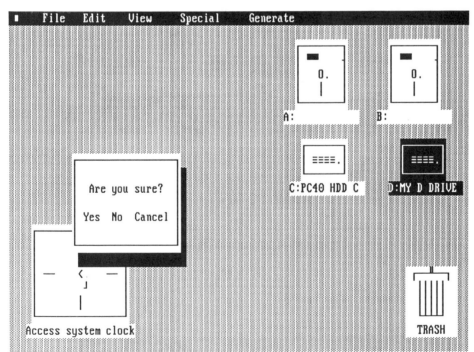

Page 7   USE THE ARROW KEYS TO MOVE THE MENU, AND PRESS PGDN WHEN FINISHED...

11-12   Place the pop-up menu where you want it on the screen with Page 7.

For the colors, set the colors to your liking. If you need help, refer to the section on setting the colors. Press PgDn to go to page 3.

On page 3, you set the border style. At this time, just accept the default border style by pressing PgDn. Once you have experience with Turbo Designer, you should experiment with setting the border style.

On page 4, you type in the entries for the pop-up menu. Type in these entries:

```
Peanuts
pOpcorn
Crackerjacks
```

Leave a space between pOpcorn and Crackerjacks and type in the entries using the capital letters exactly as shown here.

Move the selection bar to the blank line between pOpcorn and Crackerjacks and press F5. A partition appears!

Press PgDn to go to page 5.

Page 5 asks you whether or not you want a shadow. Press Enter because you want a shadow.

Page 6 shows you the pop-up menu. Move it around by pressing the arrow keys. Press PgDn after you move it to a location that you feel is good. (For example, try and put it in the center of the screen.)

You will return to the Design Menus icon menu.

Press Esc to go to the Main Menu icon menu.

Press the Up arrow key to go to the Color Constants and Environment icon (see FIG. 11-13).

Press Enter to enter the icon. Another icon menu appears.

Press the Right arrow key to move to the icon Set Program's Environment and press Enter.

Press Enter again to choose the ''Select'' option.

Press the arrow keys to move the cursor to the first letter of your name and press Enter.

Press Enter again to confirm your approval of the selection.

On page 2, type in the line This is my status line.

Press Enter to go to page 3.

On page 3, press Enter. This page should be used only when you are familiar with Turbo Designer's environment.

Press Esc to go to the Main Menu icon menu.

Press the Right arrow key to move the selection box to Design Help Screens icon menu.

Press Enter to select this icon menu.

Press Enter to select the Define Help Screens icon.

Type in Help_Me and press Enter.

Type in My help screen.

Move the cursor with your arrow keys to position (10,10).

Press Enter.

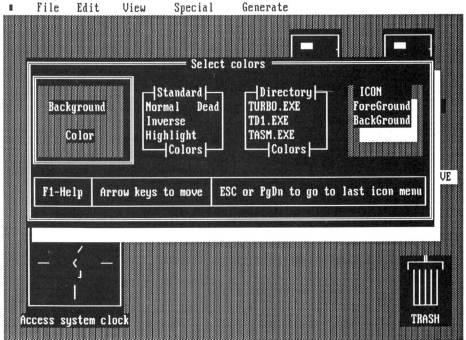

11-13 Menu to set the environment colors.

11-14 Positioning the help screen.

Move the cursor with your arrow keys to position (60,15) (see FIG. 11-14).

Press Enter.

Press Enter again.

Press PgDn. When you have more experience, you may set the colors.

Press Enter. You will use a single border.

Press Enter. You want a shadow.

Press Enter. You like that definition.

Press Enter. You want to make another help screen.

Type in More_help and press Enter.

Type in My other help screen and press Enter.

Move the cursor with the arrow keys to position (10,10).

Press Enter.

Move the cursor with your arrow keys to position (60,15).

Press Enter.

Press Enter again.

Press PgDn. When you have more experience, you may set the colors.

Press Enter. You will use a single border.

Press Enter. You want a shadow.

Press Enter. You like that definition.

Press the Right arrow key twice to move the selection box to Enter Help Text icon menu. Press Enter to select.

Press Enter to select Help_Me.

Now, type in the sentence May I help you?.

Move the cursor to the bottom left corner.

Type Yes.

Move the cursor to the Y again.

(This next stage is critical, so try not to make a mistake!)

Press F3.

Press the Right arrow key two times.

Press F3.

Press the Down arrow key.

Press Enter.

Move the cursor so that it is on the "Yes" somewhere.

Press Enter.

Type Well, tough luck!.

Press the End key.

Press F10 to go to the pull-down menus.

Press the "F" key.

Press the "S" key to save your work file.

Press the Left arrow key twice to move to the "Generate" submenu.

Press Enter to generate.

Press Enter after the code is generated.

Move to the "File" submenu, and press "Q."

Press "N" because you have already saved it.

Load Turbo Pascal

Making sure that you are in the same directory in which you created TEST1.TD1 (use Change Directory if needed), load TEST1.PAS.

Run the file

Now, you have successfully designed and executed a file from Turbo Designer. Try this a few more times, each time making your files more elaborate, and then use it for serious work.

The ProcSel procedure technical reference

This is the only section that cannot be a step-by-step tutorial (sigh). I will, however, try to make it as easy as possible to understand. Although not much, some Turbo Pascal programming skill is required here. Still, a novice shouldn't have too many problems programming PS.

The theory of pull-down menus

In TD1, a certain theory of pull-down menus is used. When a certain key is pressed, the pull-down menus are activated. These pull-down menus don't return a result but just invoke an immediate command. Therefore, when control returns to the program, the program doesn't realize that anything has happened. It will have no recollection of running the pull-down system and won't do anything different (except however the action taken by the pull-down menu might have affected it).

ProcSel—the pull-down link

ProcSel is a procedure generated in the ????UNT2.PAS file used to link the generated pull-down menus with the rest of your code. The pull-down menu procedure, also defined in ????UNT2.PAS of your code, will call it with the coordinates of the pull-down entry the user has selected. Then, using a CASE statement, ProcSel calls the procedure associated with the pull-down entry.

You must associate the procedures with the pull-down entries. Just use Turbo Pascal's text editor, load ????UNT2.PAS, and fill in the case statement.

A more formal definition of ProcSel follows with an example figure.

Definition
```
Procedure ProcSel(X, Y : Byte; Var Result : Word);
```

Parameters

X   The X-coordinate of the selection (ordinal value of the menu header) with a range of 1 to the number of headers.

Y   The Y-coordinate of the selection (ordinal value of the entry in the submenu, including partitions and dead entries) with a range of 1 to the number of entries in the submenu.

Result

A variable sent by the PDown procedure that determines whether or not the pull-down system should be deactivated.

Example

Suppose you want a directory listing in (X:1,Y:2) (First submenu, second entry) and you have designated the EXIT TO DOS procedure at (X:2,Y:3). You would modify ProcSel as shown in FIG. 11-15. (In the figure, parts added by the user are italicized, while all other parts are generated by TD1.)

```
Procedure ProcSel(X, Y : Byte; Var Result : Word);
Begin
 If Result <> 0 Then
  Begin
   Case X of
     1: Case Y of
          1:;
          2:BEGIN
             FlashAt(1,2);      { This will show the pulldown menu again }
             Directory;         { Will call the pop-up directory for (X:1,Y:2) }
            END;
        End; { Case Y }
     2: Case Y of
          1:;
          2:;
          3:BEGIN
             Halt;              { Turbo Pascal return to DOS call }
            END;
        End; { Case Y }
   End;        { Case X }
  End;
End;
```

11-15   Definition of ProcSel to create a pop-up directory and exit to DOS procedure.

This is the current way of linking procedures. With the existence of object-oriented programming in Turbo Pascal 5.5, the method is likely to change in future releases of Turbo Designer.

Using TD1 as a library

TD1 can be used as a stand-alone function library, or its library can be used in conjunction with the generated code. The files that must be "used" in the Turbo Pascal program are these (in order): Uses Dos, Crt, TD1VARS, TD1VIDEO, TD1UTILS;

The library functions that you can use are defined here:

Function CalcColor(F,B : Byte) : Byte;

This function is used to produce an *encoded color byte*, using foreground F and background B.

Usually, the foreground is stored in one byte, and the background is stored in another byte. However, you *can* put these two colors into one byte, and this byte is called an encoded color byte.

Function MonoColor(C,R : Byte) : Byte;

This function is used to ensure that colors will appear correctly on a monochrome monitor.

C The incoming color, an encoded color byte with a range of 0..255.

R The byte to change to and also an encoded color byte.

If the monitor is a monochrome monitor, MonoColor returns R; otherwise it will return C. However, if R is 255 and the monitor is a monochrome monitor, MonoColor returns an appropriate monochrome attribute to C.

Some examples are

```
Write(MonoColor(34,19));
{ Returns 19 if monochrome monitor, else returns 34 }
Write(MonoColor(CalcColor(Yellow, Black),White));
Write(MonoColor(CalcColor(Blue, Red), 255);
{Returns Blue on Red if color monitor, White on Black
    otherwise}
```

Procedure Wr(S : String; X, Y :Byte; F, B : Byte);
This procedure writes a String at coordinates (X,Y) with colors F and B.

S Any type of string.
X In the range 1..80.
Y In the range 1..25.
F Foreground color. Not encoded.
B Background color. Not encoded.

Some examples are

```
Wr('Hello',10,10,Blue, Green);
   Wr('It works!',15,15,MonoColor(Blue,255), MonoColor-
(Green,255));
```

```
{ MonoColor can also take a NON-ENCODED COLOR for its C
     parameter }
```

```
Procedure MkWin(Title   : String,
     X1,Y1,X2,Y2      : Byte;
     F, B             : Byte;
     BorderStyle      : Charray;
     Shadow           : Boolean);
```

This procedure creates a window on the screen with rectangular coordinates (X1,Y1) - (X2,Y2) with colors F and B, with a border style defined as BorderStyle. If Title < > '', then MkWin centers Title and displays it on the top border. If Shadow is true, then a shadow is displayed under the window.

The parameters are as follows:

Title	Any string.
F	Foreground color. Not encoded.
B	Background color. Not encoded.
BorderStyle	Special value of either *EmptyBorder* (no border), *SingleBorder* (single-line border), or *DoubleBorder* (double-line border).

$1 <= X1 < X2 <= 80$
$1 <= Y1 < Y2 <= 25$

Creating a window will set Turbo Pascal's WriteLn window and colors. Some examples are

```
MkWin('A window', 1,1,80,25, Blue, Red, SingleBorder,True);
MkWin('Another window',20,10,60,20,Black,White,Emptybor-
     der,False);
```

```
Procedure RmWin;
```

This procedure will remove the last window created and restore the area of the screen that the window covered.

Some examples are

```
MkWin('',10,10,70,15,White, Black, DoubleBorder, True);
     WriteLn('Look at this window.....');
     Repeat
     Until ReadKey = #27;
RmWin;
```

Procedure Help(S:Str20);

This procedure will invoke a help screen with key S.
   Some examples are

Help('Help_Screen_One');
Help('Help_Index');
Help('DoHelp');

Procedure Directory;

Making a call to this procedure will invoke a pop-up directory listing as described in section "Pop-up directory."

Procedure TrashFile;

Calling this procedure will accomplish the first step of the trash can, described in the section "Trash Can."

Procedure TrashGroup;

Calling this procedure will accomplish the trash group function, as described in the section "Trash Can."

Procedure EditTrashCan;

Calling this procedure will invoke the second step of the trash can, described in the section "Trash Can."

Procedure EmptyTrash;

Calling this procedure will complete the third step of the trash can, described previously in the section "Trash Can."

Function GetFileName : String;

Calling this procedure will accomplish the same task described in "Load Work File."

An example is

```
Var S : String;
    .
    .
    .
S := GetFileName;
```

Procedure Error(S : String);

When you call this procedure, an error box will appear with message S in it.
An example is

```
Error('No files found.');
```

Procedure Do_clock;

This procedure uses the Access system clock icon and prompts the user for the time and date.

Procedure ChangeDir;

This procedure uses the same routine that the File submenu uses in the "Change directory" option.

Procedure OSShell(Name : String);

This procedure provides a gateway to DOS. Name is the name of your program. When invoked, it will go to the DOS screen and write "Type EXIT to return to Name . . ."
An example is

```
OSShell('Turbo Designer');
```

Registration

The registration fee for Turbo Designer is $25. When you register, you will receive

☐ a disk with your registration number on it.

If you share this disk, and somebody registers with your registration number, you will get a $10 commission.

Send registration fee and any comments to

MMI Computers
Attn: SLO-0000
878 Via Seville
Livermore, CA 94550

12
Turbo-Screen System

Program title   Turbo-Screen System   *(Disk 2257)*

Special requirements   Borland's Turbo Pascal 4.0 or 5.0.

Turbo-Screen was conceived as a means to get programs running quickly while spending minimum time developing the screen panels for those programs. Turbo-Screen generates Pascal code that performs the Common User Access for your application code. Common User Access (CUA) is terminology used by the IBM Systems Application Architecture (SAA). Even though Pascal is not a language accepted within SAA, we have tried to keep our general terminology compatible with the concepts and terminology of SAA.

The Turbo-Screen System (called TSS) was developed to allow the easy definition and implementation of screen panels. Implementation requires the TSS abilities to

- locate and place messages, Entry, or Menu panel variables (fields to be edited or chosen) on the screen
- control the editing of the panel fields through the positioning of a cursor with Cursor-Movement/Editing functions (called Key-Functions)
- pass the panel field values to variables within the main program

An additional feature includes the ability to assign Key-functions to any available keystroke(s). The Key-function key assignment, as well as the Key-Functions themselves, are supported by low-level routines supplied with TSS as a Pascal Unit File called TSSLIB.TPU.

TSS contains a *code generating program* (called TSS.EXE) that generates Pascal procedures that interface your Menu Design (through a Menu Design file that you build) into a main Pascal program. TSS.EXE also produces sample test code as an example of menu inclusion in a main program. This test code allows you to quickly test menu and entry panel ideas.

Listed here are the files included with TSS:

ENTRY.PAN	Entry Panel design example file.
ENTRY.PAS	Entry Panel example program source code.
MENU.PAN	Menu Panel design example file.
MENU.PAS	Menu Panel example program source code.
SPECKEYS.H	Special keys description file.
SWAPTPU.BAT	Swaps TPU libraries from v5.0 to v4.0 and vice versa. This batch file will rename files on the diskette.
TSS.DEF	TSS definition file
TSSINST.EXE	The Turbo-Screen System installation program. This program helps the user to install the Turbo-Screen System.
TSSINST.HLP	Help file used by TSSINST.EXE.
TSSLIB04.TPU	Screen Panel Support library—Turbo Pascal 4.0.
TSSLIB.TPU	Screen Panel Support library—Turbo Pascal 5.0.
TSS.EXE	Code generating program. This program uses Panel Design files to create User Access Code for Pascal programs written using Borland's Turbo Pascal Compilers v4.0.

Installation

Follow these steps to install the Turbo-Screen System:

1. Edit CONFIG.SYS and make sure that `files = 20` is present.
2. Insert the installation diskette in the source drive.
3. Make the source drive the current drive.
4. At the DOS prompt, type `TSSINST`.
5. Ensure that Borland's Turbo Pascal Command Line Compiler is in the Path.
6. Execute SWAPTPU.BAT if you will be running Turbo Pascal 4.0 (see the section on the Version 4.0 Supporting Unit).

The installation program will then ask questions pertaining to the target drive name, directory, etc.

The TSS panel development environment

The TSS system includes an executable program called TSS.EXE that takes an Input Panel design file (See the "Panel Design" section) with an extension of PAN and produces three additional files. These files include a variable definitions file (with .CON extension), an interface procedures file (with .PRC extension), and a test file (with .TST extension). For example, if we create a Panel Design file called XX.PAN and input that file to TSS.EXE, the files XX.CON, XX.PRC, and XX.TST would be produced.

The XX.CON and XX.PRC could be included in your code for implementation. A sample call of the interface procedures is included in the XX.TST file.

See the diagram in FIG. 12-1 for an example.

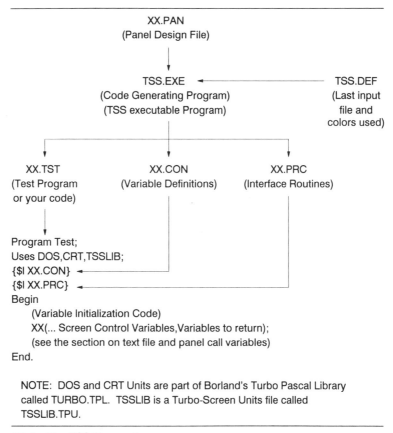

```
                          XX.PAN
                    (Panel Design File)
                            |
                            v
                        TSS.EXE  <---------------------  TSS.DEF
                (Code Generating Program)               (Last input
                (TSS executable Program)                 file and
                            |                           colors used)
          +-----------------+-----------------+
          v                 v                 v
       XX.TST             XX.CON            XX.PRC
   (Test Program     (Variable Definitions)  (Interface Routines)
    or your code)
          |
          v
  Program Test;
  Uses DOS,CRT,TSSLIB;
  {$I XX.CON}  <------------+
  {$I XX.PRC}  <---------------------------+
  Begin
        (Variable Initialization Code)
        XX(... Screen Control Variables,Variables to return);
        (see the section on text file and panel call variables)
  End.

        NOTE:  DOS and CRT Units are part of Borland's Turbo Pascal Library
        called TURBO.TPL.  TSSLIB is a Turbo-Screen Units file called
        TSSLIB.TPU.
```

12-1 The TSS file creation process.

Panel design

A panel is part of a communication link between user and program. It not only tells a program what to do but also tells the user what the program can do. The panel does this by either merely offering the user choices (such a panel is called a *Menu* panel) or by allowing the user to enter values (called an *Entry* panel).

Similar to the menus at a breakfast cafe, Menu panels can offer a list of items to pick, examine, or execute (i.e., eat, in the case of the cafe). For example, under the cafe metaphor, we might have a choice between coffee or milk, bacon and eggs, and/or pancakes with fruit. Now, in addition, after we choose our meal, we must express our quantitative desires about the chosen items. For example, how many eggs do we want? How should they be cooked? How well should they be cooked? If we speak in terms of the panel interface, these values would be communicated through an Entry panel.

Creating a panel file

Both types of panels have two important characteristics. First, we have an organized list of the items to choose or places to enter the pertinent data. Second, we have other notes, instructions, labels, explanations, and titles (such as "Breakfast Cafe") on our menu page (i.e., the computer screen). The first set of characteristics pertain to Menu or Entry variable fields (hereinafter called just fields) while the second set of characteristics refer to messages. Fields are on the screen to be chosen or interacted with (an active object) while the messages are on the screen to merely inform (a passive object).

If we are to build panels, then we must be able to place our messages and fields on our screen and return the input data to our program (or vice versa). To accomplish this, we must place specific information about our panel within a *Panel Design file*. The Panel Design file is an ASCII file with the .PAN file extension and can be created with the Borland's Turbo Pascal compiler editor or any other simple text editor. The Panel Design file holds both *message locations*, *field locations*, and contents of messages as well as *field attributes*, i.e., *field lengths* on the screen, *variable types*, and the *variable names* associated with the Fields.

To specify the locations of messages or fields, one merely must place a character (chosen by the user) in the file to denote the beginning location of the message or field. The chosen character for messages is called a *message location character*, and the chosen character for variable fields is called a *field location character*. These characters must be placed within the first 25 lines and first 80 characters to be meaningful for the normal-sized screen (See "Panel limitations").

Default location characters (which may be changed by the user) are @, Char(64), for messages and ∧, Char(94), for fields.

Messages and field attributes are entered as strings of characters within special (user-denoted) characters called *message delimiter characters* and *field delimiter characters*.

Default delimiter characters are #, Char(35), for messages and |, Char(124), for fields. An example message is

    #Here is a message!#

The message length can vary between one and eighty characters. A message must be specified for each message location character and may be placed anywhere within the Panel Design file. The messages will be assigned to message locations based on reading order (i.e., reading from left to right and down the page). This ordering rule will establish the first message, which goes with the first message location character, and so forth.

Field attributes must also be associated with each field location character. To define the field attributes, you must first specify the variable type by using the characters S, R, and I for `String`, `Real`, and `Integer` type variables. Next, you must specify the field length (between one and eighty characters in length); and, last, enter the variable name along with the closing variable delimiter character. The variable type, field length, and variable name must be separated by colons (":").

An example field attribute definition would be as follows:

```
| S:15:DATA_STRING |
```

This would define the first field as a string of length 15, and the variable name of DATA_STRING is the variable passing the string from the panel (TSS generated code) to your application code. Alternately, real and integer types would be defined as follows:

```
| R:10:Realvar |
| I:5:Intvar |
```

Sample panel design files are included for both an Entry panel and a Menu panel (named quite descriptively as ENTRY.PAN and MENU.PAN).

Complete sample panels—i.e., with variables initialized and the screen control set member `editoff` (for Menu panels; see "Advanced panel building")—are available in the files ENTRY.PAS and MENU.PAS.

Panel limitations

TSS was specifically developed for applications programmed in Borland's Turbo Pascal 4.0 and 5.0 and executed on a DOS operating system. Because of the DOS requirement, TSS can only effectively support a screen one character less than the rated screen size (coincidentally, the last character on the screen—the one in the lower right-hand corner). TSS now supports screens of the size 25 lines by 80 characters minus one character. We lose the last character because DOS scrolls the entire screen one line when we write the last character to the screen.

To overcome this limitation, one must design panels that do not write the last character. Either of these two simple rules accomplish this:

- Assume the screen is 24 lines by 80 characters in size.
- Assume the screen is 25 lines by 79 characters in size.

TSS can handle 50 messages and 50 fields along with their associated locations. A message or field length can be between one and eighty characters.

Creating the common user interface code

Running the TSS program

To create your user interface code, merely type TSS at the DOS prompt. The program then will present two entry panels for you to interact with.

The first panel (FIG. 12-2) allows you to input the filename (extension of .PAN is assumed) of your Panel Design file and alter the default field or message delimiter and location characters. You process the first panel by pressing the F3 key.

The second panel (FIG. 12-3) allows you to change the colors of the inactive Fields, the highlights or reverse video of the actively edited Fields, the colors of the background, and the colors of the Messages on the screen. You process the second panel by pressing the F3 key.

The program will then continue into an ERROR CHECKING mode and will present an opportunity to produce executable code.

```
                Turbo-Screen  by Connelly (C) 1986,87,88,89
                      V1.00 -- UNREGISTERED

       Enter Panel Design File Name ==>              entry

       Enter Message Location Character ==>            @

       Enter Message Delimiter ==>                     #

       Enter Field Location Character ==>              ▮

       Enter Field Definition Delimiter ==>            |




       Enter and/or Edit Fields, F3=Next, Esc=Cancel Program
```

12-2 The first TSS panel.

```
                    Color Attribute Choice Menu


        0  Black      4  Red        8  DarkGray    12  LightRed
        1  Blue       5  Magenta    9  LightBlue   13  LightMagenta
        2  Geeen      6  Brown     10  LightGreen  14  Yellow
        3  Cyan       7  LightGray 11  LightCyan   15  White


     Enter the above color number for the following attributes :


         Background color number              ==> 0
         Border color number                  ==> 0
         Message color number                 ==> 15
         Special character color number       ==> 0
         Variable field inactive color number ==> 15
         Variable field active color number   ==> 15

  Modify Color Types, F2=Previous, F3=Next, Esc=Cancel Program
```

12-3   The second TSS panel.

Debugging the panel file

When the Turbo-Screen System detects an error within the Panel Design file, it produces both screen error messages and a file of error messages with the extension .ERR along with the prefix name of your Panel Design file's prefix name (for example, the error file would be called XX.ERR if your Panel Design file's filename was XX.PAN).

The error file will contain error messages concerning errors of the following type:

- The number of message locations is not equal to the number of messages. This error means that either the number of message locations is incorrect or that the number of messages is incorrect. Inspect the messages and message locations for missing message delimiters and message location characters.

- The number of field locations is not equal to the number of fields. This error means that either the number of field locations is incorrect or that the number of fields is incorrect. Inspect the fields and field locations for missing field delimiters and field location characters.

- The number of messages or fields in the Panel Design file is too great for Turbo-Screen System support (see "Panel limitations").

- Variable names are *reserved words*. Change the name of the specific variables that have caused these errors.

Running the test code

The Turbo-Screen System can utilize the Turbo Pascal command-line compiler to produce Panel test code directly from the TSS.EXE or TSSUR.EXE program execution. That code (called XX.EXE, where XX.PAN is the input Panel Design file) can be executed by typing in the Panel Design file prefix name (here, XX). Ensure that Borland's Turbo Pascal command-line compiler is in the path.

You might also compile the Test Code File (XX.TST) using the standard Turbo Pascal 4.0/5.0 Compiler.

The Turbo-Screen System also creates compiler directives that will change the compiler parameters (memory allocations). These directives could be referenced if you experience memory allocation errors within your application code.

Advanced panel building

Cursor-movement and editing-control key functions

Turbo-Screen contains key functions for moving to or modifying field values. Some key functions are clear to end of field, exit panel, break out (cancel program). A Turbo-Screen user has the flexibility to change the assignment of any or all of the field movement or editing functions to any key. This enables the programmer to conform to any local key function customs or habits such as IBM's SAA function key standards. In order for Turbo-Screen to keep track of the keystrokes that perform editing or movement functions on the screen, global data is kept in TSSLIB.TPU. This data gives each keystroke an assigned key function.

Key functions are panel movement or editing functions that normal menu or entry panels would perform. Some simple editing or moving functions of an entry program would include a function that moved to the next field or deleted a field entry, etc. Turbo-Screen has a complete set of key functions for movement, editing and control (see TABLE 12-1).

As described above, these key functions are assigned to keystrokes for the panel's control. The assignment of each key function to a keystroke is completely user-configurable within the user's application code by use of the procedure set_key_fnc within TSSLIB.TPU.

Set_key_fnc changes the key function assigned to a key within TSSLIB.TPU. To assign a new key function to a key, call set_key_fnc

Table 12-1   Key functions.

Key-function literal	Definition
backspace	Backspace over a character or move backward.
break_out	When the key mapped to the break_out function is pressed, the executing program is halted.
clr_eol	Clear to the end of a field.
delete	Delete a character.
down	Move down one field. Down is calculated as the closest field below the current field occupied by the cursor.
downr	Move down one field until the cursor is at the bottom-most field, then move to the next column to the right. (*Note:* This could be a right or left downward field move.)
normal	The key value read in will be acted upon as a normal key (i.e., it will be passed to the program). For example, an ''a'' key is pressed, so an ''a'' is generated in a screen field.
exit_panel	Exit panel returns from the panel procedure to the calling program.
ins_toggle	Allow insertion of text within a field.
left	Move to the closest left most field relative to the cursor.
move_bol	Move to the beginning of a field.
move_eol	Move to the end of a field.
next_field	Move to the next field.
nullk	Do nothing when this key is struck.
prev_field	Move to the previous field.
right	Move to the closest right most field relative to the cursor.
up	Move up one field. Up is calculated as the closest field above the current field occupied by the cursor. (*Note:* This could be a right or left upward field move.)
upr	Move up one field until the cursor is at the upper-most field, then move to the next column to the right.

before calling the TSS.EXE generated panel procedure. Call the procedure as follows:

```
set_key_fnc(KEYNUMBER, KEYFUNCTION);
```

KEYNUMBER is an integer variable with the key number stored within it. Key numbers are the standard ASCII ordinal number (KEYNUMBER:=ORD(CHAR(KEYNUMBER)) or the extended ASCII ordinal number plus 256 (see TABLE 12-2 for some sample key numbers). An example of mapping the break_out key to the ^C keystroke would be accomplished by either of these two Pascal statements:

```
set_key_fnc(CTLC,break_out);
```

or

```
set_key_fnc((3+256),break_out);
```

Table 12-2   Special keys and extended key codes.

Program reference	Value	Description
CTLAT	0	Ctrl-@
CTLA	1	Ctrl-A
CTLB	2	Ctrl-B
CTLC	3	Ctrl-C
CTLD	4	Ctrl-D
CTLE	5	Ctrl-E
CTLF	6	Ctrl-F
CTLG	7	Ctrl-G
BS	8	Backspace
HT	9	Horizontal tab
CTLJ	10	Ctrl-J
VT	11	Vertical tab
CTLL	12	Ctrl-L
CR	13	Carriage return
CTLN	14	Ctrl-N
CTLO	15	Ctrl-O
CTLP	16	Ctrl-P
CTLQ	17	Ctrl-Q
CTLR	18	Ctrl-R
CTLS	19	Ctrl-S
CTLT	20	Ctrl-T
CTLU	21	Ctrl-U
CTLV	22	Ctrl-V
CTLW	23	Ctrl-W
CTLX	24	Ctrl-X
CTLY	25	Ctrl-Y
CTLZ	26	Ctrl-Z
ESC	27	Escape
BHT	271	Shift-Horizontal tab
ALTQ	272	Alt-Q
ALTW	273	Alt-W
ALTE	274	Alt-E
ALTR	275	Alt-R
ALTT	276	Alt-T
ALTY	277	Alt-Y
ALTU	278	Alt-U
ALTI	279	Alt-I
ALTO	280	Alt-O
ALTP	281	Alt-P
ALTA	286	Alt-A
ALTS	287	Alt-S
ALTD	288	Alt-D
ALTF	289	Alt-F
ALTG	290	Alt-G
ALTH	291	Alt-H

Program reference	Value	Description
ALTJ	292	Alt-J
ALTK	293	Alt-K
ALTL	294	Alt-L
ALTZ	300	Alt-Z
ALTX	301	Alt-X
ALTC	302	Alt-C
ALTV	303	Alt-V
ALTB	304	Alt-B
ALTN	305	Alt-N
ALTM	306	Alt-M
F1	315	F1
F2	316	F2
F3	317	F3
F4	318	F4
F5	319	F5
F6	320	F6
F7	321	F7
F8	322	F8
F9	323	F9
F10	324	F10
HOME	327	Home
UPA	328	Up arrow
PGUP	329	Page Up
LEFTA	331	Left arrow
RIGHTA	333	Right arrow
ENDK	335	End key
DOWNA	336	Down arrow
PGDN	337	Page Down
INS	338	Insert
DEL	339	Delete
F11	340	Shift-F1
F12	341	Shift-F2
F13	342	Shift-F3
F14	343	Shift-F4
F15	344	Shift-F5
F16	345	Shift-F6
F17	346	Shift-F7
F18	347	Shift-F8
F19	348	Shift-F9
F20	349	Shift-F10
F21	350	Alt-F1
F22	351	Alt-F2
F23	352	Alt-F3
F24	353	Alt-F4

Program reference	Value	Description
F25	354	Alt-F5
F26	355	Alt-F6
F27	356	Alt-F7
F28	357	Alt-F8
F29	358	Alt-F9
F30	359	Alt-F10
F31	360	Ctrl-F1
F32	361	Ctrl-F2
F33	362	Ctrl-F3
F34	363	Ctrl-F4
F35	364	Ctrl-F5
F36	365	Ctrl-F6
F37	366	Ctrl-F7
F38	367	Ctrl-F8
F39	368	Ctrl-F9
F40	369	Ctrl-F10
CTL_PTRSC	370	Ctrl-PrintScreen
CTL_LEFT	371	Ctrl-Left arrow
CTL_RIGHT	372	Ctrl-Right arrow
CTL_END	373	Ctrl-End
CTL_PGDN	374	Ctrl-Page Down
CTL_HOME	375	Ctrl-Home
ALT1	376	Alt-1
ALT2	377	Alt-2
ALT3	378	Alt-3
ALT4	379	Alt-4
ALT5	380	Alt-5
ALT6	381	Alt-6
ALT7	382	Alt-7
ALT8	383	Alt-8
ALT9	384	Alt-9
ALT0	385	Alt-0
ALT_	386	Alt--
ALT_EQ	387	Alt-
CTL_PGUP	388	Ctrl-Page Up
EF11	389	F11 (*enhanced 101 keyboard*)
EF12	390	F12 (*enhanced 101 keyboard*)

Note: Extended 101-102 keyboard's function keys 11, 12 might not work correctly. This is a reported and confirmed bug within Turbo Pascal 4.0 as of 4/12/88. Some AT clones work fine, but IBM-AT's do not.

So, until `break_out` is re-assigned to another keystroke, the key sequence of pressing the control key and then "C" would halt the program. See TABLE 12-3 for the default key function/key assignment upon usage of the unit TSSLIB.TPU.

**Table 12-3   Default
key-function assignments.**

Key	Key function
CTLC	break_out
BS	backspace
HT	move_eol
CR	next_field
F3	exit_panel
BHT	move_bol
UPA	up
LEFTA	left
RIGHTA	right
DOWNA	down
INS	ins_toggle
DEL	delete
char (1) . . char (255)	normal
all other keys	nullk

Screen attribute usage

Panel screen control is performed by utilizing a set of screen control variable members that mediate screen control functions. The screen control functions offer features that allow for the development of Entry, Menu, pop-up, or pull-down panels.

Panel screen control is processed by adding/deleting control word set elements to the screen control set variable `sccn`. Each control word activates/deactivates a specific menu function. To add or delete functions, use the following set operation:

```
sccn:=sccn+[editoff]-[erron];
```

This has the effect of turning off both Field editing and Field entry error checking. A list of the set elements as defined for screen control GLOBAL set variable `sccn` is available in the section on test file and panel call variables.

As a result of the earlier panel screen control set elements, the Turbo-Screen user has a complete flexibility when presenting screens and can be used to develop pop-up Panels.

See TABLE 12-4 for a list of the screen attribute set members.

Table 12-4   Screen attribute set members.

Feature	Description	Default
cpcall	Clears the entire screen when Panel is called.	ON
cpret	Clears the entire screen when Panel returns to calling procedure.	ON
cvcall	Clears all Fields when Panel is called.	ON
cvret	Clears all Fields when Panel returns to calling procedure.	ON
editoff	Turns off Field editing.	OFF
erron	Turns on default Field type error checking.	OFF
upmsg	Updates Messages only when Panel is called.	ON
upvar	Updates Fields only when Panel is called.	ON
lvcrs	Leave cursor in same Field character location when cursor moves to next Field.	OFF

The test file and panel call variables

Suppose we have the Panel Design file XX.PAN (shown in FIG. 12-4). XX.PAN will create the test file shown in FIG. 12-5. Note in the figure that comments have been added with (* and *) delimiters.

Some other things to note about the test file:

- Global `Scrn_ctl` set variable `sccn` stores the Screen Control set elements.
- Global integer variable `cerr` returns the last field number (when the panel is exited), which could not be formatted into its specific format type.
- Global integer variable `nfld` returns the field number where the cursor was located when the panel was exited. In addition, if you place the value of the Field where you want the cursor to start, and the value is a valid field number (greater than zero and less than or equal to the maximum field number), then the cursor will be located on the desired field number upon the call to the panel. If `nfld` is less than zero or greater than the maximum field number for a panel, then `nfld` is set to one upon the call to the panel.

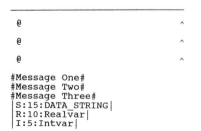

12-4 A panel design file.

```
{
Turbo-Screen V1.00A test code generation --- 1-1-1976 12:00:00
note memory allocations. Increase stack as needed for user programs
}
{$M 30500,0,655360}      (*Compiler Memory Allocation*)
Program XX_generated_code;

Uses Crt,Dos,TSSLIB;       { your code needs these units }

{$I XX.con}                (*Panel Procedure Variable Definition*)

{$I XX.prc}                (*The TSS.EXE Generated Code*)

begin
     DATA_STRING:='              ';   (*String Data Initialization*)
     Realvar:=0.0;                    (*Real Data Initialization*)
     Intvar:=0;                       (*Integer Data Initialization*)
        (* Next Variable is Global Screen Control Variable which
           is initialized here*)
     sccn:=[cpcall,cvcall,cpret,cvret,upmsg,upvar];
XX(
     sccn,            (*Global Screen Control Variable*)
     cerr,            (*Error Return Variable*)
     nfld,            (*Field Number upon Return to Calling Procedure*)
     ret_key,         (*Key Number of Exit_Panel Key*)
     DATA_STRING,     (* Your                                    *)
     Realvar,         (* Data                                    *)
     Intvar);         (* Variables from the Panel Design File*)

end.
```

12-5 The test file created by the panel design file of Fig. 12-4.

Turbo Pascal 4.0 supporting unit

Turbo Screen System supports both Turbo Pascal 4.0 and 5.0 through the use of the utility batch program SWAPTPU.BAT. TSS comes initially installed for v5.0. To switch to v4.0 unit support, use the DOS CD command to change to the directory in which TSS was originally installed. Once your current working directory has TSSLIB.TPU and either TSSLIB04.TPU or TSSLIB05.TPU within it, then merely execute SWAP-TPU.BAT at the dos prompt by typing

SWAPTPU

SWAPTPU will inform the user as to the progress and conclusion of the TPU swapping as shown in FIG. 12-6. If the user must revert back to v5.0 unit conventions, merely execute SWAPTPU again.

Possible error conditions and corrections

Two possibilities for error are mentioned here.

Error #1 This condition arises when the TSSLIB.TPU is not in the current directory. To remedy this situation, copy TSSLIB.TPU into the current working directory from the distribution diskette.

Error #2 The alternative version TPU file TSSLIB04.TPU or TSSLIB05.TPU cannot be found. To fix this error copy all TPU files from the distribution diskette by executing COPY A:*.TPU with your current working directory being the TSS installed directory.

```
Swaptpu -- V1.0
Turbo Screen System (C) 1989
by the Connelly Brothers


Swapping Version 5.0 to 4.0
Turbo Screen System is installed for Turbo Pascal Version 4.0

To swap Turbo Screen System to another Turbo Pascal Version
execute swaptpu again.

C:\>
```

12-6 Running SWAPTPU will swap v4 with v5.

Registration

If you like the results that you get from the *unregistered* version of the
Turbo-Screen System and need the library source of the *registered* version
or use Turbo-Screen System for profit or business, then you should
acquire a registered version. The registered version costs $30 and can be
obtained from

>   The Connelly Brothers
>   P.O. Box 280527
>   Lakewood, CO 80228-0527

13
Screen Debut

Program title   Screen Debut   *(Disk 2359)*

Special requirements   Graphics adapter recommended.

Screen Debut is a very powerful screen generator. It's designed as a tool to ease the development of text screens. It generates code for screens in many different ways.

- ASCII code.
- ANSI code for use with DOS and telecommunications.
- BASIC code with and without line numbers plus BSAVE.
- C code for Turbo C.
- Pascal code for use with Turbo Pascal.
- Compressed binary format for use with Snap Screen and Hammerly's ProBas.

Figure 13-1 is a graphical depiction of the major function areas in Screen Debut.

Running Screen Debut

To run Screen Debut, type the following at the DOS prompt:

```
SD [filename] [/S]
```

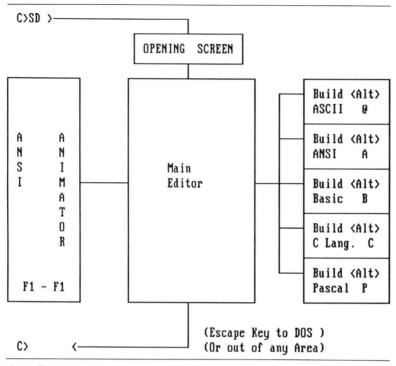

13-1 The major Screen Debut functions.

The optional parameters are

filename	Name of a screen file to be automatically loaded. Although you do not need to include the file extension in the command line, the filename should have an .SD extension.
/S	Puts the program in Snow Suppression mode. This is only useful for older CGA chips. If you don't see snow, don't use this switch; it slows the program down.

Exiting the program

Use the Esc key to exit the program. The Esc key will also exit any function within the program. With a mouse, locate the cursor in the bottom right corner and click the left key.

Editing commands

Here is a summary of how the editing commands work with Screen Debut:

- Screen Debut is mouse-supported. All commands use the left button.

- The Arrow keys move the cursor on the screen. The status bar at the bottom of the screen indicates the cursor's coordinates. To draw lines, use the F2 key to toggle between Move Cursor, Single Border, and Double Border.

- The Home, End, Pg Up, Pg Dn, and Tab also move the cursor on the screen.

- The Backspace key removes the character to the left of the cursor, moves the cursor one space to the left, and pulls all characters to the right of the cursor one space to the left.

- Pressing the Ins key will toggle between Insert mode and Overwrite mode of operation. In Insert mode, the cursor is small, allowing characters to be inserted. In Overwrite mode, the cursor is full height, allowing characters to be overwritten.

- The Del key removes characters.

- Full control key support. For example, Ctrl-A places ASCII character #1 (a happy face) at the cursor, and so on.

- Full numeric ASCII code support. Hold down the Alt key and type the ASCII code into the numeric key pad. The character will be placed at the cursor position.

- Alt-L (Letter) allows big letters to be placed on the screen. All ASCII characters from 1 to 127 are supported. The pointer on the ASCII chart (F5) is used to select the fill characters. To use the ASCII chart without putting a character at the current cursor position, set the pointer and press Escape. The fill character can be any ASCII character. The letters will be of the default color set by the (F3) or (F4) select color commands. The Tab key works very well for letter spacing. The characters are based on an 8x8 row/column matrix. To enter the big character, you can just use the normal keyboard keys, use the Ctrl-letter combination representing a control character (ASCII codes 1 to 30), or hold down the Alt-key and type in the ASCII character number.

  Note: To look at an ASCII chart, press the F5 key for a pop-up chart. Just start at the top and count from left to right. The first character is number 1 or Ctrl-A depending how you look at it. This procedure is a last-minute addition to the program and is not yet reflected in the menuing system. See Appendix A for a list of the ASCII characters.

Options

Options can be selected from the Options menu (shown in FIG. 13-2). Use the Up/Down arrow keys or press the appropriate shortcut key to select an

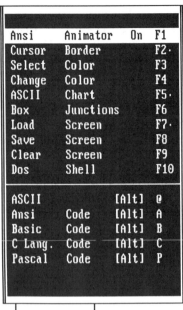

Ansi	Animator	On	F1
Cursor	Border		F2·
Select	Color		F3
Change	Color		F4
ASCII	Chart		F5·
Box	Junctions		F6
Load	Screen		F7·
Save	Screen		F8
Clear	Screen		F9
Dos	Shell		F10
ASCII		[Alt]	@
Ansi	Code	[Alt]	A
Basic	Code	[Alt]	B
C Lang.	Code	[Alt]	C
Pascal	Code	[Alt]	P

F1 OPTIONS │ [ALT] F1 X-OPTIONS   MOVE CURSOR   ←↑↓→   COL : 1 ROW : 1

13-2 Pressing the F1 key presents this menu.

option. The shortcut keys are always active for fast service. A second press of the F1 key activates the ANSI Animation Mode of operation shown in FIG. 13-3.

The **F1** key calls up the Options menu.

The **F2** key toggles between Move Cursor, Single Border, and Double Border. This is useful for moving the cursor and drawing single or double lines.

Shift-F2 is used for line modes without automatic junctions. This command is not listed on the menuing system. However, the F2 command does have a dot next to it as a reminder.

The **F3** key sets the current color, which is indicated by the color of the left half of the Status Line.

The **F4** key activates the recolor screen option. Just place the cursor over the color to reset. Notice that the red selector arrow visually differentiates this function from the F3 function.

The **F5** key calls up the ASCII character chart shown in FIG. 13-4. Characters not supported by the Keyboard are available. The selected character will be placed at the cursors current location. Shift-F5 or Alt-Z places an ASCII character selected by the ASCII chart to the current cursor position without going to the menu. *Caution:* Some ASCII characters and control codes cause unpredictable results when used in conjunction with programming languages.

```
┌─────────────────────────────┐
│ ■                           │
├─────────────────────────────┤
│ Ansi     Animator  Off  F1  │
│ Cursor   Border         F2· │
│ Select   Color          F3  │
│ Data     View           F4  │
│ ASCII    Chart          F5· │
│ Box      Junctions      F6  │
│ Step     Back           F7  │
│ Step     Forward        F8  │
│ Clear    Animator       F9  │
│ Replay   Animator       F10 │
│                             │
│ Copy     Character  [ALT] C │
│ Copy     Block      [ALT] K │
│                             │
│ ▓▓▓▓▓▓▓▓▓▓▓▓▓←↑↓→▓▓▓▓▓       │
└─────────────────────────────┘

 F1 OPTIONS │  FRAME : 0        MOVE CURSOR  ←↑↓→  COL : 1  ROW : 1
```

13-3 The menu for ANSI animation mode.

```
┌[ASCII CHART]──────────────────────────────────────────────────────┐
│                                                                    │
│                                                                    │
│                                                                    │
│                                                                    │
└────────────────────────────────────────────────────────────────────┘
```

F1 OPTIONS   [ALT] F1 X-OPTIONS   MOVE CURSOR ←↑↓→   COL : 1 ROW : 1

13-4 Any ASCII character can be chosen from this chart.

The **F6** key selects Box Junctions (see FIG. 13-5).

The **F7** key loads Screen Debut files (all of which have the .SD extension).

Shift-F7 allows for the loading of raw files. Screen Debut directs these files through the BIOS; therefore, ANSI Files are no problem as long as the ANSI Device Driver is installed. The files are loaded in line by line. To stop the process, merely hit any key. *Note:* The Screen Debut directory is limited to 110 SD files. Use subdirectories to surpass this limitation.

The **F8** key saves the screen. *Caution:* Do not keep more than 110 .SD files in one DOS directory.

The **F9** key clears the entire screen to the default colors—a grey foreground on a black background. Use the F4 key to change the foreground and background colors if desired.

The **F10** key exits to the DOS shell. Essentially, the program stays in the computer's memory while work is being done at the DOS level. *Tip:* Set the DOS Path so COMMAND.COM can be found. As an alternative, place COMMAND.COM in the current directory.

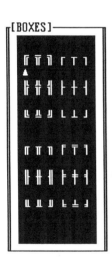

F1 OPTIONS   [ALT] F1 X-OPTIONS   MOVE CURSOR   ←↑↓→   COL : 1   ROW : 1

13-5   Pressing the F6 key allows you to choose the type of box junction.

Extended options

The pull-up Extended Options menu (shown in FIG. 13-6) provides a quick reference of the extended editing capabilities of the program. All commands have shortcut keys.

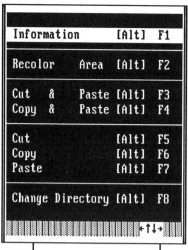

Information		[Alt]	F1
Recolor	Area	[Alt]	F2
Cut &	Paste	[Alt]	F3
Copy &	Paste	[Alt]	F4
Cut		[Alt]	F5
Copy		[Alt]	F6
Paste		[Alt]	F7
Change Directory		[Alt]	F8

F1 OPTIONS | [ALT] F1 X-OPTIONS | MOVE CURSOR ←↑↓→ COL : 1 ROW : 1

13-6 The expanded options menu can be used for editing.

Alt-F1 calls up this Extended Options menu.

Alt-F2 (Recolor Area) recolors a block (a square) on the screen. *Note:* The Block is recolored to the current selected color.

Alt-F3 (Cut and Paste) removes the selected text and allows it to be moved to another location via the arrow keys.

Alt-F4 (Copy and Paste) allows a block to be copied from one position to another.

Alt-F5 (Cut) cuts a block from the screen, storing it in memory for later recovery with Paste. Cut is also useful for erasing all or part of the Screen. The cut area assumes the current color attributes.

Alt-F6 (Copy) works much like a camera. It copies a selected area into memory, saving it for later recovery with Paste.

Alt-F7 (Paste) restores a block saved with the Cut or Copy function.

Note: The Cut, Copy, and Paste functions mainly allow the importation of screen snapshots (blocks).

Building ANSI screens

System set-up

ANSI screens use the ANSI.SYS file that comes with DOS. Make sure your CONFIG.SYS file contains the following line:

```
DEVICE = ANSI.SYS
```

It should be in the root directory on the hard disk or on the boot disk.

If it doesn't exist, you can create it with a word processor or the DOS COPY CON command (see your DOS manual for command descriptions).

Now you are ready to use the ANSI screens built by Screen Debut. All ANSI screens have the extension .ANS. Use the DOS TYPE command to post the screen to your monitor, such as

TYPE YOURFILE.ANS

Note: Alternately, you could use the Snap Screen utility (described later) instead of ANSI.SYS.

ANSI animation

Screen Debut allows for animated and non-animated screens. For information on how to create non-animated screens, see the section on editing commands. A small blinking box on the right of the status line indicates the screen is animated.

To Enter or Exit the ANSI animation mode of operation, press the F1 key twice. After doing this, you will notice a change at the bottom status line of the screen. In the Animation mode of operation, a Frame counter will appear on the Status Line.

Note: Some editing commands available under the F1 option have changed. Extended options are not used in this mode of operation.

The **F2** key toggles between Move Cursor, Single Border, and Double Border. This is useful for moving the cursor and drawing single or double lines.

The **F3** key sets the current color. The current color status changes the color on the left half of the status line at the bottom of the screen.

The **F4** key selects the Data View option, which pulls up a window containing information about the animation frames. The options available are as follows:

Up/Down arrow Scrolls data

Left/Right arrow Sets Replay Delay time in micro-seconds. This is the Animation display delay.

Ins Depressing the insert key inserts a +/– character into the frame selected by the red arrow.

Del Cuts the character selected by the red arrow.

The **F5** key selects the ASCII character chart. *Caution:* ASCII codes below 32 are used for control codes. In certain circumstances, they might cause unpredictable results.

The **F6** key selects Box Junctions.

The **F7** key steps the program one frame back.

The **F8** key steps the program one frame forward.

The **F9** key clears the animated portion of the screen.

The **F10** key causes the animator to reset to frame 1 and then replay the animation. To stop the animator, press any key.

Support for GT Power BBSs

GT Power BBSs allow uploading of ANSI code into the message areas using the ASCII protocol for uploading. Screen Debut supports these message areas in many ways.

Figure 13-7 is an example of how the ANSI code parameter window appears every time the Build ANSI code procedure is invoked.

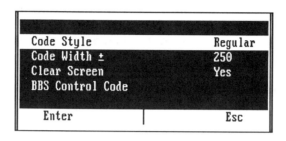

13-7 This menu allows you to choose ANSI code parameters.

The next sections describe each of the fields.

Code style Code style selects the coding routine that will code the non-animated screen. There are two flavors—Regular and Compact. Regular code is specially geared to scroll the screen as it appears, while Compact code (on the other hand) uses the different coding strategy of minimizing the number of lines of code. Compact is ideal for fairly complex screens to be used in a BBS message base.

Code width Use a width of 72 for message base work; otherwise, open it up to 250. For fine tuning, use the + or – keys. Note that these widths are only approximations; the actual code width might be wider under some circumstances.

Clear screen This controls whether or not the code to clear the screen is to be used.

Control code support GT BBSs use the ^E and ^R characters to control the "More? Y/N" prompt because it is not always desired. To add an ^E or ^R to the beginning of a file, set ANSI Code parameter window's "BBS

Control Code." An ^E will give one "More? Y/N" and then allow the file to run uninterrupted. An ^R will allow a file to run its entire length without a "More? Y/N".

Build ANSI code—Alt-A   Screen Debut use three separate algorithms to code ANSI screens. The first two code the Static (non-animated) screen. Screen Debut uses auto-sizing to adjust the size of the coded screen. Auto-sizing first determines the existence and actual size of the drawing by scanning the screen from bottom (Row 24) to top and then scans from right to left to determine the right edge of the drawing. It scans by searching for non-blank characters of the default color white on black (a blank is ASCII character 32). Once it has ascertained that a drawing does exist on the screen and determines its size, Screen Debut codes it. (See an earlier section for a discussion of the code parameter window.)

The third algorithm codes the Soft (animated) screen. It first checks to see if an animated drawing exists. If anything is in the animation buffer (memory area), it codes it. The code produced here is sensitive to screen placement because it uses the screen's (X,Y) coordinates to place each character. Furthermore, the cursor's resting position (position of the cursor when the Alt-A command was used) will be recorded into the ANSI code.

Basic   With the Alt-B option, Screen Debut codes the top 24 rows of the screen in Basic, with or without line numbers. Use Basic's MERGE command to place the code built by Debut in your program. Basic screen files end with the .BAS extension. Use Basic's RENUM command to renumber the line numbers if needed.

BSAVE   Load BSAVE files from Basic with the use of the BLOAD command. An example has been provided in the file BLOAD.BAS (FIG. 13-8). *Note:* For some reason, the BSAVE files made by this program haven't been successful on Tandy computers.

```
'Example of How to Load a BSAVE File with Quick Basic

DEFINT A-Z

'-/Modify this Line by Entering Your Own Screens/-------------------------
BSaveScreenToBeRetrived$ = "YourFile.BAS" '--Change "YourScrn"

'-/Get Video Mode/-------------------------------------------------------
DEF SEG = &H40
IF PEEK(&H49) = 7 THEN              '--PEEK to See Type of Monitor(Mono = 7)
   DEF SEG = &HB000                 '--MonoChrome Monitor(Memory Location)
ELSE
   DEF SEG = &HB800                 '--Color Monitor(Memory Location)
END IF

'-/Load the Screen into the Video Memory/--------------------------------
BLOAD BSaveScreenToBeRetrived$, &H0

END
```

13-8   The BASIC BLOAD command can be used in this way to load a screen saved with the BSAVE command.

Screen Debut files with Hammerly's ProBas

The Compressed Binary files with the .SD file extension are compatible with Hammerly's ProBas. Figure 13-9 shows the code segment needed to load and post the screens.

```
DIM SCR%(2000)                    '--- Dimension Array to 2000 integers
DIM CSCR%(2000)

'-/OPEN SCREEN FILE TO BE READ IN FROM DISK/-----------------------
CALL FOPEN("YOURFILE.SD", 0, 0, HANDLE%, ECODE%)
IF ECODE% THEN PRINT "ERROR"

'-/Get file size/-------------------------------------------------
CALL FSIZE(HANDLE%, BYTES&)
BYTES% = CINT(BYTES&)             '--- Put Long integer into short

'-/Read Data in file/---------------------------------------------
CSEG% = VARSEG(CSCR%(1))          '--- Set Pointers
COFS% = VARPTR(CSCR%(1))
CALL DFREAD(HANDLE%, CSEG%, COFS%, BYTES%, BYTESREAD%, ECODE%)
IF ECODE% THEN PRINT "ERROR"

'-/Close File/----------------------------------------------------
CALL FCLOSE(HANDLE%)

'-/UnCrunch Screen Data(Decompress)/------------------------------
DSEG% = VARSEG(SCR%(1))           '--- Reset pointers
DOFS% = VARPTR(SCR%(1))
CSEG% = VARSEG(CSCR%(1))
COFS% = VARPTR(CSCR%(1))
CALL UNSCRUNCH(DSEG%, DOFS%, CSEG%, COFS%)

'-/Put Data to the Screen/----------------------------------------
DSEG% = VARSEG(SCR%(1))           '--- Reset Pointers
DOFS% = VARPTR(SCR%(1))
CALL DSCRREST(DSEG%, DOFS%, 0, SNOW%)

NOTE: When saved, the 25th line assumes the current color attributes.
```

13-9 Hammerly's ProBas can load .SD files directly using this code segment.

C language

The C code is built on the top 24 rows of the screen and is compatible with Turbo C. C screen files end with the .C extension.

Pascal

Originally, Screen Debut was built as a Pascal-only screen code generator. The Pascal code generated by it is compatible with Turbo Pascal. Due to the use of the *CheckSnow* variable, the screens are very fast. The code can be produced as either a procedure or as a unit. See your Language manual to include the screens into your program. Pascal coded screens end with the extension .PAS.

File handling

When executing the F7 option—Load Screen—Screen Debut looks for the files with the .SD extension. When a file is selected from the menu, Screen Debut checks to see if an animated counterpart exists (the animated files having the extension .SDA). If one exists, it is loaded along with the .SD file. Screen Debut assumes that an .SDA file will not exist without an .SD file. When saving a file from one of the build code functions, the .SD file, the .SDA file (if appropriate), and the code file are all saved. If the .SD file exists, Screen Debut will challenge the user with "*.SD EXISTS OVER-WRITE ?". Select "No" to write the code to the disk without overwriting the *.SD file, and hit Escape to abort the procedure entirely. Debut guards the .SD files because they represent your work; but the coded screens are cf no concern to it and will be overwritten without notification.

File extensions

Here is a list of the meanings for each of the Screen Debut file extensions:

.SD	Debut's compressed binary file
.SDA	Debut's animated screens
.ANS	ANSI coded screens
.ASC	ASCII files
.BAS	Basic coded screens and BSAVE
.C	C language coded screens
.PAS	Pascal coded screens

Snap Screen

Snap Screen posts Screen Debut files to the screen. It is primarily intended for use with batch files and excels over ANSI in the area of speed, able to reach across a directory or even a drive and post a screen in an eye blink. All screens can be kept in one directory for easy maintenance. Snap Screen also has the ability to post screens in a dramatic split-screen way.

Snap Screen files are better than .COM screens in other ways too:

- Snap Screen saves space. It reads Screen Debuts compressed binary files typically about 800 bytes in size. On the other hand, a typical .COM screen carrying no video assistance requires over 4K of disk space!
- Snap Screen has monitor support. It checks for the monitor type (color or monochrome) and then loads the screen correctly, also setting the DOS prompt to the position you indicate.
- Snap Screen allows optional dramatic split-screen displays.
- Snap Screen is easy to maintain. All screens can be kept in the directory with Screen Debut for easy modification and still be used with batch files located elsewhere.

To use Snap Screen, type the following at the DOS prompt:

```
SNAPSCRN filename x y
```

The command-line parameters are

filename	Name of a Screen Debut file. The file should have the .SD extension, but it's not necessary to include the extension in the command line.
x	Vertical location of the cursor (range of values: 1 to 24)
y	Split screen switch (non-zero = Split Screen, 0 = Normal)

A note about color attributes

When developing a screen, you must pay attention to the hidden color attributes. Changing color attributes for no reason adds unnecessary extra code.

Errors

Many hardware and software errors have been anticipated. An example of such an error is writing to a drive while the drive door is open. In the event of an anticipated error, the program will try to recover itself. It will beep, give an error message for approximately five seconds, and then revert to where it was before the error occurred. The only action required on your part is to heed the error message.

Memory allocation

The Alt-= function checks the amount of unused memory. Without enough free memory, Screen Debut will crash. (In fact, this is the only time Screen Debut's been known to crash.) Adding TSRs improperly from the DOS shell causes a memory allocation problem. Don't load Screen Predator from the DOS shell. If you suspect the program is running out of memory, check it by pushing Alt-= while in the Main Editing environment. Storage of all the large data arrays takes place in the Far Memory. Ensure plenty of free memory here (at least 30K or more), as it is allocated on the fly.

Limitations

When using Screen Debut, you should be aware of the following program limitations:

- The program will code up to 999 lines of code.

- Line 25 has been left off coded screens. Because, when the last character of line 25 is written, it causes the cursor to move to line 26 and scrolls the screen.
- The ANSI Animator can handle up to 6000 frames (the equivalent of three full screens).

Registration

If you feel that this program would be useful and would like a copy, please register it by sending $10.00 to the following address. Your $10.00 fee earns you

☐ A free complimentary copy of Screen Predator
☐ The most recent version of Screen Debut

Send queries to

Willie Robinson
2613 Louis Blvd.
Hephzibah, GA 30815

Part Four

Other tools

14
PopText

Program title   PopText 2.1   *(Disk 1935)*

Special requirements   A hard drive is recommended.

Documentation is an essential part of any applications program. In most cases, documentation is either in the form of a separate book or else provided in documentation files on the program disk (this being common in the case of shareware). Because the documentation and the program are separate entities, a problem arises when the documentation is somehow misplaced. This happens all too often with shareware when users circulate programs among each other while neglecting to include the documentation files. The solution is to make the documentation part of the programs by providing pop-up help windows. Including well-designed help windows in your programs will give them a professional polish found in the best commercial software. Some examples of commercial programs with excellent help windows are Turbo Pascal, Wordstar 2000+, and Novel LAN services. With or without the manual, the user has some reference available on-line.

PopText is an includable Unit that allows Turbo Pascal programmers to prepare these types of help systems. With PopText, you can even design context-sensitive help systems that will make your programs much more useful to your users.

Features of PopText

PopText features an easy to use editor, a unit to include in Turbo Pascal programs, and three other units, including some fast writing routines,

routines to enhance CRT output, and a unit with all of the key definitions.

The PopText system features context-sensitive help, window linking, and an easy-to-use menubar.

PopRes is a memory-resident version of PopText that can be accessed through Interrupt 6EH.

About the help window

Each help window is a record consisting of 15 lines and 15 links. The lines are displayed on the screen, and the links are hidden in the background. In addition to being linked by line, windows are linked by the Page Up and Page Down keys. Windows are stored in a file with the extension .HLP and are accessed randomly by PopText. It is possible to access any record already existing within the helpfile. Using the Editor, you can create new files and append them up to 256 records each.

Using the editor

To use the Editor, type

    POPTX filename

at the DOS prompt, where filename is the name of the file you want to edit. If you do not supply a filename, POPTX will prompt you for one. If the file does not exist, POPTX will create a new file.

Next, you are prompted with options to Edit, Link, Test, Choose Another, and Quit (as shown in FIG. 14-1).

```
┌────Main Menu════════╗
║E)dit A Help Window  ║
║L)ink Pages          ║
║T)est the thing out. ║
║C)hoose new File.    ║
║Q)uit and Save       ║
╚═════════════════════╝
```

14-1 The PopText Main menu.

Entries In poptext.hlp: 32   13% Full

Edit

Edit allows you to place text in the windows. Here's a few helpful hints. After you have selected the Page number, use the Arrow keys (Up/Down) to select lines to Edit. Page Up and Page Down allow you to browse through the pages. Some important features of Edit are

F2	Switches you to linking Mode.
F3	Centers the Current line of text.
Enter or **Alphanumeric**	Edit the current line. (While Editing line, Esc erases line)
Esc	Return to Main menu.

Link

Linking is the key to PopText. To the right of the help box, you will see a list of numbers in another box. Most likely, in a new file, these will all be zeros. If you are editing the help file that came with this program, you will find several nonzero numbers; these represent links in the stack. The file can be looked at as a stack of cards, and the links allow you to move to any portion of the stack. Links are line-oriented, so selecting the link at the user level is as easy as moving the bar to the line containing the link and pressing Enter. This is only the first step, however. In the editing mode, you must mark the text by highlighting a keyword in the text line associated with the link. To do so, press ^Q before you type the word to be associated, and ^W after (this highlights the word). PopText will properly function only when both of these are done.

     Each box can contain up to 15 links. To establish a link, move the cursor to the line you want linked and press Enter. Respond to the prompt with the number you want linked. Pressing Alt-C clears all links, while pressing F1 returns you to the editor mode.

Test

Testing the help screen causes the program to activate the very same subroutine that you will incorporate in your program. In this manner, you can see how the help menu will look and feel, as well as check the validity of the links.

Choose Another File

This command allows you to close the current help stack and select another. If the selected file does not exist, PopText will create it.

Organizing a PopText stack

This program is most commonly used to provide context-sensitive help. Help can be best demonstrated from the Turbo Pascal Menubar. Wherever you are in the menubar, pressing F1 gives you help on that subject; the helpfile is indexed so that it calls up the exact heading needed. PopText is also popularly used as a deck. The *deck* is used when necessary to show the user a large amount of facts in small bits. You merely start at the top and browse through the cards at your leisure. Vast amounts of data can be provided through the deck.

Context-sensitive help

Context-sensitive help can be provided when a program is able to recognize what block of information is required to deliver to the user and automatically selects the appropriate card from the deck.

Example: You have six menus with 4 to 9 options on each menu. You want to maintain expandability to up to 9 items on each menu. (Menus should never have more that 9 items. If you are building larger menus, consider breaking them up.) The menus are all arranged by Topic. Pressing F1 at a Menu Header (e.g., File Options, Compiler Options, Run, Edit, etc.) will call the card 10 times the menu number. On the menu choices, pressing F1 will call 10 times the menu number plus the number of the choice. In this way, the cards are indexed automatically by topic and easy to manipulate. Should further information be needed past the first card of each topic, it would then LINK to a card further away.

Random-access deck

Random-access decks are most useful for teaching and outlines. In addition to context-sensitive help, Turbo Pascal also has a random-access deck that is called by pressing F1 twice. This places the user in a very sophisticated menu where he/she can select from the topic of his choice, some of these choices being submenus that lead down to further topics. Because those of you who will be using PopText are Turbo Pascal users, you have the opportunity to explore the Help system yourself. Doing so will give an excellent insight into the design of random-access decks.

For example, information on various topics is stored in my stacks. On the first card, I have a list of topics where, if there are more than 15 topics, I split the options over several decks with more options. (Usually, the first cards are all topic cards, so pressing Page Down immediately gives me more topics.)

On the first menu I select the topic Cars. This moves me to a card with a list of manufacturers. I select Nissan. This moves me to a list of models. I select Sentra. I am now looking at a card with information on the Nissan Sentra. In this manner, I can arrange all my data.

The help menu that comes with PopText is an example of a random-access stack. It is very detailed—perhaps more detailed than would be appropriate for most programs. When designing a stack like this, remember to inform the user of the proper way to move about the stack.

It is quite possible to combine a context-sensitive stack directly into a random-access stack. The random-access stack must eventually dig into the context-sensitive data as its final results.

Including PopText in your programs

If you are a Turbo Pascal user, you are ready to go. Simply add the statement

```
Uses Hyperhlp;
```

to your program. There are several requirements, however:

- You must call function `OpenHelpFile(S:String):Integer;`.
- Any time you want to use the help system, simply invoke the procedure `PopTextCard(NUM:BYTE);`, where num is the card number you want to begin on.
- If Openhelpfile returns a nonzero result, then either PopText was unable to find the file, or the file is bad.
- On exit, it is always wise to call the function `CloseHelpFile:integer;`
- At compile time, you must have these units available in the UNit directory or current drive:

> Keynames
> Screenio
> HLPFW
> HelpDef
> Hyperhlp

Using PopRes

PopRes is designed for those who do not have Turbo Pascal. Nearly every language enables the user access to the 8088's built-in interrupt functions. PopRes is a memory-resident program that traps a normally unused interrupt vector (6EH) and causes it to act just like unit HYPERHLP (in fact, it is the HYPERHLP unit with some surrounding code). Load PopRes before loading the program calling the PopText routines.

Note: Do not use these interrupt vectors if PopRes.EXE is not installed. If you do, your system will halt.

The PopRes routines are summarized here. You should exercise caution if you are not familiar with the use of Interrupts.

> INT 6EH — PopRes
>
> AH = 0 PopTextCard
>   Entry conditions: AH = 0
>   AL = Window to use.
>   Exit conditions: None

Activates the Help window beginning with card number Al. Control is passed back to the caller when user escapes help.

AH = 1 OPENHELPFILE
Entry conditions: Ah = 1
DS:DX = pointer to an ASCII Z string with filename
of helpfile.
Exit conditions
Al = 0 no error
Al = 1 file not found.

Prepares the help window by assigning a filevar. Required preparatory routine before calling PopTextCard.

AH = 2 Closehelpfile
Entry conditions: AH = 2
Exit conditions: None

Closes Help file and de-initializes Openhelpfile. Useful for changing help files.

A sample program using PopRes is included called ZHLP.ASM. For your convenience it has already been assembled, but you may alter it if you want and experiment with it.

PopText Files

These files are included on the PopText distribution disk:

HELPDEF.TPU	Definition of the POPTXT card
POPTX.EXE	The PopText editor
HYPERDOC.DOC	Documentation
HYPERHLP.DOC	Interface for HYPERHLP.TPU
HYPERHLP.TPU	Unit to include in your program
HYPFW.DOC	Interface for HYPFW.TPU
HYPFW.TPU	FAST screen write routines
KEYNAMES.TPU	Names of all keys
KEYNAMES.PAS	Source code for Keynames
POPRES.EXE	Memory-Resident INT 6EH version
POPTEXT.HLP	A sample of a stack, with some docs
SCREENIO.DOC	Interface to Screenio.TPU
SCREENIO.TPU	Advanced windowing and Keyboard routines
THLP.EXE	Example program
THLP.PAS	Example program source code
TSRDEMO.ASM	Example using PopRes—source code
TSRDEMO.EXE	Example using PopRes
POPTXT21.ARC	PopText units for Turbo Pascal 4.0
POPTXT22.ARC	PopText units for Turbo Pascal 5.5

Registration

By registering your copy of PopText, you will be entitled to the latest version of the program, plus one upgrade. Registered users may purchase the source code for PopText for an additional $50.00. This source code may be modified and distributed in your executable files but not in source form. Information on purchasing PopText source will be sent to registered users.

To register, send $25.00 to

Tone Zone Computing
Rt 2, TP 13
Bishop, CA 93514

15
Technojock's Turbo Toolkit

Program title   Technojock's Turbo Toolkit   *(Disk 1651)*

Special requirements   Turbo Pascal 4.0 (or greater), or Quick Pascal. See this chapter for more details.

TechnoJock's Turbo Toolkit software is a collection of procedures and functions for Turbo Pascal programmers. The Toolkit will reduce the time taken to write applications and is designed for novice and expert programmer alike.

The real purpose of the Toolkit is to provide easy-to-implement procedures that free the programmer from the more tedious and repetitive programming chores such as windows, menus, user input, string formatting, directory listing, etc. The programmer (or "software engineer," if you are from California!) then can concentrate on the main purpose of the program. The full value of the Toolkit is not limited to saving the programmer time. The final program will have a consistent easy-to-use interface, imparting a professional quality to the program.

The Toolkit is designed specifically to operate with Turbo Pascal 5.0 and 4.0 from Borland International. The full source code for all of the Toolkit is included so that the code may be reviewed and modified.

The quickest way of gaining an appreciation of the Toolkit's capabilities is to execute the program DEMOTTT.EXE. This program demonstrates most of the procedures and functions available. The demo itself was, of course, written with the Toolkit.

How to use the Toolkit

This discussion, of course, assumes that you have a basic knowledge of Borland's Turbo Pascal and understand the concepts of units. If you are new to Turbo Pascal, read the chapter "Units and Related Mysteries" in the *Turbo Pascal User's Guide* (page 65 in v5.0, page 61 in v4.0).

It is not necessary to understand the internal workings of any of the Toolkit units in order to use them—all you need to know is how to call the procedures and functions.

Example 1

The technique is best illustrated with an example. The unit FastTTT5 contains procedure called Box used for (what else?) drawing boxes. A somewhat primitive program that draws a box on the screen is as follows:

```
Program Toolkit_Demo;
Uses FastTTT5;

Begin
   Box(1,1,80,25,15,4,1);
End.
```

You only need to know what unit contains the procedure Box, as well as the syntax of the Box procedure. That's all there is to it—no need to worry about drawing horizontal and vertical lines, or what the ASCII codes are for the box corners, etc.

Example 2

Example 1 is useful to illustrate the most basic concept of the toolkit, but how often will you write five line programs? More typically, you will want to use procedures and functions from a variety of the Toolkit units. All you must do is use all the units containing the relevant procedures. For example, let's say we want to expand the previous program to draw a filled box and then write the date in a neat (!) format at the top of the screen:

```
Program Improved_Toolkit_Demo;
Uses FastTTT5, MiscTTT5;

Begin
   FBox(1,1,80,25,15,4,1);
   WriteCenter(2,14,4,Date);
End.
```

The FBox and WriteCenter procedures are in the FastTTT5 unit, and the Date function is in the MiscTTT5 unit.

Required software and hardware

The Toolkit is designed to work with v5.0 or v4.0 of Borland International's Turbo Pascal compiler for the IBM PC. To compile programs developed using the Toolkit, you will need Turbo Pascal (v4.0 or greater), as well as MS-DOS or PC-DOS (v2.0 or greater).

Programs developed with the Toolkit will function on the same hardware as specified in the Turbo Pascal compiler documentation (i.e., IBM PC, XT, AT, PS/2, and true compatibles). Any of the standard display adapters are supported, including the monochrome, CGA, EGA, and VGA. The Toolkit automatically supports a Microsoft (or true compatible) mouse. If the system does not have a mouse, no problem—the mouse features are ignored. (In other words, if you develop a program using the Toolkit, it can be run on machines with or without a mouse.)

Toolkit files

These files are included with Technojock's Turbo Toolkit:

FASTTTT5.PAS	Pascal source for the FastTTT5 unit
FASTTTT5.OBJ	Assembler object file for the FastTTT5 unit
WINTTT5.PAS	Pascal source for the WinTTT5 unit
WINTTT5.OBJ	Assembler object file for the WinTTT5 unit
KEYTTT5.PAS	Pascal source for the KeyTTT5 unit
MENUTTT5.PAS	Pascal source for the MenuTTT5 unit
PULLTTT5.PAS	Pascal source for the PullTTT5 unit
NESTTTT5.PAS	Pascal source for the NestTTT5 unit
LISTTTT5.PAS	Pascal source for the ListTTT5 unit
DIRTTT5.PAS	Pascal source for the DirTTT5 unit
READTTT5.PAS	Pascal source for the ReadTTT5 unit
IOTTT5.PAS	Pascal source for the IOTTT5 unit
STRNTTT5.PAS	Pascal source for the StrnTTT5 unit
MISCTTT5.PAS	Pascal source for the MiscTTT5 unit
READ.ME	Latest information about the Toolkit
TTT.MAK	A make file for all the units in the Toolkit
FASTTTT5.ASM	Assembler source for the FASTTTT5.OBJ file
WINTTT5.ASM	Assembler source for the WINTTT5.OBJ file
DEMO5.ARC	Demonstration files for Turbo 5.0 users
DEMO4.ARC	Demonstration files for Turbo 4.0 users
ARCX.COM	A utility file to de-archive the ARC files
BUILDTTT.PAS	A program to build the TPU files

Installation

First, you must create a subdirectory called TTT (or whatever you choose) below the compiler directory. Assuming your compiler is in a directory called TURBO, the commands would be as follows:

```
C:
MD \ TURBO \ TTT
CD \ TURBO \ TTT
```

Now place each of the disks into drive A and type the following command:

```
COPY A:*.* C: \ TURBO \ TTT
```

Put the master diskettes away in a safe place.

There are two sets of demonstration files—one for Turbo 5 users, and one for Turbo 4 users. The sets are very similar and differ only in minor ways. Next, you must extract the source code from the relevant ARC file (i.e., DEMO5.ARC or DEMO4.ARC) by using the ARCX.COM program included on the disk. For example,

```
ARCX TURBO4
```

or

```
ARCX TURBO5
```

(depending on which version you chose).

The Manual.Arc file contains an abridged version of the User Manual and is included on the diskette so that nonregistered users can evaluate the Toolkit. You will not need to keep the manual file on the hard disk. Therefore, all the arc files can be deleted from the fixed disk; type

```
DEL *.ARC
```

To save space, the Toolkit does not include the compiled TPU files. The compiler will automatically compile any required units when you build your first program. However, all the units can be recompiled using one of the following methods:

1. If you are familiar with the MAKE utility, execute the TTT.MAK file:

    ```
    MAKE -fTTT.MAK
    ```

2. Compile the program BUILDTTT.PAS or use the BUILD compiler option. This program forces the compiler to build all the TPU's. Some of the units are available in two versions; a compact unit that doesn't contain all the features but has a reduced program size, and a full featured unit. The desired version is controlled through the use of compiler directives. Instructions are included at the top of the BUILDTTT.PAS file.

Toolkit concepts

The Toolkit has been designed to be both flexible and easy to use. One of the major design criteria was to minimize the complexity of the Toolkit.

Accordingly, the number of parameters passed to each procedure has been kept to a minimum. The designers didn't want you to learn a whole new philosophy just to use the Toolkit in your programs.

Part of the flexibility has been attained through the use of global variables controlling the look and feel of many of the units. For example, the ReadTTT5 unit includes a global variable RTTT that controls the display colors, whether the user can escape, if the user is initially in input mode or overtype mode, etc. The Toolkit sets RTTT to some default values. If you prefer to use alternate settings, just change the relevant element of RTTT, like this:

```
Var Name : string;
Begin
  With RTTT Do
   begin
     Insert := False;
     WhiteSpace := ' ';
     RightJustify := True;
   end;
  Read_String( 10,5,30,'Enter Your Name ',2,Name );
End;
```

The Toolkit default settings can be automatically restored by executing the unit's Default_Settings procedure, like this:

```
READTTT5.Default_Settings;
```

The following units include global variables:

DirTTT5	DTTT
ListTTT5	LTTT
NestTTT5	NTTT
PullTTT5	PTTT
ReadTTT5	RTTT

Many of the procedures are designed to write text to the screen. The FastTTT5 unit includes a string type of StrScreen set to an 80-character string. The Turbo Pascal compiler expects these procedures to be passed only strings of exactly the same type. Sometimes, when a different string type is used, the compiler will halt and issue the message "Error 26: Type Mismatch." You do not need to change all the string types in your program to type StrScreen. Just place the following compiler directive at the top of your program:

```
{$V-}
```

This directive turns off string type checking.

User hooks

The Toolkit provides user hooks to allow the programmer to hook into the heart of the Toolkit units and customize the program. A *user hook* is basically a programmer-defined procedure called by a Toolkit unit every time a particular event occurs. For example, a programmer's procedure can be called every time a key is pressed. This hooked procedure is passed the character pressed by the user. The hooked procedure can call other procedures and can even modify the key that was pressed before returning control back to the Toolkit.

The hooks provide a mechanism to customize the Toolkit functionality without modifying the Toolkit source code.

The following units include user hooks:

KeyTTT5
MenuTTT5
PullTTT5
NestTTT5
ListTTT5
IOTTT5

Conditional compilation

Some of the units can be used in one of two modes; full featured or fewer features with smaller program size. The three units that provide the two modes are KeyTTT5, DirTTT5, and IOTTT5.

The programmer can control the mode through the use of compiler directives. Turbo Pascal's conditional compiler directives allow you to produce different code from the same source text, based on three conditional symbols: K_FULL, DIRFULL, and IOFULL (respectively).

By default, the Toolkit uses these units in their slim form. To recompile the units in their full form, use the /D switch on the command-line compiler or the menu command O/C/Conditional Defines in the integrated environment.

Once the appropriate conditional defines have been set, BUILD the program. This will force the TPUs to be recompiled. The compiler directives do not need to be set every time you compile your program, only when you want to change the units from their current state.

Registration

Registration for a copy of TechnoJock's Turbo Toolkit costs $49.95. Simply contact this address:

TechnoJock Software, Inc.
P.O. Box 820927
Houston, TX 77282
(713) 493-6354
CompuServe ID: 74017,227

16
ProStall

Program title   ProStall   *(Disk 1765)*

Special requirements   Two dual-sided diskette drives, or one diskette drive and a hard disk (highly recommended) with at least 525K disk space.

ProStall is an application installation program designed for programmers who demand maximum end-user friendliness and ease of use. This program can handle all of your application installations. ProStall includes the following features:

- automatic context-sensitive help on every field
- the purchasing company name "typed in" automatically on the main install screen
- any message the purchasing company wants to display on the ending screen
- checking for maximum DOS limits on PATH statement and various other DOS checks
- the option to specify all default settings at time of purchase

The end user has the option to accept or change the following default settings:

- which drive to install from
- which drive to install to
- which directory and/or subdirectory to install IN
- whether to add path statement or not
- whether to change buffer statement or not
- whether to change file statement or not

Installing ProStall on your hard disk

To install ProStall on your hard disk, let ProStall install itself. This is a good way to see how the program will work for your application. ProStall takes approximately 525K space on the hard disk, so be sure there is enough room. Insert Disk 1 in drive A or B and then type

    INSTALL

View the README.DOC when asked, if you haven't already. Answer all the questions on the install screen and let ProStall do the rest. When prompted to remove "Installation disk and insert Disk 1," leave Disk 1 in drive and press the Enter key. When prompted, insert Disk 2 and then press the Enter key.

Installing ProStall on a two-diskette drive

Make two disks—an INSTALL disk and a PI disk—by copying the files as shown next. The INSTALL diskette should contain the following files:

    INSTALL.EXE
    ISDC.HLP
    ISDC.DAT
    ISDC.K01
    README.DOC

The PI diskette should contain the following files:

    PI.EXE
    ISDC.HLP
    ISDC.DAT
    ISDC.K01

The file ISDC.HLP is the on-line context-sensitive help file. It is included in both disks because it is used by both the INSTALL.EXE and PI.EXE programs.

These files will be copied from PI diskette to the INSTALL diskette when data is inputted (i.e., set up by you with the PI program).

The original README.DOC file from Input Software Development Co. should be replaced for your own README.DOC. The INSTALL.EXE program will look for this file at the beginning of the install process.

For proper use of the ProStall program on a two-diskette system, see "Running on a two-diskette system."

System files

Here is a short breakdown of the system files included with ProStall:

PI.EXE is the program you will use to input data to the ISDC.DAT and ISDC.K01 files to set up the installation process. This file should NOT be sent to your customer.

INSTALL.EXE is the main install program that your customer will use to install your application.

ISDC.DAT is the data file that contains all the information necessary for the installation to take place. This file is set up with the PI.EXE program.

ISDC.K01 is a Key file for the above data file. For ISDC.DAT to work properly, this file must be present.

ISDC.HLP is the "help" file containing the on-line context-sensitive help for both the INSTALL.EXE and PI.EXE programs.

README.DOC should be read *before* the installation takes place. You should substitute your own README.DOC to relay information to your users.

Running the program from a hard disk

To run the program from a hard disk,

1. Log on to the drive and directory that contains the ProStall program.

2. Type

    PI

    at the DOS prompt.

3. The first screen is a "welcome" screen from Input Software Development Co. Read this screen and then press the Enter key.

4. The next screen, shown in FIG. 16-1, is a scrolling table containing the data necessary to make ProStall self-installing.

5. Press the F1 key to bring up the help screen and read it through. It contains necessary information on the keys used in this program. Press the F5 key to Empty the current database.

6. Figure 16-2 shows a Form screen that will appear on the lower right side of the table, along with an automatic pop-up help screen above the Form.

7. The message area in the Form will be telling you that the "Record Will Be ADDED."

8. The first prompt is for the diskette number. Start with any number you want to assign the disk that you will be sending your application out on (although the normal number to start is 01).

9. The next prompt is asking for the name of the file. Enter the *name* only, not the *extension*.

10. The next prompt is asking for the *extension* of the file. Enter the *extension* only. When you press Enter in this field, the Form will go

16-1 The scrolling table containing the names of the files to be installed.

16-2 Pressing F5 will clear the table and allow you to create a new one.

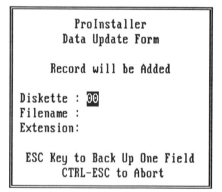

away. The table will show the data that you have entered (see FIG. 16-3 and FIG. 16-4).

11. To enter more files, press the Insert key to bring up the Form screen. Continue this until you have all the data you need to complete the installation.

12. *Important:* Pay attention to the *diskette number* you assign the files. The INSTALL program will read this data and look for the records on that *diskette number only.* If it cannot find the records, the program will inform the user and *abort.*

ProInstaller
Data Table

16-3 Type the disk number, filename, and extension in the form screen.

ProInstaller
Data Update Form

Record will be Added

Diskette : 01
Filename : OURAPP
Extension: EXE

ESC Key to Back Up One Field
CTRL-ESC to Abort

ProInstaller
Data Table

01   OURAPP   EXE

ESC Key Go to DOS
F1 for HELP

16-4 Your file will then be added to the table. Press the insert key to add another file.

13. To make the Installation Diskette that you will be sending with your application, copy the following files to a blank formatted diskette:

INSTALL.EXE
ISDC.HLP
ISDC.DAT
ISDC.K01
README.DOC

README.DOC can be any README.DOC that you want shown in the INSTALL program. It must be named README.DOC and be any legal ASCII text file.

This is the minimum number of files necessary for the INSTALL program to work. Other .DOC files can be included, but they will not be installed on the hard disk. If you want the other .DOC files installed, then include them on the other disks. Be sure to list them in the ISDC.DAT file.

Your installation system is now complete.

Registration

ProStall sells for $45.00, which covers

- ☐ Phone support
- ☐ Notification of future updates
- ☐ Shipping and handling
- ☐ A 30-day money-back guarantee

To purchase or obtain information on ProStall, call or write:

Input Software Development Co.
820 S. Walnut
Sidney, OH 45365
(513) 498-1859

17
TesSeRact

Program title   TesSeRact   *(Disk 1491)*

Special requirements   Turbo C 1.5, Turbo Pascal 4.0, Microsoft C 5.0 or
5.1, Microsoft's Macro Assembler 5.0 or 5.1, or OPTASM 1.0.

TesSeRact consists of two major parts: a library of routines (.LIB, .OBJ,
.TPU files) that allow a developer to write ram-resident or TSR (Terminate
and Stay Resident) programs; and a set of functions that attempts to
standardize communication with and between TSR-type programs.
    The TesSeRact functions and routines are listed here:

External functions
TsrMain	Entry point for popup routine
TsrBackCheck	Check to see if background processing is requested
TsrBackProc	Background processing procedure
TsrTimerProc	Periodic timer procedure
TsrUserProc	Interface for external processing
TsrCleanUp	Initialize or clean up TSR

TesSeRact library routines
TsDoInit	Initializes variables and goes resident
TsSetStack	Sets stacks to be used by resident routines
TsCheckResident	Determine if program has been loaded
TsVerify2F	Verify Interrupt 2Fh has valid handler
TessBeep	Call TesSeRact internal beep routine

TesSeRact multiplex functions

Initialization and information routines
    Check Install
    TsGetParms( )
    TsCheckHotkey( )
    TsSetUser24( )
    TsGetData( )
    TsSetExtraHot( )

TSR manipulation and status routines
    TsEnable( )
    TsDisable( )
    TsRelease( )
    TsRestart( )
    TsGetStat( )
    TsSetStat( )
    TsGetPopType( )

TSR utility routines
    TsCallUserProc( )
    TsStuffKeyboard( )

The TesSeRact libraries and modules allow developers to write ram-resident programs with little or no knowledge of the arcane art of disassembling DOS, something that has been sorely lacking for some time. Among the features provided are easy use of hotkeys, simple ram-resident routines, coresident functions, and cross-routine communication facilities. These libraries and modules provided with the TesSeRact package have been tested with Turbo C 1.5, Turbo Pascal 4.0, Microsoft C 5.0 and 5.1, Microsoft's Macro Assembler 5.0 and 5.1, and OPTASM 1.0. Also note that these routines work on the Heath/Zenith Z-100 computer (using the ZPC Hardware Modifications), with the exception of the keyboard stuff routines. This is mentioned because this computer is used extensively by government offices and is generally considered only marginally compatible.

The TesSeRact Standard for Ram-Resident Program Communication is a group of functions latched onto DOS' own Interrupt 2Fh (Multiplex). DOS uses this interrupt to communicate with its own TSRs (PRINT.COM, ASSIGN.COM, and SHARE.COM), and the TesSeRact Development Team felt it was appropriate to service TSR programs using the same interface. These functions are all accessed by generating an Interrupt 2Fh, with AX = 5453 (hex). Programs can call these multiplex functions directly or can use the functions provided in the TESS.LIB or TESS-TP.TPU modules (the assembler version of TesSeRact does not include callable functions for the Multiplex operations).

If you've never written a TSR

Writing TSR or ram-resident programs is not for the beginner, nor is it for the faint of heart. Without a product such as TesSeRact, a programmer can expect to spend a minimum of six months learning how to deal with such things as a non-reentrant operating system, hardware specifics, BIOS bugs, and more. And all this has nothing to do with writing the actual application—this work will be necessary if a resident program attempts to do any DOS or BIOS calls from within the resident program.

In developing TesSeRact and in the writing of this manual, the TesSeRact development team has made certain assumptions concerning the level of developer experience. We have assumed that developers using this product have some knowledge of the problems associated with developing resident programs. Note that it is not necessary to have this background; without it, however, certain statements will be difficult to comprehend.

Writing resident programs, in general, requires a basic understanding of both documented and undocumented DOS functions. This documentation does not attempt to detail the undocumented functions; other material provided by the TesSeRact Development Team might, at some future point, include such information.

The undocumented functions used by the TesSeRact Library routines have been documented, in some form, by Microsoft in various publications; the MS-DOS Encyclopedia in particular has about the most complete discussion on resident programs available. It is not 100% complete, and omits some facts and observations discovered by some developers, but it's the best.

The best way to learn about TSRs, in general, is to study working code. Books and articles are nice but generally omit information because of space limitations or the complexity of the subject. By combining the code for the demonstration programs along with the source code for the TesSeRact Library itself, a developer might learn more than he/she ever wanted to know about resident programming and DOS itself.

A note about DOS versions

TesSeRact has been tested on a wide variety of DOS versions, ranging in number from 2.0 to 3.3. It is important to note that Microsoft changed their OEM licensing agreements between DOS 2.x and 3.x. OEM versions of DOS 3.x must maintain certain data areas and undocumented functions in order to provide compatibility with the networking features of the operating system. For this reason, resident programs will be much more reliable when operating under DOS 3.x.

The code needed to support DOS 2.x in the TesSeRact library amounts to less than 50 bytes; this deals with known bugs and deficiencies. For this reason, support for DOS 2.x was left in; however, some OEMs might have changed some things vital to the correct functioning of a TesSeRact TSR. If this situation comes up, please contact the TesSeRact Development Team.

TesSeRact data structures and variables

A quick note about graphics modes

Although TesSeRact does not support changing video modes for resident programs (with one exception described later), there are three functions TesSeRact *does* provide to simplify how a TSR interfaces with the multitude of graphics cards available.

First, a developer can specify NOPOPGRAPH (see later) as one of the parameters to `TsDoInit( )`. This forces the TesSeRact popup routines to check to see if the current video mode is 0, 1, 2, 3, or 7. If the video mode returned by Interrupt 10h is not equal to the five standard "text modes," then TesSeRact will issue a `TessBeep( )` function call and return.

The second feature TesSeRact provides is detection of Hercules graphics modes. If the video mode returned by Interrupt 10h is 7, a check is also made for the presence of a Hercules Graphics Card (or compatible) adapter. If the HGC is present and the current mode (using routines supplied by Hercules) is graphics, the TesSeRact routines will issue a `Tess-Beep( )` function call and return to the underlying application, just as if an invalid video mode was detected.

There is one exception to this rule. If NOPOPGRAPH is specified and a graphics mode is detected, a special flag is checked to determine if the underlying application is Microsoft Word 4.0. If it is, TesSeRact sends an Alt-F9 character to the keyboard buffer and returns, causing Word to switch into text mode if possible. TesSeRact then delays a full two seconds and pops up. If Word was unable to switch to text mode (using high-resolution graphics mode on a Herc card, for example), TesSeRact beeps and returns.

The third and final provision TesSeRact makes for graphics modes is by setting two variables on popup: _TESS_VIDPAGE and _TESS_VID-MODE. These variables (one byte each) are set to the values returned by the Interrupt 10h call to get the video mode. If a Hercules card is detected and is in graphics mode, then both of these variables are set to 0FFh.

TesSeRact data structures

Four primary data structures are used by the TesSeRact library routines: `TsrIntTable`, `ExtraHot`, `TsrData`, and `TsrParms`. Each is described here in detail. Note these structures are shown in C language style (from TESS.H). TESS.INC (for assembler) and TESS.TP4 (for Turbo Pascal) have descriptions of these structures for use with other languages.

TsrIntTable The `TsrIntTable` structure shown in FIG. 17-1 is used internally by the two TesSeRact functions __TESSSETUPINTS and __TESSRESTOREINTS. These functions are used to save/restore the interrupt vectors TesSeRact uses. All occurrences of this structure are inside the TsrData structure described later.

```
struct TsrIntTable {
    void far * OldVector;        /* Old Interrupt Vector       */
    unsigned char IntNumber;     /* Interrupt Number           */
    void near * NewVector;       /* offset of new vector       */
};
```

17-1 TseIntTable structure.

ExtraHot The ExtraHot structure used by the TsSetExtraHot() function is shown in FIG. 17-2. This data area is stored within the USER data area, and the TesSeRact interrupt handlers only reference this information through a FAR pointer, stored in the TsrParms structure. Please note that the FlagByte may not be zero—that value is reserved for the PRIMARY hotkey combination, which is set up by the call to TsDoInit().

```
struct ExtraHot {
    unsigned char Hotkey;        /* hotkey to check for         */
    unsigned char ShiftState;    /* shift state for this hot key */
    unsigned char FlagByte;      /* flag value to use           */
                                 /*   MAY NOT BE ZERO!!!        */
};
```

17-2 ExtraHot structure.

TsrData The TsrData structure holds virtually all the data used by TesSeRact. For the most part, none of these should be modified by an application program (see FIG. 17-3).

RevLvl is always 1 for this release of TesSeRact. PopupType stores the current state of the INDOS flag when the _TESSDOPOPUP routine is called. Just about the only time this flag is set on entry to TsrMain() is when sitting at the DOS prompt. Some TSRs must react differently in this case (such as TSRs spawning other applications), so this information is made available.

The WasInt8 and WasInt13 bytes can be used to detect if a timer tick or a disk interrupt occurred. The TesSeRact interrupt routines only SET these flags—they never clear them—so use of the flags is totally up to the individual program developer. (See the TESSPARK assembler demonstration program for possible uses for these flags.)

IntFlags and SoftFlags are used by the TesSeRact routines to determine which interrupts are currently being executed (see definitions for these values in the section on ''Equates'' later). They should never be modified by an application program.

DosVersion stores the current MAJOR version of DOS (2, 3, etc.). Waitcount is used internally by the popup routines to delay if INDOS is set—some programs call DOS in their own Idle loop, and the delay used by TesSeRact (eight timer ticks) appears to be sufficient to ensure popup.

```
struct TsrData {                        /* PUBLIC Symbol TESS_GLOBALS      */
    unsigned char RevLvl;               /* Revision Level of TESS Lib      */
    unsigned char PopupType;            /* Type of popup in effect         */
    unsigned char WasInt8;              /* An Interrupt 08h occurred       */
    unsigned char WasInt13;             /* An Interrupt 13h occurred       */
    unsigned char IntFlags;             /* Which interrupts are active     */
    unsigned char SoftFlags;            /* Which soft ints are active      */
    unsigned char DosVersion;           /* Current major revision of DOS   */
    unsigned char waitcount;            /* Count to wait before popping up */
    void far * InDosFlag;               /* Pointer to DOS INDOS flag       */
    void far * DosCritErr;              /* Pointer to DOS Critical Error   */
    unsigned short UserPSP;             /* PSP segment of user program     */
    unsigned short User28PSP;           /* PSP segment of user program     */
    void far * UserDTA;                 /* DTA of interrupted program      */
    void far * User28DTA;               /* DTA of interrupted program      */
    unsigned short UserSS;              /* Stack segment of user program   */
    unsigned short UserSP;              /* Stack pointer of user program   */
    unsigned short User28SS;            /* Stack segment of user program   */
    unsigned short User28SP;            /* Stack pointer of user program   */
    void far * UserInt24;               /* Pointer to use INT 24 handler   */
    unsigned short OldExtErr[3];        /* Storage for old DOS 3 extended  */
                                        /*      error information          */
    unsigned char OldBreak;             /* Old Break Setting               */
    unsigned char OldVerify;            /* Old Verify Setting              */
    unsigned char InWord4;              /* Flag to indicate in WORD 4.0    */
    unsigned char WasWord4;             /* Word 4 special popup flag        */
    unsigned char NewKbdFlag;           /* Enhanced Keyboard Call in use   */
    unsigned char Word4Delay;           /* Delay for Word 4                */
        /* Interrupt vector tables        */
    struct TsrIntTable Int8;
    struct TsrIntTable Int9;
    struct TsrIntTable Int13;
    struct TsrIntTable Int16;
    struct TsrIntTable Int1C;
    struct TsrIntTable Int21;
    struct TsrIntTable Int28;
    struct TsrIntTable Int2F;
    struct TsrIntTable Int1B;
    struct TsrIntTable Int23;
    struct TsrIntTable Int24;
    };
```

17-3 TsrData structure.

The next two pointers, InDosFlag and DosCritErr, point to data areas inside DOS. The INDOS flag is a byte signifying whether an Interrupt 21h function is active; and the Critical Error is normally zero, unless DOS is currently servicing an Interrupt 24h (critical error) request.

Next comes a number of storage areas that are fairly self-explanatory. The variables with "28" in their names are used by the background procedures, and the others are used by the popup procedures.

UserInt24 is a far pointer (normally set to 0) to a user-defined Interrupt 24h handler. This value is set when a user calls the TsSetUser24() function (TesSeRact Multiplex Function 03h).

The OldExtErr, OldBreak, and OldVerify areas are used to store information during popup; and the InWord4, WasWord4, and Word4Delay variables are used by the popup routines for the special graphics "flip" described earlier. The NewKbdFlag variable is generally 0—however, if an application program calls one of the "extended" keyboard functions (Interrupt 16h, Functions 10h, 11h or 12h), this byte gets set to 10h during the interrupt call.

At the end of this structure are the interrupt tables used by TesSeRact routines.

TsrParms The `TsrParms` structure is used to store information about the TSR necessary for hotkey detection and popup control. All of the information in this structure is placed there by the TesSeRact initialization routines—users should not directly write into this area except under controlled circumstances and under *very* controlled conditions. For the most part, these variables are self-explanatory, but some comments are in order. (See FIG. 17-4.)

```
struct TsrParms {                       /* PUBLIC Symbol TESS_USERPARMS    */
   char IdCode[8];                      /* Unique TSR Identification String*/
                                        /* NOTE -- NOT NULL-TERMINATED     */
   unsigned short IdNum;                /* Unique TSR Identification Number*/
   unsigned long FuncFlags;             /* Bit map of supported functions  */
   unsigned char HotKey;                /* Hotkey used by TSR for popup     */
   unsigned char ShiftState;            /* ShiftState used by this TSR pop  */
   unsigned char HotKeyFlag;            /* Which hotkey is in use           */
   unsigned char ExtraHotCount;         /* Number of Extra Hotkeys to use   */
   void far * ExtraHotKeys;             /* Pointer to extra hotkeys         */
   unsigned short TsrStatus;            /* Current TSR Status Flags         */
   unsigned short TsrPSP;               /* TSR's PSP Segment                */
   void far * TsrDTA;                   /* Pointer to TSR's DTA region      */
   unsigned short TsrDSeg;              /* TSR's Default Data Segment       */
   void far * PopupStack;               /* Pointer to Popup Stack Area      */
   void far * BackStack;                /* Pointer to Background Stack      */
   };
```

17-4 `TsrParms` structure with comments.

The `IdCode` area is eight bytes long—with no null-terminator required and no length byte (as used by Pascal). Eight bytes are copied from the string passed during `TsCheckResident( )`. *It is absolutely vital that the identification string be padded to a minimum of eight bytes*; if the identification string is less than eight bytes, your TSR will not be able to find itself in memory. Please note that the `IdNum` is assigned based on the number of other TesSeRact-aware programs currently installed in the system.

`FuncFlags` is a bit-mapped, four-byte variable describing which Tes-SeRact Multiplex Functions are supported by this TSR. For all programs written using the TesSeRact library, this is (hex) FFFFFFFF. Developers of programs supporting the TesSeRact standard should use this double-word to identify which Multiplex functions they support (for more details, see "Writing TesSeRact-compatible programs").

`HotKey` and `ShiftState` are used in combination to determine when the program should call `TsrMain( )`. If your program does not use a popup, set both of these values to Hex 0FFh on the call to `TsDoInit( )`. Do not set `HotKey` to *zero*—this signifies that the program is to pop up when the current shift states match the value of `ShiftState`, without checking for a hotkey value.

The correct value for `HotKey` is the Scan Code (listed in Appendix B) of the key—not the value returned by Interrupt 16h.

The `HotKeyFlag` byte can be used by a program to determine which hotkey the user hit (if extra keys are set with `TsSetExtraHot( )`). This value is *zero* if the primary hotkey was used; otherwise, this is set to the `FlagByte` specified for the appropriate hotkey in the `ExtraHotKeys` array.

The `ExtraHotCount` tells TesSeRact how many "extra" hotkeys are used. These hotkeys are stored in an array of `ExtraHot` structures; `TsSetExtraHot()` receives a pointer to this array, and stores it here.

The `TsrStatus` flag word is a bit-mapped value described in more detail in the description of the various equates below.

Other public, global variables

The variables shown in FIG. 17-5 are other public symbols available. The `newint` variables point to TesSeRact's interrupt handlers. `_TESS_END OFDATA` is the end of TesSeRact's internal data, and the beginning of the copyright notice. `_TESS_CPYRT` is a pointer to the second part of the copyright notice.

```
newint??                /* TesSeRact Interrupt Vectors    */
_TESS_ENDOFDATA         /* Top of TesSeRact Data Area     */
                        /* Beginning of Copyright Notice  */
_TESS_CPYRT             /* Second Part of Copyright Notice */
_TESS_VIDMODE           /* Video Mode when TsrMain() called*/
_TESS_VIDPAGE           /* Video Page when TsrMain() called*/
_TESS_INTERRUPTRETURN   /* Dummy 'IRET' instruction        */
_TESS_ERROR24           /* Interrupt 24h Error Code        */
_TESS_TEMPPARMS         /* Temporary Data Storage Location */
```

17-5   Other available PUBLIC symbols.

_TESS_VIDMODE and _TESS_VIDPAGE are used to store the current video mode information on entry to `TsrMain()` and are described in more detail earlier.

_TESS_INTERRUPTRETURN is used by the POPFF macro to avoid the problems that can be caused by the infamous "popf" bug on early 80286 chips.

_TESS_ERROR24 is used by TesSeRact's default Interrupt 24h handler to store the error code passed by DOS, and _TESS_TEMPPARMS is used for some temporary data storage.

Equates and definitions

Two shift state and hotkey flags are

```
TSRHOT_??    /*   Definitions for (scan code)     */
TSRPOP???    /*   Definitions for shift state     */
```

Appendix B lists equates for various scan codes and shift states that can be used by TesSeRact programs for calling `TsDoInit()` and `TsSet-ExtraHot()`. These definitions are included in TESS.H, TESS.INC, and TESS.TP4.

TsrFlags Figure 17-6 shows the equates, described in the various include files, that are used for the `TsrFlags` parameter in the call to `TsDoInit()`. These values are bit-mapped and correspond directly to the equates described below for the bit-mapped values of `TsrStatus`.

TsrStatus The equates in FIG. 17-7 describe the bit-mapped contents of the `TsrStatus` flag word. The actual equates are described in more detail in each include file.

```
TSRUSEPOPUP              /* User Requests Popup Routine    */
TSRUSEBACK               /* User Requests Background Routine*/
TSRUSETIMER              /* User Requests Timer Routine    */
TSRUSEUSER               /* User Requests User Procedure   */
NOPOPGRAPH               /* User Requests No Pop on Graphics*/
NOPOPCOMMAND             /* User Requests No Pop if INDOS==1*/
```

17-6 `TsrFlags` structure.

```
HOTKEYON                 /* Hotkey pressed                 */
SHIFTSON                 /* Shift states match             */
TSRACTIVE                /* TSR is running in foreground    */
INT28ACTIVE              /* Background routine is active    */

POPUPSET                 /* Popup resident routine installed*/
BACKSET                  /* Background routine installed    */
TIMERSET                 /* Timer procedure installed       */
EXTRAHOTSET              /* Extra hot keys installed        */

USERPROCON               /* User-defined procedure installed*/
TSRENABLED               /* TSR currently enabled          */
TSRRELEASED              /* TSR has been released          */
EXTRAINT24               /* User installed replacement INT24*/
```

17-7 `TsrStatus` structure.

TesSeRact external functions

The routines described in this section are *required* user entry points called by the TesSeRact library routines. If you are using the TP4 Unit, the `TsSetAdrTP4` procedure must be called with appropriate flags for *every* function you intend to use. Unused functions are initialized by the Unit to point to far returns. (See "Language specifics" later for a complete description of `TsSetAdrTP4`.)

Users of the C Library should note that there are dummy functions for each of these routines in the library (users of Microsoft LINK should use the /NOE linker option)—it is only necessary to include those routines that you actually intend to use. Users of the assembler version *must* have an entry point for each of these public symbols; at a minimum, these entry points must have a near return.

TsrMain *Entry point for popup routine*

This is the main entry point for your TSR procedure. If you specify TSR USEPOPUP for the `TsrFlags` parameter, this routine is called whenever your Shift State and HotKey are pressed. (Note that if extra hotkeys are specified using the `TsSetExtraHot( )` function, the `ExtraHotCount` byte of the TsrParms data area is set to the appropriate value for the hotkey selected.) On entry to this routine, DS and ES are the default data segment for your program; all other registers are undefined. The PSP and DTA have been setup for your application, and it is safe to call any runtime library functions as long as your application uses the default stack or avoids functions with built-in stack-checking (see other discussion about stack-checking in the description of `TsSetStack( )`), as well as any DOS functions.

Note that ^C and ^Break are *completely* disabled while this routine is in action. The scan codes are intercepted by the TesSeRact Keyboard handler and prevented from ever reaching the BIOS or DOS.

Parameters
None.

Returns
None.

C usage
void far pascal TsrMain(void);

Pascal usage
{$F+} PROCEDURE TsrMain; {$F-}

Assembler usage
PUBLIC TSRMAIN
TSRMAIN proc near
ret
TSRMAIN endp

TsrBackCheck   *Check to see if background processing is requested*

This function is a simple one—and should be as small as possible. The purpose of this routine is to check appropriate status flags to determine if background processing is needed. This is user-specific, but the following guidelines should be taken into account: this routine is called when it is safe to interrupt DOS; but the stack is the DOS stack, so C runtime routines should not be used. The DS and ES registers point to your default data segment, so it is possible to access your own data; you can also call BIOS and DOS functions safely (at some point, a full list of safe DOS functions might be available—at the present time, we know of none that do *not* work here).

As mentioned above, the primary purpose of this routine is to determine if full background processing is needed. If so, a non-zero value is returned; otherwise, a value of zero is returned. If non-zero, the Tsr-BackProc( ) procedure is called immediately. TSRUSEBACK must be set for this function to be called.

Parameters
None.

Returns
Zero signals that no background processing is desired.
Non-zero results in an immediate call to `TsrBackProc`.

C Usage
`unsigned far pascal TsrBackCheck(void);`

Pascal usage
`{$F+} FUNCTION TsrBackCheck : word; {$F-}`

Assembler usage
```
PUBLIC TSRBACKCHECK
TSRBACKCHECK proc near
mov ax,word ptr ShouldProcess    ;0 if no
background, 1 for
ret                              ; background
    processing
TSRBACKCHECK endp
```

TsrBackProc   *Background processing procedure*

This function is called if `TsrBackCheck( )` returns a non-zero value. It is safe to call the C runtimes, DOS, and virtually anything you want. On entry, ES and DS point to your default data segment; you are operating on the stack you specified for background operations, the PSP and DTA are yours, and all the DOS status has been saved. Processing here can be identical to `TsrMain( )` processing, except that this interrupt occurs asynchronously rather than as the result of a hotkey.

Parameters
None.

Returns
None.

C Usage
`void far pascal TsrBackProc(void);`

Pascal usage
`{$F+} PROCEDURE TsrBackProc; {$F-}`

```
PUBLIC TSRBACKPROC
TSRBACKPROC proc near
ret
TSRBACKPROC endp
```

TsrTimerProc   *Periodic timer procedure*

This function is called approximately 18.2 times per second (unless the routine takes too long—re-entrancy is not permitted). The DS and ES registers point to your default data segment, but no other modifications are made—you are operating off of the stack that was interrupted by the Interrupt 08h Timer Tick. DOS functions and runtime functions are generally not safe, so be careful. This routine should be as small and fast as possible in order to receive the maximum number of ticks from the processor and avoid slowing down other background operations.

"Too long" is very subjective. It completely depends on the hardware being used and other factors that can hurt interrupt latency. In general, spend as little time as possible in this procedure.

Parameters
None.

Returns
None.

C Usage
```
void far pascal TsrTimerProc(void);
```

Pascal usage
```
{$F+} PROCEDURE TsrTimerProc; {$F-}
```

Assembler usage
```
PUBLIC TSRTIMERPROC
TSRTIMERPROC proc near
ret
TSRTIMERPROC endp
```

TsrUserProc   *Interface for external processing*

This function is designed to allow an external program or procedure to interface with your TSR. You receive DS (in the non-assembler version, ES=DS as well) pointing to your data segment, and SS is the background stack. If a call to `TsrBackProc()` is currently being processed when an application calls this function, the TesSeRact functions loop until the background stack is free. This is generally used for interprocess communication between applications. This routine is called when a program issues TesSeRact Multiplex Function 20h.

Note that the PSP in effect when `TsrUserProc()` is called is the PSP belonging to the CALLER, not the PSP of the TSR. Although it is safe to use DOS functions, the TSR's file handle table and other PSP data areas are not available.

Parameters
UserPtr   FAR pointer to user-defined data

Returns
None.

C Usage
```
void far pascal TsrUserProc( void far *UserPtr );
```

Pascal usage
```
{$F+} PROCEDURE TsrUserProc( UserPtr : pointer ); {$F-}
```

Assembler usage
```
PUBLIC TSRUSERPROC
TSRUSERPROC proc near
;
; ES:DI contains FAR pointer to user data
;
ret
TSRUSERPROC endp
```

TsrCleanUp   *Initialize or clean up TSR*

This function is called by the TesSeRact routines to tell the TSR that it is initializing or releasing. On entry, DS and ES is set to the correct segment, and SS:SP is set to the stack pointer *unless* it is already set correctly. (For example, the first time this routine is called—from inside `TsDoInit()`— the stack is correct and thus is not adjusted.) It is safe to call DOS from inside this routine.

The initialization portion of this procedure should be used to call "configuring" functions, such as `TsSetExtraHot()` or other TesSeRact Multiplex Functions that cannot be called until the Interrupt handlers have been installed. The shutdown procedure should be used to close any open files and call the high-level language exit procedures.

Note: TP4s exit procedures are called from within TESSTP.TPU.

Parameters
InitOrShutdown: 0 = Initialize, 1 = ShutDown

Returns
None.

C Usage
```
void far pascal TsrCleanUp(unsigned InitOrShutdown);
```

Pascal usage
{$F+} PROCEDURE TsrCleanUp (RemoveTSR:Boolean); {$F-}

Assembler usage
```
PUBLIC TSRCLEANUP
TSRCLEANUP proc near
;
; on entry, AX contains the initialize or shutdown flag
or ax,ax
jz do_init
do_release:
 ....
jmp cleanup_exit
do_init:
 ....
cleanup_exit:
ret
TSRCLEANUP    endp
```

TesSeRact library routines

The TesSeRact library routines described in here are the functions a program should call before going resident. They are presented in the order in which they should be called: TsSetStack(), TsCheckResident(), and then TsDoInit(). TsVerify2F() and TessBeep() are utility functions also included in this section.

TsSetStack   *Sets stacks to be used by resident routines*

This function tells the TesSeRact functions what data areas to use as stacks. A value of NULL for the PopUpStack parameter means to use the current (default) stack segment and stack pointer of the application that calls this function. If you use NULL for the PopUpStack, this should be the first call inside main(), and you should use as few local variables in main() as possible to allow the use of the maximum amount of stack. Do not specify a value of NULL for the BackGroundStack parameter unless you do not have a background procedure.

To use the C or Pascal runtime routines within your TSR, you should use stacks of *at least 2K*. Also, all high-level language users should note that unless the default stack is used, stack-checking will fail. Many routines in the standard runtime libraries provided with Turbo C, Microsoft C, and Turbo Pascal have been compiled with stack-checking enabled (printf() being a good example) and will *fail* unless the stack is within the limits defined by the runtime library.

The demonstration programs show sample code (using undocumented variables) of how to "split" the default stack. Please note that with

Microsoft C, you cannot directly set the size of the default stack from within the program—you must use the EXEMOD program (or the /STACK option to LINK) in order to enlarge the stack.

Parameters
PopUpStack   Pointer to stack for popup procedure.
BackGroundStack   Pointer to stack for background procedure.

Returns
None.

C Usage
```
extern void far pascal TsSetStack(
void far * PopUpStack,
void far * BackGroundStack
);
```

Pascal usage
```
procedure TsSetStack(
var PopUpStack,
BackGroundStack
);
```

Assembler usage
```
EXTRN TSSETSTACK:NEAR
mov   di,offset PopUpStack
mov   si,offset BackGroundStack
call  TSSETSTACK
```

TsCheckResident   *Determine if program has been loaded*

This function serves two primary purposes. First, it checks to make sure that the program identified by the passed IDStr has not previously been loaded. Then it begins setting up the TesSeRact data structures for this TSR, in preparation for a call to TsDoInit( ). Programs that will not go resident may either use this function call or may call the TesSeRact Multiplex Function (00h) directly.

Parameters
IDStr   Pointer to unique 8-byte identification string for this program. *All eight* bytes are significant when comparing strings!

IDNum   Pointer to WORD (two-byte) data location where returned TSR identification number will be placed.

Returns
FFFFh indicates the TSR has already been loaded and may be identified by the identification number returned in IDNum.

0 (zero) indicates the specified TSR was not found and a new TSR may be installed using the identification number returned in IDNum.

If this function returns FFFFh, and the high byte of IDNum is FFh, it signifies that the TSR has previously been loaded, but has a "release" command pending. This TSR may be restarted with the TsRe-start( ) function or TesSeRact Multiplex Function 13h.

C Usage
```
extern unsigned far pascal TsCheckResident(
char far * IDStr,
unsigned far * IDNum
);
```

Pascal usage
```
function TsCheckResident(
var IDStr,IDNum
) : word;
```

Assembler usage
```
EXTRN TSCHECKRESIDENT:NEAR
 push  cs
 pop   es
 mov   si,offset IdStr
 mov   di,offset IdNum
 call  TSRCHECKRESIDENT
 ;
 ;      result returned in AX
 ;
```

TsDoInit   *Initializes variables and goes resident*

This function initializes the TSR variables and 'goes resident' with the amount of memory you specify and initializes the flags for user routines that you specify.

Parameters

HotKey	Scan Code of Key to use as HotKey (see Appendix B).
ShiftState	Shift State to be used in combination with HotKey.
TsrFlags	Which Routines are enabled (see "TesSeRact data structures and variables").
MemoryTop	Number of 16-byte Memory Paragraphs to keep resident (in the ASM version, this is the offset of the top of program's memory that will be kept resident).

Returns

Should *never* return, unless DOS' INDOS flag or Critical Error Flag could not be found, in which case the return value is 0xFFFF.

C Usage
```
extern unsigned far pascal TsDoInit(
```

```
          unsigned char HotKey,
          unsigned char ShiftState,
          unsigned short TsrFlags,
          unsigned short MemoryTop );
```

Pascal usage
```
function TsDoInit(
HotKey,
ShiftState,
TsrFlags,
MemoryTop : word
) : word;
```

Assembler usage
```
EXTRN  TSDOINIT:NEAR
 mov   ah, HotKey
 mov   al, ShiftState
 mov   bx, TsrFlags
 mov   dx, offset MemoryTop
 call  TSDOINIT
 ;
 ;     Remember that this function ONLY returns on an
       error
 ;
```

TsVerify2F *Verify Interrupt 2Fh has valid handler*

This function is called internally by TsCheckResident() and is used to ensure that the existing Interrupt 2Fh handler is valid. This function is only needed under DOS versions 2.x—beginning with v3.0, DOS pointed this interrupt vector to an IRET instruction. It is only necessary to call this function if an application is not using the TsCheckResident() library routine.

Parameters
None.

Returns
None.

C Usage
```
extern void far TsVerify2F(void);
```

Pascal usage
```
procedure TsVerify2F;
```

Assembler usage
```
EXTRN   TSVERIFY2F:NEAR
 call   TSVERIFY2F
```

TessBeep   *Call TesSeRact internal beep routine*

This function is used to allow a routine to call the same BEEP procedure used by TesSeRact when it is unable to popup. In the assembler version of TesSeRact, TessBeep( ) is provided in a separate OBJ module so that it may be completely replaced by a user-defined procedure. In the C library, TessBeep( ) is in the TSDOBEEP module and also may be replaced by the user.

> **Parameters**
> None.
>
> **Returns**
> None.
>
> **C Usage**
> extern void far pascal TessBeep(void);
>
> **Pascal usage**
> procedure TessBeep;
>
> **Assembler usage**
> EXTRN TESSBEEP:near
> call TESSBEEP

TesSeRact Multiplex functions

These functions can be accessed in one of two ways: you can call either the library routine described next (not available in the assembler version) or the appropriate Interrupt 2Fh Multiplex Function call described later.

Initialization and information routines

The initialization and information routines are designed to be called by a TSR during the initialization portion. The Check Install function may be used instead of the TsCheckResident( ) Library routine described in the last section. The *only* Multiplex Functions that may be called *before* TsDoInit( ) are Check Install or Check Hotkey. The other functions in this section should be called from inside the TsrCleanUp( ) procedure (initialization portion).

Check Install   *(Function 00h)*

This function must be called before TsDoInit( ). It checks to see if this TSR has already been loaded by comparing the passed IDStr with other compatible TSRs. The primary difference between CheckInstall and TsCheckResident( ) is that Check Install does no initialization of internal data structures and should *only* be used by a program to *find* a TSR in memory and get its handle—*not* to determine if the TSR you are trying to install has already been loaded. Please note that under DOS 2.x, the Interrupt 2Fh vector is initialized to zero—a program calling Interrupt 2Fh will cause the machine to crash if a TesSeRact TSR has not been loaded. `TsVerify2F()` should be called prior to calling this function, or the application should make its own check for the validity of Interrupt 2Fh.

Parameters
IDStr   Pointer to unique 8-byte ID string for this program. All eight bytes are significant when comparing strings, so make sure you specify the values for *all* eight bytes.

Returns
AX=0FFFFh indicates the TSR has already been loaded, and may be identified by the ID Number returned in the CX register.

Any other value for AX indicates that it is safe to install this TSR, using the identification number returned in the CX register.

C Usage
See Assembler usage.

Pascal usage
See Assembler usage.

Assembler usage
```
mov ax,5453h
mov si,offset IDStr xor cx,cx
xor bx,bx
int 2fh
;
; result returned in AX
;
```

Return user parameter pointer   *(Function 01h)*

This function returns a pointer to the specified TSR's parameter block, which contains important information about the TSR. The structure is described in detail at this chapter's beginning as the `TsrParms` structure. Note that other TesSeRact Multiplex Functions provide information also available from the data contained in this structure; they are designed to be used as an alternative method for getting information about the TSR.

Parameters
TsrIdNum   Identification number of TSR to call.

Returns
NULL = No matching TSR ID number found. Otherwise, FAR pointer to `TsrParms` structure.

C Usage
```
extern struct TsrParms far * far pascal TsGetParms(
unsigned short TsrIdNum
);
```

Pascal usage
```
function TsGetParms(
TsrIdNum : word
) : ParmPtr;
```

Assembler usage
```
mov    ax,5453h
mov    bx,01h
mov    cx,TsrIdNum
int    2fh
or     ax,ax
jnz    not_found
;
;      Pointer to data returned in
;      ES:BX
;
```

Check Hotkey   *(Function 02h)*

This function is used to determine if the selected hotkey is not in use by any other TesSeRact-compatible TSR. At present, this function checks only for primary hotkeys and does not compare the "shift state" required for activation, assuming that a TSR that uses Alt-T to pop up would conflict with a TSR that uses Shift-Alt-T.

Parameters
HotKey   Scan Code of key to use for HotKey.

Returns
FFFFh—HotKey conflicts with TSR already loaded.

Anything else signifies it is safe to install a TSR with this hotkey.

C Usage
```
extern unsigned far pascal TsCheckHotkey(
unsigned char HotKey
);
```

Pascal usage
```
function TsCheckHotkey(
HotKey : word
) : word;
```

Assembler usage
```
mov    ax,5453h
mov    bx,02h
```

```
mov    cl,HotKey
int    2fh
;
;      result returned in AX
;
```

Replace Default Interrupt 24h Handler   *(Function 03h)*

This function is used to replace the TesSeRact default Critical Error Handler routine. The default procedure returns a FAIL code to the calling program. This routine allows the developer to replace that function with his own. Registers on entry to this routine are the same as described in the *DOS Technical Reference Manual*, and all conditions described there are in effect. Once control has been passed to this routine, it is the developer's responsibility to return back to DOS or the calling program. Please note that this routine, if implemented by the developer, cannot be called until the TSR has been enabled by TsDoInit( ); this should be called during the initialization phase of TsrCleanup( ).

Parameters
TsrIdNum   Identification number of TSR to call.
UserCritErrProc   Pointer to function to call.

Returns
Zero means success.
Non-zero means Unable to Install Handler—invalid ID number.

C Usage
```
extern unsigned far pascal TsSetUser24(
unsigned short TsrIdNum,
void(far *UserCritErrProc)(void)
);
```

Pascal usage
```
function TsSetUser24(
TsrIdNum : word;
UserCritErrProc : pointer
) : integer;
```

Assembler usage
```
mov    ax,5453h
mov    bx,03h
lds    si,UserCritErrProc
int    2fh
;
;      result returned in AX
;
```

Return TesSeRact data pointer   *(Function 04h)*

This function returns a pointer to the specified TSR's internal data areas. This block contains internal information about the TSR.

The structure is described in detail in Section 1 as the TsrData structure. Note that other TesSeRact Multiplex Functions provide information also available from the data contained in this structure; they are designed to be used as an alternative method for getting information about the TSR.

Parameters
TsrIdNum   Identification number of TSR to call.

Returns
NULL means no matching TSR ID number found.
Otherwise, FAR pointer to TsrData structure.

C Usage
```
extern struct TsrData far * far pascal TsGetData(
unsigned short TsrIdNum
);
```

Pascal usage
```
function TsGetData(
TsrIdNum : word
) : DataPtr
```

Assembler usage
```
mov    ax,5453h
mov    bx,04h
mov    cx,TsrIdNum
int    2fh
or     ax,ax
jnz    not_found
;
;      Pointer returned in ES:BX
;
```

Set multiple hot keys   *(Function 05h)*

This function is used to set multiple hotkeys for a TSR. The TsDoInit() function only has facilities for a single hotkey/shift-state combination, which should suffice for the majority of resident programs. However, many programmers want the ability to set up multiple hotkeys. Please note that this routine, if implemented by the developer, cannot be called until the TSR has been enabled by TsDoInit(); this should be called during the initialization phase of TsrCleanup().

Parameters

TsrIdNum	Identification number of TSR to call.
count	Number of extra keys to install.
ExtraHotKeys	Pointer to an array of struct ExtraHots.

Returns

Zero means success.
Non-zero means Unable to Install Hotkeys—invalid ID number.

C Usage

```
extern unsigned far pascal TsSetExtraHot(
unsigned short TsrIdNum,
unsigned char count,
struct ExtraHot far *ExtraHotKeys
);
```

Pascal usage

```
function TsSetExtraHot(
TsrIdNum : word;
Count : byte;
ExtraKeys : pointer
) : word;
```

Assembler usage

```
mov   ax,5453h
mov   bx,05h
mov   cx,TsrIdNum
mov   dl,count
lds   si,ExtraHotKeys
int   2fh
;
;     result returned in AX
;
```

TSR manipulation and status routines

The TesSeRact Multiplex Functions in this group are designed to be called by both resident and non-resident portions of applications. Appropriate use of these functions, many of which can be directly applied to the TesSeRact data areas, makes communication and manipulation of TesSeRact programs simple.

Enable TSR   *(Function 10h)*

This function calls the TesSeRact Multiplex interrupt to turn on the "enable" flag for a TSR. It is the functional opposite of the TsDisable() function.

Parameters

TsrIdNum   Identification number of TSR to call.

Returns

Zero means success.
Non-zero means Unable to Enable TSR—invalid ID number.

C Usage

```
extern unsigned pascal TsEnable(
unsigned short TsrIdNum
);
```

Pascal usage

```
procedure TsEnable(
TsrIdNum : word
);
```

Assembler usage

```
mov ax,5453h
mov bx,10h
mov cx,TsrIdNum
int 2fh
;
; result returned in AX
;
```

Disable TSR   *(Function 11h)*

This function turns off the "enable" flag for a TSR. The TSR remains in memory; but it cannot pop up, nor will any of its other operations be active. As soon as it is enabled again, actions on "hold" (like keys stuffed into the buffer) will immediately take place. It is the functional opposite of the TsEnable( ) function.

Parameters

TsrIdNum   Identification Number of TSR to call.

Returns

Zero means success.
Non-zero means Unable to Disable TSR—invalid ID number.

C Usage

```
extern unsigned pascal TsDisable(
unsigned short TsrIdNum
);
```

Pascal usage

```
procedure TsDisable(
TsrIdNum : word
);
```

Assembler usage
```
mov    ax,5453h
mov    bx,11h
mov    cx,TsrIdNum
int    2fh
;
;        result returned in AX
;
```

Release TSR [unload]   *(Function 12h)*

This function allows for releasing a TSR from memory at the earliest possible moment. In order for a TSR to remove itself, it must be the last interrupt in the interrupt chain for every interrupt it uses. If another program is
loaded that interferes with the interrupt chain, the TesSeRact Library will
wait until it is safe to remove your TSR from RAM.

Parameters
TsrIdNum   Identification number of TSR to call.

Returns
Zero means success.
Non-zero means Unable to Release TSR—invalid ID number.

C Usage
```
extern unsigned pascal TsRelease(
unsigned short TsrIdNum
);
```

Pascal usage
```
procedure TsRelease(
TsrIdNum : word
);
```

Assembler usage
```
mov    ax,5453h
mov    bx,12h
mov    cx,TsrIdNum
int    2fh
;
;        result returned in AX
;
```

Restart TSR   *(Function 13h)*

This function is used to "restart" a TSR that has been released but is still
physically in memory. Note that TsrCleanUp( ) is NOT called again for
initialization, because the program has never been notified through the
same routine that it was removed.

Parameters

TsrIdNum Identification number of TSR to call.

Returns

Zero means success.
Non-zero means Unable to Restart TSR—invalid ID number.

C Usage

```
extern unsigned pascal TsRestart(
unsigned short TsrIdNum
);
```

Pascal usage

```
procedure TsRestart(
TsrIdNum : word
);
```

Assembler usage

```
 mov   ax,5453h
 mov   bx,13h
 mov   cx,TsrIdNum
 int   2fh
 ;
 ;     result returned in AX
 ;
```

Get TSR status word *(Function 14h)*

This function is used to determine what the current status flags are for the specified TSR. The possible values are the same as for the TsrFlags parameter to TsDoInit( ). Note also that this status word can also be accessed directly by modifying the TsrStatus word from the TsrParms data structure. The high-level language functions specifically return the status flags if no error occurred; the assembler version is atypical in that this value is not returned in AX, as expected.

Parameters

TsrIdNum   Identification number of TSR to call.

Returns

FFFFh—invalid TSR ID code.
Any other value is current status flags.

C Usage

```
extern unsigned far pascal TsGetStat(
unsigned short TsrIdNum
);
```

Pascal usage
```
function TsGetStat(
TsrIdNum : word
) : word;
```

Assembler usage
```
mov   ax,5453h
mov   bx,14h
mov   cx,TsrIdNum
int   2fh
or    ax,ax
jnz   invalid_idnum
;
;       result returned in BX
;
```

Set TSR status word   *(Function 15h)*

This function is used to modify the existing status flags for the specified TSR. The possible values are the same as for the TsrFlags parameter to `TsDoInit( )`. Please note that the `NewStatus` parameter will *override* the existing status flags; it is recommended that the user call `TsGet-Stat( )` prior to this call and only make the necessary changes to the status word.

Parameters

TsrIdNum   Identification number of TSR to call.
NewStatus   New status WORD for specified TSR.

Returns

Zero means success.
Non-zero means Unable to Set Status Word—invalid ID number.

C Usage
```
extern unsigned far pascal TsSetStat(
unsigned short TsrIdNum,
unsigned short NewStatus
);
```

Pascal usage
```
function TsSetStat(
TsrIdNum : word
NewStatus : word
) : word;
```

Assembler usage
```
mov   ax,5453h
mov   bx,15h
```

```
mov   cx,TsrIdNum
mov   dx,NewStatus
int   2fh
;
;     return code returned in AX
;
```

Get Indos state at popup   *(Function 16h)*

This function is used to determine what the state of DOS was at the time of
the popup. Under some conditions, certain things cannot be done while
INDOS is 1 (like SHELLing to a new copy of COMMAND.COM) but are per-
fectly valid when INDOS is 0. The value returned by this routine is only
valid when called during `TsrMain( )`, `TsrBackCheck( )`, or `TsrBack-`
`Proc( )` procedures. Also note that the value returned here is the same as
the PopupType member of the `TsrData` structure.

Parameters
TsrIdNum   Identification number of TSR to call.

Returns
FFFFh—invalid TSR ID code.
Any other value is current status flags.

C Usage
```
extern unsigned far pascal TsGetPopType(
unsigned short TsrIdNum
);
```

Pascal usage
```
function TsGetPopType(
TsrIdNum : word
) : word;
```

Assembler usage
```
mov   ax,5453h
mov   bx,16h
mov   cx,TsrIdNum
int   2fh
or    ax,ax
jnz   invalid_idnum
;
;     result returned in BX
;
```

TSR utility routines

This group of TesSeRact Multiplex Functions was designed specifically for
communication and action of resident programs. With this release of Tes-

SeRact, there are only two functions in this category—Call User Procedure and Stuff Keyboard.

Call User Procedure   *(Function 20h)*

This function is designed to allow an external application (or a second invocation of the application) to call into the primary TSR. This should generally be used to change status, such as turning a feature on or off, adding files to a print queue, etc. The UserPtr parameter is passed to the `TsrUserProc( )` function of the specified TSR. No specifications or recommendations are made as to what this pointer should reference.

Parameters
TsrIdNum   Identification number of TSR to call.
UserPtr   User-defined, FAR pointer to *anything*.

Returns
Zero means success.
Non-zero means Unable to Pass Pointer—invalid ID number.

C Usage
```
extern unsigned far pascal TsCallUserProc(
unsigned short TsrIdNum,
void far *UserPtr
);
```

Pascal usage
```
function  TsStuffKeyboard(
TsrIdNum  : word;
KbdPtr    : pointer;
KbdLen    : word;
Speed     : word
)         : word;
```

Assembler usage
```
mov   ax,5453h
mov   bx,21h
mov   cx,TsrIdNum
les   di,KbdPtr
mov   si,KbdLen
mov   dx,Speed
int   2fh
;
;     result returned in AX
;
```

Writing a TesSeRact TSR—a tutorial

This section is intended to briefly describe the steps needed to create a TesSeRact TSR. Language-specific differences are covered in the "Language specifics" section—this section serves only as an outline to the general procedure.

First, you must design your program. Write it, test it, debug it—all without ever considering a TSR. Put your main procedural statements *outside* the primary execution loop—main() for C programmers—possibly in a separate function or such.

Once you've got the application debugged, you must set up your stack areas. The stack should be split into two parts, for both background and popup processing. If you only use one type of processing in your TSR, you should specify a small (4 bytes, or so) area for the other stack. Also, if you are using a high-level language, it is strongly recommended that you use a stack within the default stack area provided by your compiler—many functions assume certain things about the stack.

Now determine what kind of TSR processing you need—background, popup, timer, or a combination of the three. Also determine if you must be able to communicate with the resident portion of the program through a user-procedure.

Define the TesSeRact entry points: TsrBackCheck(), TsrBack-Proc(), TsrTimerProc(), TsrMain(), TsrUserProc(), and Tsr-CleanUp(). Note that users of the assembler version must define *all* these entry points in their code in order to resolve linker references. High-level language users will find dummy procedures provided to handle these references.

Your primary loops of execution should be placed in either Tsr-Main() or TsrBackProc(). Small bits of code to test flags or other status should be placed in TsrBackCheck() and TsrTimerProc()—and remember that TsrBackCheck() returns a flag determining whether TsrBackProc() should be called.

Now it's time to set up your data structures. Variables for hotkey and shift state values should be set up so that they can be easily changed. An eight-byte array of characters should be defined, which will become your TSR identification string. *Use eight characters!* Pad the string to eight bytes if needed, because the TesSeRact routines check all eight bytes for a match. Also define a data area that will be used to store your identification number.

If you plan to use multiple hot keys, set up an ExtraHot structure that contains the scan code, shift state, and flag byte for each additional hotkey you want.

Next, you must add the TesSeRact code to your program. As early in execution as possible, set up pointers to your internal stack areas and call TsSetStack(). Next, call TsCheckResident(), passing pointers to your identification string and identification number. This routine will pace the appropriate identification number in the data area you indicate. This identification number will be used on all future calls to TesSeRact once you call TsDoInit().

This is a good place to call `TsCheckHotkey()` to ensure that another TSR is not already using the hotkey combination you want.

Finally, a call is made to `TsDoInit()`, passing it the appropriate parameters as described in the documentation. The most important parameter to this function is the resident size; calculating it correctly will solve many problems.

If you're using multiple hotkeys, or need to communicate through the TesSeRact Multiplex interface, the time to do it is inside the initialization portion of `TsrCleanUp()`. This function is called *after* the TesSeRact interrupts have been installed. In my TSRs, I generally do all my initialization (except for memory allocation) inside this routine. Please note that it is not possible to call a TesSeRact Multiplex Function before `Tsr-CleanUp()` is called. The Multiplex routines are dependent on the interrupt handler being installed.

And that's all there is to it. Of course, you can do many other things—for example, if when you call `TsCheckResident()`, you determine that your program is already resident, you can pass new parameters to the resident portion using `TsrUserProc()`, etc. You also can modify the hotkeys, status, or anything as needed.

For more specific examples of this, see the next section "Language specifics," and also see the demonstration programs.

Language specifics

This section is designed to explain how to compile/assemble/link your ram-resident programs with the appropriate version of TesSeRact. It also will describe any language-specific variables or procedures that must be called. Examining in detail the demonstration code would be useful to you while reading this section.

Turbo C

Writing a TSR with Turbo C is very straightforward. Developers remembering that the stack is *above* the heap in tiny and small models can use a routine such as the `SizeOfCode()` module provided in the demonstration program. This routine allows developers to determine how much of the heap and stack the developer wants to be resident. If you specify ALL-STACK, it is totally possible to use Turbo C's normal dynamic memory allocation routines (`malloc`, `free`, etc.) in tiny or small model (`farmal-loc()` and dynamic memory under other memory models is a different subject entirely). Developers should set the size of the heap and stack they desire by setting `_heaplen` and `_stklen` to appropriate values.

The Turbo C demonstration program was compiled with the following command line:

```
TCC -C -M -w -K -O -Z -k -d TESSDEMO
tlink /m /l /s /c c0s+tessdemo,tessdemo,tessdemo,tess+cs
```

One other item of consideration for TC is the need to call the _restorezero() function from the termination portion of Tsr-CleanUp(). This is needed to restore the Interrupt 0 vector to its former position. Other packages or library routines may install their own termination handlers; please note that at present, TC 1.5 does not provide a mechanism for easily detecting their presence, other than by actually searching and modifying the _atexit() chain.

Microsoft C

From a functional standpoint, using Microsoft C for a TSR as opposed to Turbo C differs only in that instead of calling _restorezero(), you instead call _ctermsub(). Note that this function DOES call all procedures in the _atexit() chain, safely unlinking anyone who must be unlinked. Also, because the stack is *below* the heap in MSC small and medium models, using dynamic memory allocation functions is a chancy thing; the runtime library code has no way of knowing that you've put an arbitrary limit on the size of the heap.

TESSDEMO can be compiled with MSC using the following command lines:

```
CL /W3 /Ox /DMSC5 TESSDEMO.C
```

By defining the variable MSC5, compiled programs are provided with the Turbo C runtime library, allowing the program to execute.

Some problems have been noted concerning the console I/O functions of Microsoft C 5.0 and 5.1. We are currently unclear as to what exactly the problems are, but we recommend you do not use cputs() and cprintf() from inside your TSR. Note that the problem is not due to a DOS re-entrancy problem, because making the DOS function calls directly works just fine.

You also should be aware that many MSC functions call malloc() without being documented to do so (one being printf()). Be careful about your heap management with MSC.

Finally, note that the size of the stack under MSC can be controlled either by using the EXEMOD program and directly modifying the EXE header information, or by using the /STACK parameter at the link step.

Turbo Pascal

To use TesSeRact with Turbo Pascal 4.0, you need simply add the line

```
Uses TESSTP;
```

to your program. The various function, procedure, and CONST declarations are located in the TESS.TP4 file.

Please note that when using TP4, you must call one additional procedure before any of the other TesSeRact routines. Because of the organization of TP4 units, you cannot have code in the unit directly call routines in the main section of the code. To get around this, the TP unit has been written with indirect calls to these locations, which are initialized to far returns. In order to set the appropriate addresses into these data locations, TP4 users must call the `TsSetAdrTP4` procedure:

```
procedure TsSetAdrTP4(
ProcAdr : pointer;
Index : integer
);
```

This procedure exists only in the TP4 version; it is used to set the TesSeRact pointers to permit popup of your own routines. During initialization of the unit, all six pointers are set to a FAR RET within the unit; your code must reset those you want to use, via `TsSetAdrTP4( @TsrMain, 2 );`, etc. The index codes to use are

```
0 = TsrTimerProc
1 = TsrBackProc
2 = TsrMain
3 = TsrBackCheck
4 = TsrUserProc
5 = TsrCleanUp
```

Assembler

Writing a TesSeRact program using the assembler version affords the programmer the most compact code (because near calls are used, rather than far), as well as the most flexibility. The TesSeRact routines in this version assume that CS = DS, and any function that references the DI register also assumes that ES = CS. This version will work only for .COM-style programs. The developer, however, does not need to use the following common code sequence

```
ORG 100h
start:
jmp begin
.....
END START
```

because the TesSeRact library already has the code embedded within it. The program must have a public variable called TESSINITSTART. The TesSeRact library gets control of the program and does a near jmp to that label. All registers normally in effect at the beginning of a .COM program are still as they were.

Other than this label, there are some minor differences in calling some of the TesSeRact library routines; most notably, `TsDoInit( )` takes the offset of the top of memory (the common practice for .COM programs) as opposed to the number of paragraphs of RAM required. The `TsDoInit()` module will convert to paragraphs.

Please note also that all entry points must exist in the code. See the example program for more details.

The TESSPARK demonstration program was assembled/linked using SLR Systems OPTASM 1.0 and Borland International's TLINK 1.1, as noted next. Microsoft's MASM and LINK utilities work just as well.

```
OPTASM /Mx tesspark;
TLINK /M /L /S /C tess_asm+tess_bp+tesspark+tess_
    end,tesspark;
```

The functions located in TESS_END.OBJ are not used after the TSR is initialized and should therefore be placed in the .EXE file past the end of the resident portion of your program. TESS_BP.OBJ has been provided as a separate module to allow ease in replacing it with your own BEEP routine.

Communicating with the TesSeRact

In order for a program to communicate with routines using the TesSeRact standard, it must use the TesSeRact multiplex functions.

The TesSeRact standard for ram-resident program communication is a group of functions latched onto DOS' own Interrupt 2Fh (Multiplex). DOS uses this interrupt to communicate with its own TSRs (PRINT.COM, ASSIGN.COM, and SHARE.COM); and the TesSeRact Development Team felt it was appropriate to service TSR programs using the same interface. These functions are all accessed by generating an Interrupt 2Fh, with AX = 5453 (hex).

Important: In versions of MS-DOS and PC-DOS prior to 3.0, the Interrupt 2Fh vector was initialized to zero rather than being pointed into the DOS service area. With such DOS versions, a program calling Interrupt 2Fh will crash the machine if a TesSeRact TSR has not been loaded. `TsVerify2F()` should be called prior to calling this function, or the application should make its own check for the validity of Interrupt 2Fh.

To determine whether any routine is in fact using the TesSeRact standard, use multiplex function 00h (Check Install). Check Install determines whether a TesSeRact program has been loaded and is called as shown. (The assembler interface is required if the TesSeRact library is not available. If it is, refer to the section on multiplex functions for details of its use in high-level languages.)

```
mov    ax,5453h        ;   the  TesSeRact   Multiplex
                           signature
mov    si,offset IDStr ;   FAR pointer to 8-character
                           name of
mov    ds,seg IDStr    ;   routine being checked for
```

```
        xor   cx,cx                ; will count TesSeRact using
                                     CX
        xor   bx,bx                ; specify Function 00h
        int   2fh
```

IDStr is an eight-byte data area containing the TSR identification string unique to the particular TSR program. All eight bytes are significant when comparing strings, so make sure you specify the values for *all* eight bytes. If necessary, pad an IDStr array with spaces to ensure eight unique bytes.

If no TesSeRact routine is present in the system, the interrupt will return with the signature in the AX register unchanged. If the routine being sought is present, AX will contain 0FFFFh, and the CX register will contain its identification number. This ID number is used by all the remaining TesSeRact multiplex functions rather than the full identification string and should be saved for use.

Note that Check Install will *always* return an identification number for the routine being sought if *any* TesSeRact TSR is present, even though the routine might not yet be present in the system. To double-check that the routine is present, request a pointer to its data area.

Check Install does no initialization of internal data structures and should only be used by a program to find a TSR in memory and get its handle—*not* to determine if a TSR has already been loaded.

In the TesSeRact standard, multiplex function 01h returns a far pointer to a data area containing the TsrParms pointer—including the identification string, identification number, and FuncFlag members for the TSR bearing the IdNum passed into the function. This function is called as follows:

```
        mov   ax,5453h
        mov   bx,01h
        mov   cx,TsrIdNum
        int   2fh
```

If the identification number in CX matches the TSR's ID number (which was returned by multiplex function 00h), the TSR returns with ES:BX pointing to the TsrParms area and AX equal to zero. Any other value in AX upon return indicates that the TSR could not be located.

Once the pointer to the user parameter area is obtained, most of the critical information used by the routine is available to the calling program.

Any developer wanting a copy of the source code for TesSeRact's Interrupt 2Fh multiplex handler can receive it by sending a self-addressed, stamped envelope to

TesSeRact Development Team
c/o Chip Rabinowitz
2084 Woodlawn Av.
Glenside, PA 19038

For more information, contact the TesSeRact Development Team either at the above address, at CompuServe 70731,20, or at MCIMAIL 315-5415 (TESSERACT).

Writing TesSeRact-compatible programs

The current TesSeRact product consists of both a library of routines enabling developers to write safe ram-resident programs and an interface permitting developers to communicate with their own (and other) TSRs.

The TesSeRact standard for ram-resident program communication is a group of functions latched onto DOS' own Interrupt 2Fh (Multiplex). DOS uses this interrupt to communicate with its own TSRs (PRINT.COM, ASSIGN.COM, and SHARE.COM), and the TesSeRact Development Team felt it was appropriate to service TSR programs using the same interface. These functions are all accessed by generating an Interrupt 2Fh, with AX = 5453 (hex).

In order for a program to support the TesSeRact Standard, it *must* provide the following multiplex functions:

```
Function 00h (Check Install)
Function 01h (Return User Parameter Pointer)
```

Check Install is used by TesSeRact programs to determine if the program has been loaded before and is called in the following fashion:

```
mov     ax,5453h
mov     si,offset IDStr
mov     ds,seg IDStr
xor     cx,cx
xor     bx,bx
int     2fh
```

IDStr is an eight-byte data area containing a unique TSR identification string. The Interrupt 2F routine should compare the passed string (as shown in the next example) with its own eight-byte string. If the two strings match, the TSR should return with the CX register set to its own TSR "handle" and the AX register set to 0FFFFh.

If the identification strings do not match, all the registers should be restored, the CX registers should be *incremented*, and the interrupt handler should call down the chain.

You might wonder why it is done this way. Basically, if every TesSeRact-compatible TSR on a particular system increments the CX register when no match occurs, then when the interrupt procedure returns to the caller, the CX register will contain the next available handle.

The code shown in FIG. 17-8 is taken directly from the TesSeRact library's Interrupt 2Fh handler.

The other requirement for TesSeRact compatibility is to support the TsrParms data area (Multiplex Function 01h). The UserParms area is shown in FIG. 17-9.

```
finish_2f:
     add    sp,4                           ;get rid of two words on stack
     xor    ax,ax                          ;clear AX to show we got it
done_2f:
     iret

next_one:
     inc    cx                             ;try next higher ID code
get_out_2f:
     pop    bx
     pop    ax
not_our_2f:
     jmp    DPTR [oldint2F]

overparms:
     cmp    ax,5453h                       ;ax=5453h for TesSeRact
     jne    not_our_2f
     cmp    bx,MAXENT
     ja     not_our_2f
     push   ax
     push   bx
     or     bx,bx                          ;do check for install first,
     jz     check_install                  ;so we can check ID number only
                                           ;one time!
     ....                                  ; other code .....

check_install:
                                           ;DS:SI points to ID string
                                           ;DI contains hotkey for check
                                           ;CX is current number in chain
                                           ;    must be 0 from caller

     push   cx
     push   si                             ;save SI for next one
     lea    di,[USERPARMS]
     push   cs
     pop    es
     mov    cx,8
     rep    cmpsb
     pop    si
     pop    cx
     jnz    next_one                       ;no match, not us
     pop    bx
     pop    ax
     mov    cx,es:[di]                     ;return ID number in CX
     test   WPTR [STATUS],TSRRELEASED
     jz     return_idnum
     or     cx,0ff00h                      ;say we're released!
return_idnum:
     xor    ax,ax
     dec    ax                             ;AX=-1 means already here
     jmp    short done_2f
```

17-8 Tsr code taken from Interrupt 2Fh handler.

```
UserParms         db    8 dup (0)
IdNum      dw    0              ;TSR Identification Number
FuncFlag   dd    0ffffffffh     ;supported functions
HotKey     db    0              ;Scan code of hotkey to use
ShiftSt    db    0              ;shift state to use for popup
HotFlag    db    0              ;Which hotkey is in use
ExtCnt     db    0              ;number of extra hotkeys
ExtHot     dd    0              ;pointer to extra hot keys
Status     dw    0              ;TSR status flags
OurPSP     dw    0              ;our PSP segment
OurDTA     dd    0              ;our DTA region
DSeg       dw    0              ;User's Default Data Segment

NOTE:  This  is  only  a  partial  listing  of  the  full  TsrParms
structure.
```

17-9 UserParms area.

For minimal support of the TesSeRact Standard, multiplex function 01h should return a far pointer to a data area containing the identification string, identification number, and `FuncFlag` members. It is called as follows:

```
mov     ax,5453h
mov     bx,01h
mov     cx,TsrIdNum
int     2fh
```

If the identification number in CX matches the TSR's ID number (which was returned by multiplex function 00h), the TSR should return with ES:BX pointing to the `TsrParms` area and AX equal to zero.

The `FuncFlag` is a bit-mapped, four-byte variable showing all multiplex functions supported by this TSR. This variable is mapped as shown in FIG. 17-10.

```
Bit  0          Function 00h (check install -- REQUIRED)
Bit  1          Function 01h (return userparms -- REQUIRED)
Bit  2          Function 02h (check hotkey)
Bit  3          Function 03h (replace INT 24h)
Bit  4          Function 04h (return Data Pointer)
Bit  5          Function 05h (set extra hotkeys)
Bits 6-7        Undefined -- reserved for future use
Bit  8          Function 10h (enable TSR)
Bit  9          Function 11h (disable TSR)
Bit 10          Function 12h (release TSR from RAM)
Bit 11          Function 13h (restart TSR)
Bit 12          Function 14h (get current status)
Bit 13          Function 15h (set TSR status)
Bit 14          Function 16h (get popup type)
Bit 15          Undefined -- reserved for future use
Bit 16          Function 20h (Call user procedure)
Bit 17          Function 21h (stuff keyboard)
Bits 18-31      Undefined -- reserved for future use
```

17-10   The mapping of `FuncFlag`.

If the TSR supports the particular function, the bit should be SET (1); otherwise, it should be zero. Note that a product using TesSeRact's library will return with `FuncFlag` set to (hex) FFFFFFFF. Other TSRs should set the undefined variables to 0 to differentiate themselves.

Registration

Registration for the TesSeRact library, in any form, is a one-time fee of $25. Payment of this fee entitles you to the following:

☐ A disk with the latest version of the TesSeRact library
☐ Printed documentation
☐ The right to use the TesSeRact Library with any ram-resident program you sell or distribute, provided the appropriate copyright notices appear in your code and documentation
☐ Upgrades to future versions of TesSeRact for $10

The complete, commented source code to TesSeRact is also available to registered users for a fee of $25.

For an additional $10 per year, registered users can receive a monthly newsletter consisting of a list of all registered products, their associated TSR Identification Strings, and level of support of the TesSeRact Ram-Resident Program Communication Standard. This newsletter will also contain information about new versions of TesSeRact, supported languages, new documentation, etc.

To register, send to

TesSeRact Development Team
2084 Woodlawn Av.
Glenside, PA 19038

18
Mouse Tools

Program title   Mouse Tools   *(Disk 2278)*

Special requirements   Turbo Pascal 5.5

Using a mouse as an input device is becoming increasingly common in many types of programs. While this (usually) makes life easier for the user, it certainly does make the programmer's job harder. This package contains utilities allowing you to incorporate mice into your Turbo Pascal 5.5 programs.

This set of utilities provides most of the necessary procedures to use a mouse in your own programs, including

- the displaying of the mouse cursor.
- the reading of mouse and button positions.
- the displaying of various prompts with "push buttons."
- the selecting of filenames.

To use these tools, you will need Turbo Pascal 5.5 as well as the TP5.5 units Crt, Dos, Drivers, Fonts and Graph. Included here are two sample programs (MAPEDIT.PAS and CGAEXP.PAS) along with the .TPU files for all the mouse tools; these should give you enough to get started writing mouse programs in Turbo Pascal. The source code for the units, however, is not included.

New in v1.1 is support for MCGA graphics mode. To use this mode, you'll need the driver that Borland has made available in the BGIKIT because it was not included in the standard Turbo Pascal package.

The following files are included in MouseTools:

MOUSE.TPU	Mouse driver interface and other basic mouse tools
MOUSERS2.TPU	Mouse response tools
CONVERT.TPU	Some conversion tools used by MAPEDIT.PAS
PALETTE.TPU	Graphics initialization used by MAPEDIT.PAS
BOX.TPU	Graphics utilities for popup boxes
CGAEXP.PAS	Sample program using MouseTools (CGA)
CGAEXP.EXE	Run-able version of sample program
MAPEDIT.PAS	Sample program using MouseTools (EGA)
MAPEDIT.EXE	Run-able version of sample program
CCMAP.PIC	Sample data for MAPEDIT.EXE

Using MouseTools

Probably the best way to understand how the tools work is to examine the sample programs MAPEDIT.PAS and CGAEXP.PAS. You should refer to them for actual examples of how things are used as they are described here.

First, some basic concepts. Most of your interface to the mouse is actually done by the mouse driver supplied by the mouse manufacturer. The interface to the mouse driver is done through interrupts similar to the way MS-DOS or BIOS functions are accessed. If you've never used MS-DOS /BIOS functions, don't worry: MouseTools handles all the messy details for you.

Once the mouse is activated and you can read positions from it, your program needs to display something on the screen to echo the mouse's actions. MouseTools allows you to use any shape as a mouse cursor and comes with an arrow, finger, and hand cursor already drawn. With the registered version, you can add your own cursor shapes. Tools are provided for displaying and moving the cursor around the screen.

In addition to movement, you must determine when the user wants to do something either by just being over a particular part of the screen or by using the mouse buttons. These are the basic tools of the mouse interface.

In addition to the basics, tools are provided to display prompts of several types and return the selections the user made. One of the most sophisticated prompts is the file selection tool, which allows the user to select files through a scrolling list and includes the ability to change directories and drives.

OK, so all these tools are available. Now you're probably wondering exactly how to use them. Let's go through that step by step.

Initialization

First, you must enter graphics mode as you would any Turbo Pascal program. Then the mouse itself must be initialized. The functions to do this are as follows:

MReset   Resets the mouse and returns – 1 if a mouse driver is
               installed.
MLimit (x1,x2,y1,y2)
               Sets the limits of the mouse coordinates.
MPut(x,y)   Positions the mouse at coordinates (x,y).

If MReset doesn't return a value of – 1, no mouse driver is installed and your program won't be able to do any mouse functions. MLimit is used to control the range of values the mouse returns to you. These limits will probably be equal to the size of the screen (i.e., x=0 thru 639, y=0 thru 349 for EGA graphics mode). MPut sets the starting mouse coordinates. (You'll probably want to either put the mouse in a corner or in the middle of the screen.)

Several Pascal variables are used to keep track of what the mouse has been doing:

Mx   Last mouse x coordinate
My   Last mouse y coordinate
Button   Last mouse button value

Initially, you should set Mx and My to the values you used in MPut(x,y), and you should initialize Button to 0.

You'll also need some memory on the heap to save the portion of screen under the mouse cursor. The variable MCurs (in MOUSE.TPU) is used to point to this memory. Set it up by using

```
GetMem(MCurs,ImageSize(0,0,MW,MH));
{reserve memory for mouse cursor}
```

There's still no visible indication on the screen that a mouse is in use. You can now turn on the mouse cursor using the procedure:

```
MouseCursorOn(Mx,My,HAND);
{display a hand cursor}
```

The first two parameters determine where the mouse cursor will be. The third parameter determines the shape of the mouse cursor, with the available cursor shapes being HAND, FINGER, and ARROW.

Now everything is set, and you can start the main body of your program.

Using the mouse in your main program

The main body of your program will need a loop where the mouse is polled allowing its displayed position to be updated and to check for command requests from the user.

The main procedure in this loop is

```
MStatus(NewButton,NewX,NewY);
{get mouse status}
```

This returns the current position of the mouse buttons followed by the x and y mouse coordinates. There are several things you can then do with this information:

- Compare NewX to Mx and NewY to My to see if the mouse has moved. If it has, use

```
MouseCursor(NewX,NewY,Mx,My,HAND);
{move mouse cursor}
```

to move the mouse cursor to its new position. After moving, save NewX into Mx and NewY into My.

- See if the mouse is over something significant by using

```
MouseLocate(NewX,NewY,18,@mt)
```

This function uses a table ("mt" in this case, containing 18 items) of coordinates and returns a value indicating which, if any, sets of coordinates NewX/NewY are within. MouseLocate() is described in more detail later.

- See if a button is being pushed by comparing NewButton with Button. Detecting a button push will usually mean a call to MouseLocate() to find what item the user is selecting. Then a case statement can be used to call the appropriate procedure.

MouseTools detailed descriptions

Once you understand the basics of initializing the mouse and detecting what it's doing in the body of the program, you'll need to know what tools are available for using it further. This section describes in detail all the available mouse functions and procedures, in order by the unit they are in.

MOUSE.TPU

This unit provides the interface to the mouse driver, plus the basic routines for displaying the mouse cursor and determining what the mouse is pointing to.

```
function MReset: INTEGER;
```

MReset initializes the mouse. It returns an integer value of − 1 if a mouse is detected. If MReset does not return − 1, you cannot use mouse functions in the remainder of the program.

```
procedure MPut(mx,my: INTEGER);
```

MPut sets the current mouse position to mx,my. Thus, if you were to immediately read the mouse position using MStatus() before the user had a chance to move it, the values you'd receive back would be mx,my.

```
procedure MStatus(var button,xpos,ypos: INTEGER);
```

MStatus returns the current state of the mouse. Button is a bit-mapped value indicating which buttons are pressed (i.e., Button is 1 if button 1 is pressed, 2 if button 2 is pressed, 3 if both buttons 1 and 2 are pressed). xpos,ypos are the current position of the mouse.

```
procedure MLimit(xmin,xmax,ymin,ymax: INTEGER);
```

You can limit the coordinate values returned by MStatus using this procedure. To prevent the mouse from going off the screen in EGA 640x350 mode, you could set xmin=0, xmax=639, ymin=0, ymax=349. Smaller values can be used to limit mouse travel to only a portion of the screen.

```
procedure MouseCursor(x,y,Oldx,Oldy,Num: INTEGER);
```

MouseCursor moves the displayed mouse cursor from one position—Oldx,Oldy—to a new position—x,y. Make sure the mouse cursor is actually being displayed when you call this function, otherwise you will leave blocks of garbage on the screen.

```
procedure MouseCursorOn(x,y,Num: INTEGER);
```

MouseCursorOn is basically one half of MouseCursor(). Use it when the mouse cursor is not currently being displayed but now should be, such as at the beginning of the program. MouseCursorOn() must be used before MouseCursor() is first called.

```
procedure MouseCursorOff(Oldx,Oldy: INTEGER);
```

MouseCursorOff removes the mouse cursor from the screen and restores whatever was under it to view.

```
function MouseLocate(x,y,size: INTEGER; mt: mtptr):
   INTEGER;
```

MouseLocate is the key to making the mouse do useful things within your program. It uses a table mt with size entries in it to determine what the user is pointing to. x and y should be the current mouse coordinates (Mx and My).

To use MouseLocate, you must set up a table of integers—4 numbers per entry—that describe rectangles on the screen. Here is a sample table:

```
Const
mt: array[1..2,1..4] of INTEGER = (
(400,620,68,81), {save}
(400,620,82,95) ); {read}
```

The sample shows two possible functions—save and read—that the user can select. If the x coordinate of the mouse is between 400 and 620 and the y coordinate is between 68 and 81, then "save" is being selected. MouseLocate will check all entries in the table and will return the number of the first table entry found containing the specified coordinates.

Note that when calling MouseLocate, you must actually pass a pointer to the table rather than the table itself, so a sample call to Mouse-Locate might look like this:

```
i := MouseLocate(Mx,My,18,@mt);
```

MOUSERS2.TPU

This unit provides several ways of prompting the user for input and using the mouse to get his response.

---

function MGetFile(FileSpec,Heading: STRING): STRING;

MGetFile is a very sophisticated routine for allowing the user to select filenames. A box is popped up containing a list of files that the user can select from. The list can be scrolled if all valid files do not fit and the user can switch between directories and disks.

FileSpec specifies what filenames will be shown. You'd use "*.*" to show all files, but if you only wanted files with the suffix .PIC, you could set FileSpec to "*.PIC". Many possibilities are available for FileSpec.

Heading is a prompt to the user that will be at the top of the box showing the filenames. MGetFile returns a string containing the filename that was selected. If character 0 of the returned string is equal to #255, however, the user aborted the file selection.

---

function MouseYN(x,y: INTEGER; Heading: STRING): BOOLEAN;

MouseYN displays a question contained in Heading along with a yes and no button. If the user selects the yes button, the function returns a TRUE value; otherwise, it returns false.

```
function MouseQuestion(Size: INTEGER;Heading: STRING;
      Ques:QTable): INTEGER;
```

MouseQuestion displays a question and a list of answers for the user to choose from, returning the number of the user's choice. Size is the number of possible answers. Ques is an array of strings containing the possible responses. A sample Ques might look like:

```
PalQues: array[1..5] of STRING = ( {palette questions}
'Save','Load','Change','Rotate','Default');
```

Note that, when calling MouseQuestion, you must actually pass a pointer to the table rather than the table itself, so a sample call to Mouse-Question might look like this:

```
case MouseQuestion(5,'Select a palette function',@Pal-
      Ques) of
```

```
function MouseReadKey(Heading: STRING): CHAR;
```

MouseReadKey displays a heading (actually, the heading is optional) and waits for the user to hit a single key or click the mouse. If a key is hit, its value is returned; otherwise, if the mouse is clicked a value of #0 is returned.

BOX.TPU

This unit has a couple of tools used for popup boxes and other things:

```
procedure OutlineBox(x1,y1,x2,y2,boxcolor,rectcolor:
      INTEGER);
```

This procedure draws a box using boxcolor as the background color of the box, and using a single pixel wide outline of color rectcolor around the edge. This is the standard box used for mouse prompts.

```
procedure XPutPixel(x,y,color: INTEGER);
```

Plot a pixel at x,y by XOR'ing its current color with color.

```
procedure XLine(x1,y1,x2,y2,color: INTEGER);
```

Draw a line from x1,y1 to x2,y2 by XOR'ing its current color with color.

```
procedure Input(var temp: STRING);
```

String input routine for graphics mode. Handles echoing of the string using the currently selected font as well as displaying a cursor and backspacing.

PALETTE.TPU

This unit is not strictly part of the mouse tools but is needed to use EGA graphics mode. Its only procedure initializes graphics mode.

```
procedure Initialize;
```

As currently set up, Initialize sets up EGA 640x350 mode graphics. This routine is right out of the Turbo Pascal sample programs, so if you need other modes, you should be able to make your own version of it.

CONVERT.TPU

This unit isn't really necessary for a mouse interface either but contains some functions used in MAPEDIT.PAS that you might find useful.

```
function RtoI(number: REAL): INTEGER;
```

Takes the real variable number and returns it as an integer.

```
function ItoS(number: LONGINT): STRING;
```

Takes the integer variable number and returns it as a string.

```
function ItoFS(number: LONGINT; a: INTEGER; fill: CHAR):
STRING;
```

Takes the integer variable number and returns it as a formatted string, exactly a characters long with unneeded character positions set to the character fill.

```
function RtoS(number: REAL; a,b: INTEGER): STRING;
```

Takes the real variable number and returns it as a formatted string, exactly a characters long with b characters after the decimal point.

```
function NoSpace(s: STRING): STRING;
```

Takes the string s and returns it with leading spaces removed.

```
function GetVal(s: STRING): REAL;
```

Takes the string s and returns it as a real number.

Sample programs

MapEdit, one sample program demonstrating MouseTools, is actually a utility written for a programmer who needed to draw icons that would be combined to create a map display. Since then, he has also used it to draw the keys for a calculator program he is writing. The author is working on an adventure game that will use maps and creatures created with Map-Edit. Thus, in addition to a sample of the mouse tools, you're getting a potentially useful program because graphical icons have so many possible uses.

Also included is a sample icon file called CCMAP.PIC for you to play around with. This is some of the icons for the author's future adventure game. Try using the various functions of MapEdit to see what the mouse tools actually look like on the screen.

By the way, if you want to see an actual program that used MapEdit, look for BassTour by Dick Olsen, currently available on BBS's as BASSTR 42.ZIP.

CGAExp, the other sample program, doesn't actually do anything useful but demonstrates that the MouseTools can be used in CGA graphics as well as EGA. Because there's less actual program surrounding the tools, you might find it more useful for understanding the tools than MapEdit.

Registration

MouseTools is provided as shareware. You may use it, copy it for friends, upload it to BBS's, etc. If you continue to use MouseTools and would like to reward the author for his work, you can send a donation ($10 suggested) to

Nels Anderson
92 Bishop Dr.
Framingham, MA 01701

Registered users will get the latest updates on the tools as well as the source code for all the mouse units. Support is also available through the author's BBS, at (508) 875-3618 or (617) 449-7322, 300/1200/2400/9600HST. You are encouraged to send anything you create using these tools. You can either mail a copy or upload it to the BBS.

A
ASCII character charts

This is the ASCII character set. The standard set, which includes codes from 0 to 127, is used by all ASCII devices. The extended set, which includes codes from 128 to 255, is used by all IBM-compatible PCs and printers.

Standard ASCII chart (character codes 0-127)

ASCII control codes

Code	Function	IBM character	Code	Function	IBM character
000	NUL	(none)	016	DLE	▶
001	SOH	☺	017	DC1	◀
002	STX	☻	018	DC2	↕
003	ETX	♥	019	DC3	‼
004	EOT	♦	020	DC4	¶
005	ENQ	♣	021	NAK	§
006	ACK	♠	022	SYN	▬
007	BEL	•	023	ETB	↨
008	BS	◘	024	CAN	↑
009	TAB	○	025	EM	↓
010	LF	◙	026	EOF	→
011	VT	♂	027	ESC	
012	NP	♀	028	FS	∟
013	CR	♪	029	GS	↔
014	SO	♫	030	RS	▲
015	SI	☼	031	US	▼

Standard ASCII characters

Code	Character	Code	Character
032	sp	074	J
033	!	075	K
034	"	076	L
035	#	077	M
036	$	078	N
037	%	079	O
038	&	080	P
039	'	081	Q
040	(	082	R
041	)	083	S
042	*	084	T
043	+	085	U
044	,	086	V
045	–	087	W
046	.	088	X
047	/	089	Y
048	0	090	Z
049	1	091	[
050	2	092	\
051	3	093	]
052	4	094	^
053	5	095	_
054	6	096	`
055	7	097	a
056	8	098	b
057	9	099	c
058	:	100	d
059	;	101	e
060	<	102	f
061	=	103	g
062	>	104	h
063	?	105	i
064	@	106	j
065	A	107	k
066	B	108	l
067	C	109	m
068	D	110	n
069	E	111	o
070	F	112	p
071	G	113	q
072	H	114	r
073	I	115	s

Code	Character	Code	Character
116	t	122	z
117	u	123	{
118	v	124		
119	w	125	}
120	x	126	
121	y	127	(bs)

Extended ASCII chart (character codes 128 - 255)

Code	Character	Code	Character
128	Ç	162	ó
129	ü	163	ú
130	é	164	ñ
131	â	165	Ñ
132	ä	166	ª
133	à	167	º
134	å	168	¿
135	ç	169	⌐
136	ê	170	¬
137	ë	171	½
138	è	172	¼
139	ï	173	¡
140	î	174	«
141	ì	175	»
142	Ä	176	░
143	Å	177	▒
144	É	178	▓
145	æ	179	│
146	Æ	180	┤
147	ô	181	╡
148	ö	182	╢
149	ò	183	╖
150	û	184	╕
151	ù	185	╣
152	ÿ	186	║
153	Ö	187	╗
154	Ü	188	╝
155	¢	189	╜
156	£	190	╛
157	¥	191	┐
158	₧	192	└
159	ƒ	193	┴
160	á	194	┬
161	í	195	├

Code	Character	Code	Character
196		226	Γ
197		227	π
198		228	Σ
199		229	σ
200		230	μ
201		231	τ
202		232	Φ
203		233	Θ
204		234	Ω
205		235	δ
206		236	∞
207		237	ϕ
208		238	ϵ
209		239	
210		240	
211		241	$\pm$
212		242	$\geq$
213		243	$\leq$
214		244	$\int$
215		245	
216		246	$\div$
217		247	$\approx$
218		248	$\circ$
219		249	$\bullet$
220		250	$\cdot$
221		251	$\sqrt{}$
222		252	n
223		253	2
224	α	254	$\blacksquare$
225	β	255	(null)

B
Keyboard scan codes

These are the scan codes used for each of the keyboard keys. The codes are shown in decimal.

Character keys

Key	Scan code	Key	Scan code
1	2	I	23
2	3	O	24
3	4	P	25
4	5	[	26
5	6	]	27
6	7	A	30
7	8	S	31
8	9	D	32
9	10	F	33
0	11	G	34
–	12	H	35
=	13	J	36
Q	16	K	37
W	17	L	38
E	18	;	39
R	19	'	40
T	20	`	41
Y	21	\	43
U	22	Z	44

Key	Scan code		Key	Scan code
X	45		'	51
C	46		.	52
V	47		/	53
B	48		(PrtSc)	55
N	49		(Space)	57
M	50			

Function keys

Key	Scan code
F1	59
F2	60
F3	61
F4	62
F5	63
F6	65
F7	65
F8	66
F9	67
F10	68

Control keys

Key	Scan code
Esc	1
Backspace	14
Num Lock	69
Scroll Lock	70
Tab	15
Enter	28
Ctrl	29
Left Shft	42
Right Shft	54
Alt	56
Caps Lock	58

Numeric keypad

Key	Scan code
7	71
8	72
9	73
–	74
4	75
5	76
6	77
+	78
1	79
2	80
3	81
0	82
.	83

Index

Other Bestsellers of Related Interest

WORDPERFECT® 5.1 MACROS
—Donna M. Mosich, Robert Bixby, and Pamela Adams-Regan

Get everything you need to know about macros in any version of WordPerfect through 5.1. Create and use macros to generate form letters, automate mailing list production, index manuscripts, and more! There are more than 300 usable macros covered in this guide (and available on disk), with explanations and illustrations on how the macro command language is used. 480 pages, 162 illustrations. Book No. 3617, $26.95 paperback, $34.95 hardcover

BUILDING C LIBRARIES: Windows, Menus & User Interfaces—Len Dorfman

Improve the quality of your programs while drastically reducing development time with this new guide from expert Len Dorfman. He shows you how to use the library manager to create your own professional window, screen, and keyboard handling libraries. *Building C Libraries* emphasizes interfaces and library development. You get line after line of well-documented source code for menus, pop-up windows, Macintosh-style pull-downs, bounce bars, and more. 432 pages, 198 illustrations. Book No. 3418, $26.95 paperback, $34.95 hardcover

80386: A Programming and Design Handbook—2nd Edition—Penn Brumm and Don Brumm

"This book has all the information you require to design, build, and program your own 80386-based system."
—*Computing Magazine*

Now, with the guidance of system applications experts Penn and Don Brumm, you can exploit this advanced processor. Revised and expanded, this book explains and demonstrates such advanced features as: 32-bit instruction enhancements, memory paging functions, debugging applications, and Virtual 8086 Mode. 480 pages, 108 illustrations. Book No. 3237, $24.95 paperback, $34.95 hardcover

ACCPAC PLUS USER'S GUIDE, Covers Version 5.0—Esther Deutsch

This is the most comprehensive work available on ACCPAC PLUS, ACCPAC's hot new top-of-the-line general accounting package. The text simplifies functions through keystroke-by-keystroke instructions and sample company data in the order you will actually use the functions in practice. Plus it offers a working accounting system you can customize. You get valuable how-to-use-it data for all the major modules: general ledger, financial reporter, accounts payable, and accounts receivable. 672 pages, illustrated. Book No. 3758, $26.95 hardcover only

HANDBOOK OF DATA COMMUNICATIONS AND COMPUTER NETWORKS
—2nd Edition—Dimitris N. Chorafas

Completely revised and updated, this results-oriented reference—with over 125 illustrations—progresses smoothly as theory is combined with concrete examples to show you how to successfully manage a dynamic information system. You'll find applications-oriented material on networks, technological advances, telecommunications technology, protocols, network design, messages and transactions, software's role, and network maintenance. 448 pages, 129 illustrations. Book No. 3690, $44.95 hardcover only

WORDPERFECT POWER: Word Processing Made Easy—2nd Edition—Jennifer de Lasala

This guide is the ultimate nontechnical learning tool. Use it to understand 5.1's new features such as optional, mouse-operated pull-down menus and equation-oriented graphics, and to find information on: commands, file management, merging, style sheets, printing, document layout, function key usage, macros, graphics, and much more. 432 pages, illustrated. Book No. 3679, $24.95 hardcover only

COMBATING COMPUTER CRIME: Prevention, Detection, Investigation
—Chantico Publishing Company, Inc.

This timely handbook outlines practical solutions for identifying, preventing, and detecting computer crimes, and represents the experiences of over 2,000 participating organizations from industry, commerce, and government. Step by step, the authors show you how to establish a computer crime policy and provide a management plan of action for implementing that policy. Detailed checklists and worksheets are included. 350 pages, 100 illustrations. Book No. 3664, $39.95 hardcover only

DISASTER RECOVERY HANDBOOK
—Chantico Publishing Company, Inc.

Could your company survive if a tornado struck today? You'll find everything you need for coping with your worst-case scenario in this book. Among the other issues covered are plan formulation and maintenance; data, communications, and microcomputer recovery procedures; emergency procedures. Action-oriented checklists and worksheets are included to help you start planning right away—before it's too late. 276 pages, 88 illustrations. Book No. 3663, $39.95 hardcover only

ASSEMBLY LANGUAGE SUBROUTINES FOR MS-DOS® —2nd Edition—Leo J. Scanlon

Use this collection of practical subroutines to do high-precision math, convert code, manipulate strings and lists, sort data, display prompts and messages, read user commands and responses, work with disks and files, and more. Scanlon gives you instant access to over 125 commonly needed subroutines. Never again will you waste valuable time wading through manuals or tutorials. 384 pages, 211 illustrations. Book No. 3649, $24.95 hardcover only

ENHANCED MS-DOS® BATCH FILE PROGRAMMING—Dan Gookin

This new guide leads you through the development of versatile batch files that incorporate the features of the latest DOS versions, commercial batch file extenders, and utilities written in high-level languages such as Pascal and C. The companion diskettes packaged with the book include all the significant batch file programs described—plus all the utilities and their source codes. 360 pages, 71 illustrations. Two $5^1/4''$ diskettes. Book No. 3641, $34.95 hardcover only

BUILD YOUR OWN 80486 PC AND SAVE A BUNDLE—Aubrey Pilgrim

With inexpensive third-party components and clear, step-by-step photos and assembly instructions—and without any soldering, wiring, or electronic test instruments—you can assemble a 486. This book discusses boards, monitors, hard drives, cables, printers, modems, faxes, UPSs, memory, floppy disks, and more. It includes parts lists, mail order addresses, safety precautions, troubleshooting tips, and a glossary of terms. 240 pages, 62 illustrations. Book No. 3628, $26.95 hardcover only

STRATEGY, SYSTEMS, AND INTEGRATION: A Handbook for Information Managers—George M. Hall

Now you can successfully plan new data processing systems and integrate existing systems. Hall shows you how you can get beyond basic strategic problems and concentrate on mastering the techniques that will meet the increasing demands of your system. From an in-depth analysis of database requirements to key management issues, you'll follow the logical order in which systems should be designed and developed. 384 pages, 118 illustrations. Book No. 3614, $39.95 hardcover only

BIT-MAPPED GRAPHICS—Steve Rimmer

This is one of the first books to cover specific graphic file formats used by popular paint and desktop publishing packages. It shows you how to pack and unpack bit-map image files so you can import and export them to other applications. It helps you sort through available file formats, standards, patches, and revision levels, using commercial-quality C code to explore bit-mapped graphics and effectively deal with image files. 504 pages, 131 illustrations. Book No. 3558, $38.95 hardcover only

AUTOCAD™ Methods and Macros
—2nd Edition—Jeff Guenther and Ed Ocoboc

With 275 illustrations, this completely revised and updated guide takes you step by step through dozens of useful techniques for working through Release 11 of AutoCAD. Twenty new chapters outline object selection, lines, editing and viewing documents, inserting drawings into documents, working with text, sketching, printer plots, dialogue boxes, the new multi-purpose menu, and much more. 464 pages, 275 illustrations. Book No. 3544, $34.95 hardcover only

Prices Subject to Change Without Notice.

Look for These and Other TAB Books at Your Local Bookstore

To Order Call Toll Free 1-800-822-8158
(in PA, AK, and Canada call 717-794-2191)

or write to TAB Books, Blue Ridge Summit, PA 17294-0840.

Title	Product No.	Quantity	Price

☐ Check or money order made payable to TAB Books

Charge my ☐ VISA ☐ MasterCard ☐ American Express

Acct. No. _____ Exp. _____

Signature: _____

Name: _____

Address: _____

City: _____

State: _____ Zip: _____

Subtotal $ _____

Postage and Handling
($3.00 in U.S., $5.00 outside U.S.) $ _____

Add applicable state and local
sales tax $ _____

TOTAL $ _____

TAB Books catalog free with purchase; otherwise send $1.00 in check or money order and receive $1.00 credit on your next purchase.

Orders outside U.S. must pay with international money order in U.S. dollars.

TAB Guarantee: If for any reason you are not satisfied with the book(s) you order, simply return it (them) within 15 days and receive a full refund.　　　　　　　　　　　　　　　　　　**BC**

FREE DISK OFFER

One free disk with your initial order of disks from PC-SIG's Library, the world's largest shareware source!

Use the order form on the reverse side of this page and choose your disks from the PC-SIG shareware collection listed below or call PC-SIG's Toll Free Hotline: 800-245-6717. Ask for operator #2275.

Don't miss the bargain membership offer that includes *The PC-SIG Encyclopedia of Shareware*, also listed on the order form.

800-245-6717

TM

PC-SIG Laptop Shareware Collection

CAD (Computer Aided Design) and Designing

☐ **#1587, 1588 VGACAD** VGACAD is an all-purpose graphics editor, image processor and paint program to create, enhance, or colorize digitized images. *Requires VGA or EGA. A hard drive is recommended. Registration Fee: $27.95 or $42.95 outside USA.*

Communication Programs

☐ **#1206, 1343 Boyan Communications** Communicate via modem at 300 to 9600 baud with menued ease. Access bulletin boards or E-mail. A 20 number redialing queue, on-line chat mode, usage log, automated calling and more! *Requires a modem. A hard drive is recommended. Registration Fee: $55.00*

☐ **#499 Procomm** PROCOMM provides easy and convenient access to a wide array of telecommunications tasks. *Requires a modem. Registration Fee: $75.00*

☐ **#310, 1022, 1023, 1483 QMODEM SST** A top-rated telecommunications package. Fast and versatile, it supports Hayes, Racal-Vadic and other modems and runs at up to 9600 Baud. *Requires a modem. A hard drive is recommended. Registration Fee: $30.00*

☐ **#2300 Telix** A full-featured communications program designed to meet the needs of almost any user. This program offers a large range of file transfer protocols and many features. *Requires hard drive and a modem. Registration Fee: $39.00*

Databases

☐ **#830 WAMPUM** Fully-relational, menu-driven, dBASE-compatible GRAPHICS DBMS ...now supports .PCX graphics fields and can be loaded as a 20K TSR. *Requires 512K RAM a hard drive and a Hercules graphics card. Registration Fee: $50.00 per PC or $150.00 per network, User's Guide $20.00*

Games, Arcade

☐ **#293 Arcade Series 3** A diskful of arcade games: Breakout in BRICKS, three-dimensional pakman in 3-DEMON, jump barrels and watch out for KONG, squish killer bees in PANGO, and more! *Requires CGA. Registration Fee: None.*

☐ **#274 Brian's Games** Arcade selections: BREAKOUT, CASTLE, PACMAN, SPACE INVADERS, LUNAR LANDER, and others! *Some programs require a version of BASIC and CGA. Registration Fee: None.*

Reference Materials (books/articles/information/data)

☐ **#1127 Terra*Time** TERRA*TIME tracks and displays the current local time in hundreds of cities around the globe. Calculate time zone differences and great- circle distances between cities. *Registration Fee: $20.00*

Sales and Prospect Management

☐ **#1880 Contact Tracker** The answer to a sales manager's dream, CONTACT TRACKER gives you the tools to track prospects, appointments and clients. It is a mail merger, labeler, phone dialer and letter writer. *Requires two floppy drives. Hard drive recommended. Registration Fee: $50.00*

☐ **#687, 688, 2686, 2687 IN-CONTROL** Sales prospecting and business contact tracking that has high-speed data sort, an appointment tickler and an extensive sort system. *Requires 512K RAM and two floppy drives. Registration Fee: $99.00 (required after 50 prospects entered).*

☐ **#1790 Phoebe** Manage your contacts so they grow into clients and manage your clients to grow your sales potential with them. PHOEBE is a contact/client control system designed to help you manage contacts effectively. *Requires 384K RAM and two floppy drives. Registration Fee: $69.00*

☐ **#1610 Sales Call Reports** SALES CALL REPORTS (SCR) enables a sales representative to easily and effectively use a computer to automate the reporting and customer list functions that are usually performed manually or not at all. *Requires 512K RAM. Registration Fee: $35.00*

See Other Side For More Disks.

To Order Call 800-245-6717, Operator#2275

Software Order Form

Enter Disk Numbers You Wish To Order:

✳ ▢▢▢▢ **Free Disk** (with initial order of five disks or membership)

1. ▢▢▢ 13. ▢▢▢
2. ▢▢▢ 14. ▢▢▢
3. ▢▢▢ 15. ▢▢▢
4. ▢▢▢ 16. ▢▢▢
5. ▢▢▢ 17. ▢▢▢
6. ▢▢▢ 18. ▢▢▢
7. ▢▢▢ 19. ▢▢▢
8. ▢▢▢ 20. ▢▢▢
9. ▢▢▢ 21. ▢▢▢
10. ▢▢▢ 22. ▢▢▢
11. ▢▢▢ 23. ▢▢▢
12. ▢▢▢ 24. ▢▢▢

Please send: (USA Prices Only)

☐ **$39 Super Saver Membership Special** —
Includes 2 years of *Shareware Magazine* (12 issues), *The PC-SIG Encyclopedia of Shareware*, One free disk of your choice, technical support, periodic mailings on the newest and most popular shareware, and special member pricing on future purchases @ $39 $ _____

☐ 1 year subscription to *Shareware Magazine* @ $12.95   _____

☐ _____ Disks @ $2.49 each (members)   _____

☐ _____ Disks @ $3.49 each (non-members)   _____

☐ $.50 per disk surcharge for 3.5" disks   _____

☐ CD ROM @$299.00 (entire Library on disc)   _____

☐ *The PC-SIG Encyclopedia of Shareware* - @ $19.95   _____

☐ Other _____   _____

Subtotal   _____
CA residents add 7% sales tax   _____
Shipping and Handling $5.00

Payment by: ☐ Check ☐ Visa ☐ MC   **TOTAL** _____

Card No _____
Exp. Date _____ Sig. _____
Name _____
Address _____

1030 D East Duane Ave., Sunnyvale, CA 94086, FAX: 408-730-2107   **PC-SIG**

Visa/MasterCard Phone Orders: 800-245-6717 Ask for Operator #2275

☐ **#1582 Sales Tools** If you are looking for a dBase program that keeps track of your sales calls, appointments and expenses, try SALES TOOLS. *Requires dBase III or compatible, and two floppy drives or a hard drive. Registration Fee: $20.00*

Schedulers, Calendars, To Do Lists, and Ticklers

☐ **#1792 APPTracker** Keep track of all of your appointments whether they're this afternoon, next month or next year. Clean, crisp screens and a direct, effective approach make this datebook a pleasure to use. *No special requirements. Registration Fee: $20.00*

☐ **#1900 Big Event** BIGEVENT warns you 10 days in advance of special events such as birthdays, anniversaries and special days of the year such as Mother's Day. After all, it's your memory, not your heart, that needs a hand. *No special requirements. Registration Fee: $10.00*

☐ **#1571 Calendar Program** CALENDAR PROGRAM is a quick, no nonsense way to help people whose lives are tied to dates. *Registration Fee: None.*

☐ **#1963 Calendar Program by Small** Print a three-page calendar for any year from 1990 through 1999. *Requires Epson or compatible printer. Registration Fee: $5.00*

☐ **#1106 Flexical** Stay on top of your business or social engagements with efficient and flexible engagement calendars and keep track of your running with the runner's diary. *Requires 384K RAM, hard drive, and a printer. Registration Fee: $20.00*

☐ **#618 MakeMyDay** A complete, computerized time management system — An appointment calendar, a job scheduler, a time log and an expense account manager. *No special requirements. Registration Fee: $50.00*

☐ **#1716 MOMSYS** Throw away those hand-written reminders and turn your activity calendar over to MOMSYS, the ideal program for tracking re-occuring activities. *No special requirements. Registration Fee: $20.00*

☐ **#1530 Phone Message** PHONE MESSAGE is a memory-resident utility that allows you to quickly record phone messages. Once the program is installed in memory, press the "hot-key" to activate this handy phone jotter. *Registration Fee: $10.00*

Sports Management

☐ **#1659 Fish-N-Log Plus** FISH-N-LOG helps you log important facts about your fishing trips by simply answering questions asked by the program. *No special requirements. Registration Fee: $9.95*

☐ **#1358 FishBase II** Keeps track of all the cold, hard facts of up to 800 fishing trips. It also prints such reports as which lure worked best for which fish, and where your best fishing spots are and when. *Requires graphics card. Registration Fee: $15.00*

Spreadsheets

☐ **#751 AsEasyAs** A well-rounded spreadsheet system with on-line help, macros, financial and statistical functions, date arithmetic, database functions and graphs. Direct access to Lotus 1-2-3 files. *Requires 384K RAM. Registration Fee: $50.00*

Utilities, System or Hardware

☐ **#1682 Capacity** CAPACITY is a simple, but helpful program that graphically displays free disk space as well as a computer's hardware information. *No special requirements. Registration Fee: $10.00*

☐ **#2357 Within & Beyond DOS** Check out these four programs to help you transfer complete disks via modem, and transfer odd or unused disk formats to DOS. *Requires a modem for Teledisk. High density drives required for the rest. Registration Fee: Teledisk $20.00 Raindos, Eagle16, HP150, & Sharp56 each $15.00.*

Wordprocessors, Text Editors, and Outliners

☐ **#2090, 2091 PC-WRITE LITE** PC-WRITE LITE is a simpler, easier, faster version of the wordprocessor PC-WRITE. It requires less memory to run but remains file and keystroke compatible with PC-WRITE. *Requires 384K RAM (256k without speller). Registration Fee: $79.00 plus $5.00 shipping.*

☐ **#1783 QEdit Advanced** QEDIT is an extremely fast, easy-to-use text editor for entering program code, letters and small documents. Load and go. *Registration Fee: $44.00*

To order use the order form above or call Toll Free 800-245-6717 and ask for operator #2275.

PC-SIG
1030 D East Duane Ave.
Sunnyvale, CA 94086   FAX: 408-730-2107

FREE DISK OFFER

One free disk with your initial order of disks from PC-SIG's Library, the world's largest shareware source!

Use the order form on the reverse side of this page and choose your disks from the PC-SIG shareware collection listed below or call PC-SIG's Toll Free Hotline: 800-245-6717. Ask for operator #2275.

Don't miss the bargain membership offer that includes *The PC-SIG Encyclopedia of Shareware,* also listed on the order form.

800-245-6717

PC-SIG Business Shareware Collection

Accounting, Billing

☐ **#1147 Fast Invoice Writer** FAST INVOICE WRITER is for the small business owner. Produce invoices, P.O.'s, requisitions, or any document similar in format. Compute taxes or bill by the hour — the program does all the calculations. *Requires 512K RAM, DOS 2.11 or greater. Registration fee: $39.95*

☐ **#1216 Fast Statement Writer** Print monthly totals of invoices, statement labels, and inserts. Handle many details about shipping charges and taxes. *Requires 384K RAM. Registration fee: $29.95*

Accounting, G/L, A/P, A/R, Payroll

☐ **#1115 C-A-S-E Accounting** Accounting system for small to mid-size companies which includes: cash and credit sales journals, invoicing, accounts payable, general ledger, payroll and capital equipment. *Requires 640K RAM and two floppy drives. Registration fee: $75.00*

☐ **#785 CheckMate-GL** A powerful multiple-entry general ledger package that operates on the principles of classical accounting. *Requires two floppy drives or a hard drive. Registration fee: $39.95*

☐ **#331 Medlin Accounting** The General Ledger, Accounts Payable, Accounts Receivable, and Payroll accounting program for the small business. Top-rated software! *Requires two floppy drives. Registration fee: $35 for PC-GL; PC-AP; PC-AR; PC-PR. $25 for PCINV*

☐ **#2059, 2060, 2061 Painless Accounting** If you are looking for a full-featured accounting program, then PAINLESS ACCOUNTING may be your program. It is like Dac Easy Accounting in the way the account numbers are used and in the way the menus are laid out. On the other hand, PAINLESS ACCOUNTING is more business oriented than Dac Easy Light, which is good for those small businesses looking for an inexpensive accounting program. *Requires 640K RAM, and a hard drive. Registration fee: $125.00*

☐ **#565 PC-Payroll** The complete payroll system for mid-sized companies (40-140 employees). Everything from time records and 401(K) plans to tax computations and paycheck printing. *Requires 384K RAM and two floppy drives, hard disk recommended. Registration fee: $145.00*

☐ **#1762 W2/1099-Misc Generator** Let W211 print your W2 and 1099 tax forms this year. W211 is designed for the small business owner or tax preparer who needs to prepare these forms for their employees or clients. *No special requirements. Registration fee: $49.00*

Accounting, Inventory Control

☐ **#1910 PC-Inventory+** An inventory program — not an accountant, not a cash register — just an inventory program. But if that's all you want, then this one is easy to use with lots of screen help and good report features. *No special requirements. Registration fee: $25.00*

Accounting, Job Costing and Bill of Materials

☐ **#1230, 2674 Job Cost** A job-cost control system for multiple job cost centers. Do variance studies with budget controls, project profit and loss estimates and cost entire job. *Requires 640K RAM, a hard disk, and a printer. Registration fee: $45.00*

Accounting, Purchase Orders

☐ **#741 Purchase Order System** Track all P.O.'s, open and cleared, and list all your vendors with this system. *Requires 640K RAM, a hard drive. Registration fee: $69.00*

See Other Side For More Disks.

To Order Call 800-245-6717, Operator#2275

Software Order Form

Enter Disk Numbers You Wish To Order:

✳ ▢▢▢▢ **Free Disk** (with initial order of five disks or membership)

1. ▢▢▢▢   13. ▢▢▢▢
2. ▢▢▢▢   14. ▢▢▢▢
3. ▢▢▢▢   15. ▢▢▢▢
4. ▢▢▢▢   16. ▢▢▢▢
5. ▢▢▢▢   17. ▢▢▢▢
6. ▢▢▢▢   18. ▢▢▢▢
7. ▢▢▢▢   19. ▢▢▢▢
8. ▢▢▢▢   20. ▢▢▢▢
9. ▢▢▢▢   21. ▢▢▢▢
10. ▢▢▢▢   22. ▢▢▢▢
11. ▢▢▢▢   23. ▢▢▢▢
12. ▢▢▢▢   24. ▢▢▢▢

Please send: (USA Prices Only)

☐ **$39 Super Saver Membership Special** —
Includes 2 years of *Shareware Magazine* (12 issues), *The PC-SIG Encyclopedia of Shareware,* One free disk of your choice, technical support, periodic mailings on the newest and most popular shareware, and special member pricing on future purchases @ $39 .... $ _____

☐ 1 year subscription to *Shareware Magazine* @ $12.95 _____

☐ _____ Disks @ $2.49 each (members) _____

☐ _____ Disks @ $3.49 each (non-members) _____

☐ $.50 per disk surcharge for 3.5" disks _____

☐ CD ROM @ $299.00 (entire Library on disc) _____

☐ *The PC-SIG Encyclopedia of Shareware-* @ $19.95 _____

☐ Other _____ _____

Subtotal _____

CA residents add 7% sales tax _____

Shipping and Handling __$5.00__

Payment by: ☐ Check ☐ Visa ☐ MC   **TOTAL** _____

Card No _____

Exp. Date _____ Sig. _____

Name _____

Address _____

1030 D East Duane Ave., Sunnyvale, CA 94086, FAX: 408-730-2107   **PC-SIG**

Visa/MasterCard Phone Orders: 800-245-6717 Ask for Operator #2275

Accounting, Time-Billing Management

☐ **#1168 BillPower Plus** Integrated timekeeping, bookkeeping and billing system. A single-entry program, it tracks 15 employees and thousands of clients. *Requires 512K RAM and a hard drive. Registration fee: $150.00*

☐ **#825 Time Tracker** Automated billing system tracks accounts receivable and prints itemized invoices ready for mailing! Also documents time spent on client work. A professional time billing program that does it all — simply. Prints plain paper invoices and plenty of reports. Includes complete A/R. *Requires 512K RAM. A hard drive is recommended. Registration fee: $69.00*

Databases

☐ **#2082, 2083, 2084 PC-File** PC-FILE — A flexible database with the unbeatable combination of ease of use, power and versatility. *Requires 512K RAM, DOS 3.0, and a hard drive or two high density floppy drives. Registration fee: $149.95*

Desktop Organizers

☐ **#405 PC-DeskTeam** Pop-up desktop productivity tools — An appointment calendar, an alarm, a phone book with auto-dialer, DOS access, printer controls and a calculator. All there when and where you need them. *No special requirements. Registration fee: $29.95*

Form Creation Programs

☐ **#2329 FormGen - Business Form Collection** A collection of business forms for use with FormGen. Standard invoices, purchase orders, credit applications, accounting forms, fax letters, etc. that you can use "as is", or modify to suit your needs. Over 70 commonly used business forms. *Requires Formgen, PC-SIG Disk #1695. Registration fee: $15.00*

Graphing Programs

☐ **#669, 670 Graphtime-II (CGA/EGA)** A business and technical graphics system with text and font editors. Designed for use with dBASE II/III, Multiplan, Lotus 1-2-3 and ASCII files, it can also be used on its own with data entered from the keyboard into the built-in spreadsheet. *Requires 640K RAM, CGA, and hard drive. Registration fee: $49.95*

Hard Drive Utilities

☐ **#1188 Point & Shoot Backup/Restore** Make fast, easy backups of your hard disk! *Requires 320K RAM and hard drive. Registration fee: $35.00*

Label Makers

☐ **#1150, 1679 Simply Labels III** Design labels any size or format for mailing, files, VCR tapes or anything else that needs a label. *Requires printer. Registration fee: $25.00*

Menu Programs

☐ **#608 Automenu** Let AUTOMENU help you find your way around DOS. With or without a mouse, create your own "point-and-shoot" menus to find and run all your programs. *Requires hard drive recommended. Registration fee: $69.95*

Resumes and Job Search

☐ **#1097 Resumebest** The first thing most employers see of us is our resume. Use RESUMEBEST to create a good-looking, properly prepared resume. *Requires a version of BASIC and a printer. Registration fee: $29.95*

To order use the order form above or call Toll Free 800-245-6717 and ask for operator #2275.

PC-SIG
PC-SIG
1030 D East Duane Ave.
Sunnyvale, CA 94086   FAX: 408-730-2107